D0945262

Grace Church Library
Pottstown, Pennsylvania

THE DAILY STUDY BIBLE

(OLD TESTAMENT)

General Editor: John C. L. Gibson

ISAIAH
Volume 1

ISAIAH

Volume I

JOHN F. A. SAWYER

THE WESTMINSTER PRESS
PHILADELPHIA

Grace Church Library.
Pottstown, Pennsylvania

Copyright © John F. A. Sawyer 1984

All rights reserved—no part of this book may be reproduced in
any form without permission in writing from the publisher,
except by a reviewer who wishes to quote brief passages in
connection with a review in magazine or newspaper.

Scripture quotations from the Revised Standard Version of the
Bible are copyright 1946, 1952, © 1971, 1973 by the Division
of Christian Education of the National Council of the Churches
of Christ in the U.S.A. and are used by permission.

Published by
The Saint Andrew Press
Edinburgh, Scotland
and
The Westminster Press®
Philadelphia, Pennsylvania

Printed in the United States of America
2   4   6   8   9   7   5   3

Library of Congress Cataloging in Publication Data

Sawyer, John F. A.
    Isaiah.

    (The Daily study Bible series)
    Bibliography: p.
    1. Bible. O.T. Isaiah—Commentaries. I. Bible.
O.T. Isaiah. English. Revised standard. 1984.
II. Title. III. Series: Daily study Bible series
(Westminster Press)
BS1515.3.S28 1984   224'.1077   84-22098
ISBN 0-664-21812-1 (v. 1)
ISBN 0-664-24579-X (pbk. : v. 1)

MATRI MEAE IN MEMORIAM

GENERAL PREFACE

This series of commentaries on the Old Testament, to which this first volume on *Isaiah* by Professor Sawyer belongs, has been planned as a companion series to the much-acclaimed New Testament series of the late Professor William Barclay. As with that series, each volume is arranged in successive headed portions suitable for daily study. The Biblical text followed is that of the Revised Standard Version or Common Bible. Eleven contributors share the work, each being responsible for from one to three volumes. The series is issued in the hope that it will do for the Old Testament what Professor Barclay's series succeeded so splendidly in doing for the New Testament—make it come alive for the Christian believer in the twentieth century.

Its two-fold aim is the same as his. Firstly, it is intended to introduce the reader to some of the more important results and fascinating insights of modern Old Testament scholarship. Most of the contributors are already established experts in the field with many publications to their credit. Some are younger scholars who have yet to make their names but who in my judgment as General Editor are now ready to be tested. I can assure those who use these commentaries that they are in the hands of competent teachers who know what is of real consequence in their subject and are able to present it in a form that will appeal to the general public.

The primary purpose of the series, however, is *not* an academic one. Professor Barclay summed it up for his New Testament series in the words of Richard of Chichester's prayer—to enable men and women "to know Jesus Christ more clearly, to love Him more dearly, and to follow Him more nearly." In the case of the Old Testament we have to be a little more circumspect than that. The Old Testament was completed long before the time of Our Lord, and it was (as it still is) the sole Bible of the Jews, God's first people, before it became part of the Christian Bible. We must take this fact seriously.

Yet in its strangely compelling way, sometimes dimly and sometimes directly, sometimes charmingly and sometimes embarrassingly, it holds up before us the things of Christ. It should not be forgotten that Jesus Himself was raised on this Book, that He based His whole ministry on what it says, and that He approached His death with its words on His lips. Christian men and women have in this ancient collection of Jewish writings a uniquely illuminating avenue not only into the will and purposes of God the Father, but into the mind and heart of Him who is named God's Son, who was Himself born a Jew but went on through the Cross and Resurrection to become the Saviour of the world. Read reverently and imaginatively the Old Testament can become a living and relevant force in their everyday lives.

It is the prayer of myself and my colleagues that this series may be used by its readers and blessed by God to that end.

New College   JOHN C. L. GIBSON
Edinburgh   General Editor

CONTENTS

CONTENTS

SOME USEFUL DATES FOR REFERENCE

765 B.C.   birth of Isaiah (?)

736 B.C.   death of Uzziah (=Azariah), king of Judah (787–736)

732 B.C.   Assyrian conquest of Syria (capital: Damascus)

727 B.C.   death of Tiglath-Pileser III (=Pul), king of Assyria (744–727)

725 B.C.   death of Ahaz (=Jehoahaz), king of Judah (736–725)

722 B.C.   Assyrians conquer Israel (=Ephraim; capital: Samaria)

712 B.C.   Assyrian campaign against Ashdod (Philistine city)

701 B.C.   Assyrian defeat of Egyptians at Eltekeh

701 B.C.   Assyrian conquest of Judah and siege of Jerusalem

695 B.C.   death of Isaiah (?)

622 B.C.   fall of Nineveh, capital of Assyrian Empire

609 B.C.   death of Josiah, king of Judah (640–609)

586 B.C.   Nebuchadnezzar, king of Babylon (605–562), conquers Jerusalem

560 B.C.   release of Jehoiachin, king of Judah (609–598), in Babylon

538 B.C.   Cyrus, king of Medes and Persians (550–530), conquers Babylon

515 B.C.   Second Temple at Jerusalem built

323 B.C.   death of Alexander the Great, king of Macedon (336–323)

167 B.C.   desecration of Temple by Antiochus IV, Seleucid king (175–163)

164 B.C.   rededication of Temple at Jerusalem by Judas Maccabaeus

145 B.C.   Jewish Temple founded at Leontopolis in Ptolemaic Egypt (?)

INTRODUCTION

The aim of this commentary is to present the meaning of the text of the Book of Isaiah as clearly as possible. The variety of material contained in the book is immense. In some places we can hear the actual voice of Isaiah himself addressing his contemporaries in eighth century B.C. Jerusalem. More often than not, we shall be reading "Isaianic" literature, that is to say, prophetic messages inspired by Isaiah, although composed a century or more after he died. But since we are concerned with the meaning of the book as a whole, this distinction between "Isaiah" and "Isaianic" is an academic one and for our purpose not of great import: our primary interest is in the rich and enormously influential "Isaianic" literature, all sixty-six chapters of it, not simply in what the great individual who started it off said.

Similarly, in some cases the precise historical circumstances referred to in the text can be quite convincingly reconstructed, as in the case of Sennacherib's invasion of Judah in 701 B.C. (chs. 36–37) or the rise of Cyrus, king of the Medes and Persians, in the middle of the sixth century B.C. (e.g. 45:1–7). But the text is seldom if ever concerned with history as such, and for that reason I have been concerned not so much with the question of what actually happened as with why the account is told in this way and not that way; not so much with whether the author is historically accurate as with what he is getting at.

To put this another way, reading the Book of Isaiah from cover to cover, one acquires a basic vocabulary of "Isaianic" terms such as faith, righteousness, salvation, Zion, the Holy One of Israel and the Lord of hosts. One also becomes familiar with graphic images such as the vineyard, and with prophetic formulae such as "Thus says the Lord..." and "Woe to...!" I have tried to concentrate on these, explaining the allusions and associations present in the original Hebrew and so letting the text speak for itself as much as possible. This has seemed to me preferable to spending time on historical matters which are important to the scholar but have not greatly concerned the millions of readers and listeners down the ages, in Jewish and Christian communities all over the world, for whom the Book of Isaiah has been a source of interest and inspiration.

Finally, we must remember that the book is an integral part of Biblical tradition, the first of the five prophetic books (Isaiah, Jeremiah, Ezekiel, Daniel and the "Twelve"), and must be read in that larger context too. In explaining difficult words and phrases, I have therefore paid particular attention to parallels in other Biblical texts, in the modest hope that readers of this commentary will become more sensitive to a wide range of Biblical words and phrases and ways of thinking, not only Isaianic ones.

ISAIAH

A PROPHET'S VISION

Isaiah 1:1

¹The vision of Isaiah the son of Amoz, which he saw concerning Judah and Jerusalem in the days of Uzziah, Jotham, Ahaz, and Hezekiah, kings of Judah.

The heading at the beginning of the Book of Isaiah has a very important purpose and repays careful study before we turn to the prophecies themselves. It asks us, in the first place, to think of this enormous collection of prophecies, the longest in the Bible, as a "vision", the "vision" of an eighth-century B.C. prophet by the name of Isaiah ben Amoz. As we shall see, there are good reasons for dating parts of the book to the seventh and sixth centuries, possibly even later. In particular, many of the later chapters in the book were probably first written in the time of the Babylonian Exile in the mid-sixth century B.C. Consequently, if we look for historical information in the heading, we will miss its point. The book is a "vision", it tells us, and so, whenever the prophet lived, his "words" go beyond the immediate historical circumstances of his day. They are addressed not only to the citizens of eighth-century B.C. Jerusalem or to the Babylonian exiles in the sixth century, but to "us who are all of us here alive this day" (Deut. 5:3). From the ox and the ass that recognize their master's crib in 1:3 to the vision of a new Jerusalem in chapter 65, from the "Virgin" Birth in 7:14 to the "man of sorrows, and acquainted with grief . . . wounded for our transgressions . . . bruised for our iniquities" in chapter 53, it is we who are addressed by this, the first and, from the Church's point of view, the most influential of the Old Testament prophets.

The originator of this astonishingly virile Isaianic tradition lived in Jerusalem throughout most of the second half of the eighth century B.C. (c. 765–695). We shall have occasion to examine what biographical details there are later on (they are found especially in chapters 6–8; 20; 36–39), as well as the political, social and religious circumstances of his time (see esp. 2 Kings 15–20). For the moment it will suffice to note that the prophet witnessed, from a position of some influence at the royal court, a devastating series of Assyrian invasions resulting in the destruction of most of the major cities of the region, including Samaria, capital of Judah's northern neighbour, Israel. The cities of Judah were last to fall, but Jerusalem survived—only just—in 701 B.C. There were some feeble attempts to throw off Assyrian domination on the part of some of the states and, under Hezekiah, Judah and Jerusalem retained some degree of national pride reflected in many of Isaiah's prophecies "concerning Judah and Jerusalem". There is also some evidence that the reign of Hezekiah was characterized by literary and religious activity (cf. Prov. 25:1; 2 Chron. 29). About the death of Isaiah there is nothing in the book that bears his name, but a second-century A.D. Jewish work known as "The Martyrdom of Isaiah" assumes, not without good reason, that he was put to death under Manasseh, Hezekiah's evil son (cf. 2 Kings 21:16)—"sawn in two", if we are to believe the tradition referred to as well in the list of martyrs in Hebrews 11:37.

The prophet's name *Yesha'yahu*, "the Lord [Yahweh] saves, helps", enshrines two elements of immense theological significance. The last part stands for Yahweh, the name of Israel's God, and marks out as distinctively "Yahwistic" all those names ending in -jah or -iah (e.g. Elijah, Jeremiah, Zephaniah, Zechariah, Isaiah). The other element, *yesha'*, appears in the names Joshua, Elisha and Hosea, as well as Jesus (*Yeshua'*) and in the triumphant cry "Hosanna!" (= *hoshi'a-na*, "save!"; Ps. 118:25; cf. John 12:13). The word *yeshu'ah* ("salvation") and related words are unusually frequent in the Book of Isaiah (see on 12:3). The name of Isaiah's father, Amoz, is otherwise unknown, but has nothing to do with the prophet Amos.

Firstly, then, the Book of Isaiah contains the vision of a prophet who lived in the eighth century B.C., "in the days of Uzziah, Jotham, Ahaz and Hezekiah, kings of Judah". But secondly, it takes in, as we shall discover later, many sayings which Isaiah cannot have uttered but which are nevertheless in a real sense included within the "vision" which he saw. The third feature of this huge collection of Isaianic traditions to which the heading draws attention is that they are about Judah and Jerusalem.

Nowhere in the Bible are the hopes centred on the city of Zion and the house of David more prominent than in the Book of Isaiah. The Saviour figure in chapters 9 and 11 is of David's line; the exiles in far-off Babylon are addressed as "Jerusalem" or "daughters of Zion" (e.g. 51:17–52:2); the vision of a new world with which the book concludes has at its centre, like the Apocalypse of John of Patmos (Rev. 21–22), "the New Jerusalem" (65:17–66:21). Not a few Psalms, such as 48, 122, 125, 126 and 137, have Zion as their chief subject; Ezekiel and Amos end with visions of a New Jerusalem and a Davidic hope too; even the Book of Jeremiah concludes with a glimmer of hope for Jerusalem. But, as our heading points out, it is the Book of Isaiah, firmly rooted in eighth-century B.C. Jerusalem, that gathers together sixty-six chapters of Jerusalem-centred prophetic traditions, and concentrates on "the city of righteousness, the faithful city" (1:26), "Ariel, the city where David encamped" (29:1), "the holy city" (52:1), "my holy mountain Jerusalem" (66:20), from beginning to end. It is the Book of Isaiah that lays the foundation for Jewish and Christian beliefs about Jerusalem, and the Messiah who will reign there

> upon the throne of David and over his kingdom,
>   to establish it, and to uphold it
> with justice and with righteousness,
>   from this time forth and for evermore. (9:7)

A PEOPLE LADEN WITH INIQUITY—I

Isaiah 1:2–9

2Hear, O heavens, and give ear, O earth;
    for the Lord has spoken:
"Sons have I reared and brought up,
    but they have rebelled against me.
3The ox knows its owner,
    and the ass its master's crib;
but Israel does not know,
    my people does not understand."

4Ah, sinful nation,
    a people laden with iniquity,
offspring of evildoers,
    sons who deal corruptly!
They have forsaken the Lord,
    they have despised the Holy One of Israel,
    they are utterly estranged.

5Why will you still be smitten,
    that you continue to rebel?
The whole head is sick,
    and the whole heart faint.
6From the sole of the foot even to the head,
    there is no soundness in it,
but bruises and sores
    and bleeding wounds;
they are not pressed out, or bound up,
    or softened with oil.

7Your country lies desolate,
    your cities are burned with fire;
in your very presence
    aliens devour your land;
    it is desolate, as overthrown by aliens.
8And the daughter of Zion is left
    like a booth in a vineyard,
like a lodge in a cucumber field,
    like a besieged city.

⁹If the Lord of hosts
   had not left us a few survivors,
we should have been like Sodom,
   and become like Gomorrah.

Like the heading in verse 1, chapter 1 as a whole serves as a valuable introduction to all sixty-six chapters of Isaianic material which make up the Book of Isaiah. It sets the scene for the whole book: a scene of disease, desolation and despair, in which what hope there is centres on the city of Jerusalem. The first part of the chapter reflects the Assyrian period, possibly the year 701 B.C., when only Jerusalem survived by the skin of its teeth and all the fortified cities of Judah were taken by Sennacherib, king of Assyria (36:1; cf. 2 Kings 18:13).

It is interesting to contrast the prophetic denunciation of the people here, faced by almost total destruction, with the prophecies of salvation and miraculous victory in chapter 37. Here Assyria is represented as the rod of God's anger (cf. 10:5ff.) and Sennacherib's devastating invasion as God's punishment on a sinful nation; in chapter 37 Sennacherib mocks the Living God (37:17) and is ignominiously assassinated by his sons after a miraculous defeat (37:36–38). Here there are but few survivors, but in chapter 37 "the surviving remnant of the house of Judah shall again take root downward, and bear fruit upward; for out of Jerusalem shall go forth a remnant, and out of Mount Zion a band of survivors. The zeal of the Lord of hosts will accomplish this" (37:31–32). Here in chapter 1 the villain of the piece is Israel and the Assyrian invasion nothing but just punishment; in chapter 37 Assyria is totally in the wrong, and "shall not come into this city, says the Lord. For I will defend this city to save it, for my own sake and for the sake of my servant David" (37:34f.).

Such contrasts enable us to distinguish between how things really were in 701 B.C. and how they came to be interpreted later, under the influence of the national achievements or aspirations of another age and the unshakable Zion tradition discussed in the previous section.

The first section begins, like the second (vv. 10–20), with a call to "Hear the word of the Lord": heaven and earth are summoned like witnesses to hear the charges against Israel. This law-court scene, in which Israel stands accused before God, is a very common rhetorical device in the prophetic literature. It has the effect of emphasizing the justice of God and at the same time provides an opportunity for arguments (cf. v. 18) and appeals (v. 17). Possibly the device is derived from those glimpses into the heavenly court which prophets are described as having had as part of their prophetic experience (cf. Isa. 6:1–8; 1 Kings 22:19–23; Job 1:6–12; 2:1–6; Jer. 23:18–22). At all events it provides an impressive opening to the book and, like the ending (66:22), sets the prophecies of Isaiah in a universal context.

It is significant that the very first "oracle" (= direct words of God) calls not for justice or love or piety or faith, but for reason (cf. v. 18). Even dumb animals have more sense than Israel: they can recognize their master, while the people of Israel have ignored their own father. The appeal to nature is another very common rhetorical device, especially in the Wisdom literature: e.g.

> Go to the ant, O sluggard;
> consider her ways and be wise. (Prov. 6:6)

It is stupidity as much as disobedience that is being attacked, and the messianic hope in later chapters will contain "the spirit of wisdom and understanding, the spirit of counsel and might, the spirit of knowledge and the fear of the Lord" (11:2). The early Church found in this verse a telling image for the recognition of their Lord and Saviour in a manger, while Israel, that is to say the Jews, could not or would not see him there. The route taken by this image from the crisis of eighth-century B.C. Jerusalem to the nativity scenes on present day Christmas cards is a long one, but nonetheless illuminating.

The prophet then turns to address the evildoers themselves. We must remember that he was concerned with the leaders of his city, not the ordinary people. This is evident from the specific reference to "rulers" (v. 10), "princes" (v. 23), "judges" and "counsellors" (v. 26), "the nobility" (5:14) as well as to their victims, the fatherless and the widows (vv. 17, 23). In fact the citizens of Jerusalem were for the most part well off, the owners of "large and beautiful houses" (5:9; cf. Amos 3:15), their wealth and security built up over the previous one hundred years or so. Affluence and iniquity need not be connected, but it is evident from the examples singled out for prophetic attacks, in chapters 2–5 especially (cf. Amos 3–6), that they were in eighth century B.C. Jerusalem. Wealth was used to finance foreign soothsayers and idols, drunkenness and greed, wantonness and the perversion of justice. Above all it was arrogance he was attacking, the arrogance of those with the power to grind the faces of the poor, while at the same time religiously observing the festivals and rituals of the Temple.

These are the sins and iniquities to which the opening prophecy refers. Verse 4 accumulates no less than seven terms to describe the "nation": first, the general terms "sin" and "iniquity", then two words that suggest "causing damage and wanton destruction" (cf. NEB), and finally three phrases that refer to the religious implications of what they were doing. The Lord (Heb. *Yahweh*), the Holy One of Israel, has been abandoned in favour of foreign, pagan commitments: the last word, "estranged", has definite idolatrous associations (cf. Ezek. 14:5). The Isaianic title, "Holy One of Israel" (*qedosh yisra'el*), points forward to chapter 6 where the concept of holiness will be discussed in full. Wherever it occurs, it highlights both the terrifying, transcendent power of Israel's God and the demands for moral and spiritual purity alongside, or even in preference to, ritual purity.

A PEOPLE LADEN WITH INIQUITY—II

Isaiah 1:2–9 (cont'd)

The two gruesome pictures that follow, the one of somebody suffering from a hideous, untreated disease (vv. 5–6), the other of a land destroyed by enemy invasion (vv. 7–8), illustrate the devastating consequences of sin. To put this another way, they teach that suffering is due to sin; it is divine judgment upon those who rebel against the Holy One of Israel. Thus the catastrophe of 701 B.C. is interpreted as punishment on Jerusalem, at the hands of the Assyrian army. The word translated "smitten" in verse 5 means "smitten by God"; a normal word for "plague, affliction" (*makka*) comes from the same root. The whole idea of reward and punishment, portrayed in these grisly terms, is perhaps best summed up in the words of Deuteronomy:

> If you are not careful to do all the words of this law . . . that you may fear this glorious and awful name, the Lord your God, then the Lord will bring on you and your offspring extraordinary afflictions [*makka*], afflictions severe and lasting, and sicknesses grievous and lasting. And he will bring upon you all the diseases of Egypt, which you were afraid of; and they shall cleave to you. (28:58–60; cf. Lev. 26:21)

Obviously this is not the only explanation of suffering in the world, natural and man-made, but it certainly has a powerful rhetorical effect—especially when the sin and the suffering are there for all to see. There could be no question of "What have I done to deserve this?" in 701 B.C. on the part of the "sinful nation, a people laden with iniquity".

This twofold account of suffering with which the Book of Isaiah opens has a curious sequel in a more familiar passage later in the book. In chapter 53 suffering is again represented by two horrifying descriptions, the first in terms of a hideous disfiguring disease (vv. 2–6), the second as due to man's inhumanity to man (vv. 7–10). Again both types of suffering are due to divine intervention—"he was smitten by God, and afflicted" (v. 4) . . . "it was the will of the Lord" (v. 10). But while chapter 1 presents suffering as punishment for sin, chapter 53 interprets it as a means of healing and forgiveness: "with his stripes we are healed" (v. 5), and a road to victory and exaltation (v. 12; cf. 52:13). Chapter 1 presents us with the problem; the solution comes later.

The tender phrase "daughter of Zion" (v. 8) reminds us of the whole web of Zion traditions that had grown up around Jerusalem by the time of Isaiah. The names of cities in Hebrew are feminine and this makes it possible for prophets and poets to address Jerusalem (and her citizens) in suitably tender and affectionate language; thus "Arise, shine; for your light is come" (60:1), with the verbs in the feminine gender, has a distinctive sound in Hebrew, which cannot be represented in English. Elsewhere Jerusalem is a mother, bereft of her children and amazed to see them return (49:21); and a wife convinced she has been divorced, but in fact still loved and cherished by her divine husband (50:1). In the present context it is her vulnerability amongst aliens bent on her destruction that gives the expression its particular force.

The section ends with a cry of despair on behalf of the people themselves. We are probably to envisage the prophet identifying himself with his people here and speaking on their behalf. Taking up the phrase "overthrown by aliens" in verse 7, which is very much associated with the spectacular destruction of Sodom and Gomorrah (cf. 13:19; Deut. 29:23; Amos 4:11; Jer. 49:18; 50:40), he is perhaps quoting from a community lament such as we have in Psalm 124:

> If it had not been the Lord who was on our side,
>   when men rose up against us,
> then they would have swallowed us up alive . . .

The phrase "few survivors" was scarcely a sign of hope in 701 B.C.; rather it was like the "two legs or a piece of an ear" which is all that is left of a sheep mauled by a lion (Amos 3:12). But the whole idea of a saving remnant certainly does appear in the eighth-century parts of the book, particularly in the name of Isaiah's son, Shear-jashub, "a remnant will return" (7:3), and probably quite early on such passages as 1:9 were reinterpreted more optimistically. Just as the defeat of 701 was transformed into miraculous victory (cf. chapter 37), so passages like this one, and the one concerning the smouldering stump remaining after a forest fire (6:13), were transformed into sources of hope after destruction.

Like the "Holy One of Israel", "the Lord of hosts" is a highly emotive term in the language of the eighth-century prophets. Alongside a militaristic sense of armies, "hosts" in Isaianic tradition is closely associated with the idea of God as creator: the Lord is not only the divine commander of Israel's armies, responsible for their victories "as on the day of Midian" (9:4), but also that same transcendent creator God who rules over the armies of heaven and whose terrifying powers, summed up in the word "holiness", make rebellion against him futile. That is the force of the cry of the seraphim in chapter 6. The forces of nature are under his control as well as the military and political forces of history. Just look at what he did to the cities of Sodom and Gomorrah (Gen. 19:24–29).

BLOODSTAINED HANDS

Isaiah 1:10–20

¹⁰Hear the word of the Lord,
     you rulers of Sodom!
Give ear to the teaching of our God,
     you people of Gomorrah!
¹¹"What to me is the multitude of your sacrifices?
     says the Lord;
I have had enough of burnt offerings of rams
     and the fat of fed beasts;
I do not delight in the blood of bulls,
     or of lambs, or of he-goats.

¹²"When you come to appear before me,
     who requires of you
     this trampling of my courts?
¹³Bring no more vain offerings;
     incense is an abomination to me.
New moon and sabbath and the calling of assemblies—
     I cannot endure iniquity and solemn assembly.
¹⁴Your new moons and your appointed feasts
     my soul hates:
they have become a burden to me,
     I am weary of bearing them.

¹⁵When you spread forth your hands,
    I will hide my eyes from you;
even though you make many prayers,
    I will not listen;
    your hands are full of blood.
¹⁶Wash yourselves; make yourselves clean;
    remove the evil of your doings
    from before my eyes;
    cease to do evil,
¹⁷   learn to do good;
seek justice,
    correct oppression;
defend the fatherless,
    plead for the widow.

¹⁸"Come now, let us reason together,
    says the Lord:
though your sins are like scarlet,
    they shall be as white as snow;
though they are red like crimson,
    they shall become like wool.
¹⁹If you are willing and obedient,
    you shall eat the good of the land;
  ²⁰But if you refuse and rebel,
    you shall be devoured by the sword;
    for the mouth of the Lord has spoken."

Our first full-scale prophecy of judgment begins with the usual introductory formula, "Hear the word of the Lord" (cf. Jer. 7:2; Ezek. 13:2), by which the prophet indicates that what follows is not just his own words, but divine proclamation; and it ends with another conventional formula, "for the mouth of the Lord has spoken" (cf. 40:5; 58:14), which has the effect of underlining the final warning: "But if you refuse and rebel, you shall be devoured by the sword" (v.20).

The divine proclamation itself is in two parts: the first a blistering attack on the whole sacrificial system at the Temple (vv.10–14), and the second an appeal for justice and obedience (vv. 16–20*a*). The two are linked by the gruesome verse 15 in which the blood on worshippers' hands stretched out in prayer to God points back to the blood of bulls which does not please the Lord of hosts (v. 11), and on to the bloodguilt and the sins that are "like scarlet . . . red like crimson" (v. 18), which he hates even more.

Verse 10, as well as introducing the prophecy, links it with what goes before, since Sodom and Gomorrah are symbols of gross immorality as well as destruction. "Rulers of Sodom" and "people of Gomorrah" remind us of the enormity of Israel's crimes, but also of their fate: the whole city has been contaminated by the crimes of its leaders and one judgment awaits them all as it did "the cities of the plain" in Genesis 18–19.

The Temple rituals, sacrifice, incense, festivals and so on were a major theme of the eighth-century prophets. Amos 5:21–24 is one of the bitterest examples:

> I hate, I despise your feasts,
>   and I take no delight in your solemn assemblies . . .

They were obviously familiar with all the details of temple worship, and it is most unlikely that they were advocating the abolition of all the ceremonial side of their religion. The temples of the northern cities were destroyed, as it turned out, by the end of the eighth century and the Temple of Solomon at Jerusalem in 586 B.C., and it is interesting to note that, without a Temple and thus without a sacrificial system, the religion of the Babylonian exiles flourished, as has orthodox Judaism to this day after the destruction of the second Temple in A.D. 70.

No doubt the emphasis on spiritual values and the moral purity of the worshipper is one that can be found in the teaching of prophets and sages of all ages. In Biblical tradition it appears in the stories of Saul (1 Sam. 15:22f.), and in proverbial wisdom (e.g. Prov. 21:27; 28:9). Even in the extended ritual legislation of Leviticus there is provision for confession of sin (5:5) and the payment of restitution (5:16) along with the cultic acts; sacrifice of animals alone is not enough. A spiritual alternative to ritual as a road to forgiveness is envisaged most poignantly in Psalm 51, a sinner's confession:

For thou hast no delight in sacrifice;
   were I to give a burnt offering, thou wouldst not be pleased.
The sacrifice acceptable to God is a broken spirit;
   a broken and contrite heart, O God, thou wilt not despise.

(vv. 16–17)

The ethical demands of the eighth-century prophets, including Isaiah, are therefore unlikely to be a new phenomenon; but the emphasis certainly is. The gap between worship and life, between Sunday and the rest of the week, is what the prophet is attacking, not just what we do on Sunday.

The colourful language of the prophecy comes straight out of temple talk. The chief types of sacrifice are enumerated: communion sacrifice (v. 11a), holocaust (11b), cereal offering (13a) and incense (13b), all of which are described in the early chapters of the Book of Leviticus. The fat and the blood are singled out for special mention (v. 11), as are the festivals, from the weekly sabbath to the monthly and annual feasts celebrated in ancient Israel (13–14). But with penetrating originality the prophet turns the cultic language on its head: the word "abomination" is a technical term for pagan practices, forbidden throughout Israel's legislation (e.g. Lev. 18:22; Deut. 7:25; 2 Kings 23:13). Here it is daringly applied to the regular worship at the Temple in Jerusalem. The blood which plays so important a role in sacrifice (Lev. 17:11; Heb. 9:22) is rejected because it is mingled with the blood of innocent victims (vv. 15–17). The horror of blood-guilt and violent death surfaces again in the prophetic attacks on Edom later in the book (chapters 34 and 63). Hands outstretched to God in prayer, like Solomon's at the dedication of the Temple (1 Kings 8:22,54), are stained with innocent blood, symbol of oppression and violence.

Most significant of all, perhaps, there is the language of washing and ritual cleanness which is here given a moral meaning instead of its usual ritualistic one: like holiness, purity is a matter of the heart. "Wash yourselves; make yourselves clean" (v. 16), not in preparation for some cultic act at the Temple (cf. Exod. 30:17–21), but in order to live up to the ethical demands of your religion. Psalm 51 is again our major parallel to this:

Purge me with hyssop, and I shall be clean;
  wash me and I shall be whiter than snow. (v. 7)

Forgiveness is possible, but it requires moral courage and obedience rather than ritual.

It is a curious fact about the prophets of the eighth century B.C. that the test of obedience is not whether you keep the Ten Commandments or any other of the laws in the Pentateuch, which are nowhere mentioned as such in eighth-century writings, but to what extent you "seek justice, correct oppression; defend the fatherless, plead for the widow" (v. 17). The same message comes across in Hosea (e.g. 12:6), Amos (e.g. 5:24) and Micah: e.g.

  and what does the Lord require of you
but to do justice and to love kindness,
  and to walk humbly with your God? (6:8)

Whether Isaiah was familiar with the laws in the Pentateuch or not, there is no doubt that his moral imperatives belong more to the universal ethical teaching of the Wisdom literature than to the more distinctively Israelite laws. It is in Job and Proverbs that we find the closest parallels: e.g.

. I delivered the poor who cried,
  and the fatherless who had none to help him . . .
  and I caused the widow's heart to sing for joy. (Job 29:12f.)

Job's righteousness was not the righteousness of the priests, but the righteousness that the prophets demanded: justice, kindness, humility. There are a good many proverbs on the same subject: e.g. "He who mocks the poor insults his Maker" (17:5). It is from the Wisdom traditions that the appeal to "*learn* to do good" (v. 17) comes too, and the call to "reason together" (v. 18). You remember the prophet's first words to Israel: even dumb animals have more sense (v. 3)!

One last theme from the Wisdom tradition concludes the section: retribution. If you obey, you will be rewarded; if you rebel you will be punished (vv. 19–20). All through the books of Job and Proverbs, and incidentally Deuteronomy which in many respects belongs to the same educational context, the choice is laid before us: "See, I have set before you this day life and good, death and evil" (Deut. 30:15). In the proverbial language:

> . . . the upright will inhabit the land,
>   and men of integrity will remain in it;
> but the wicked will be cut off from the land,
>   and the treacherous will be rooted out of it. (Prov. 2:21f.)

The assumption that prosperity and peace depend on obedience, while defeat is the result of disobedience, is basic to the prophet's teaching, and provides both an incentive to do good and an interpretation of history. While it may have had little effect on Isaiah's stubborn and unresponsive contemporaries, in a later age it provided an explanation for the destruction of Jerusalem in 586 B.C. and a basis on which to build a new theology (see later on chapter 40).

THE FAITHFUL CITY

Isaiah 1:21–31

21How the faithful city
    has become a harlot,
    she that was full of justice!
Righteousness lodged in her,
    but now murderers.
22Your silver has become dross,
    your wine mixed with water.
23Your princes are rebels
    and companions of thieves.
Every one loves a bribe
    and runs after gifts.
They do not defend the fatherless,
    and the widow's cause does not come to them.

24Therefore the Lord says,
    the Lord of hosts,
    the Mighty One of Israel:

"Ah, I will vent my wrath on my enemies,
   and avenge myself on my foes.
²⁵I will turn my hand against you
   and will smelt away your dross as with lye
   and remove all your alloy.
²⁶And I will restore your judges as at the first,
   and your counsellors as at the beginning.
Afterward you shall be called the city of righteousness,
   the faithful city."

²⁷Zion shall be redeemed by justice,
   and those in her who repent, by righteousness.
²⁸But rebels and sinners shall be destroyed together,
   and those who forsake the Lord shall be consumed.
²⁹For you shall be ashamed of the oaks
   in which you delighted;
and you shall blush for the gardens
   which you have chosen.
³⁰For you shall be like an oak
   whose leaf withers,
   and like a garden without water.
³¹And the strong shall become tow,
   and his work a spark,
and both of them shall burn together,
   with none to quench them.

This is the first of many Isaianic poems on the theme of "Jerusalem". The next chapter begins with one (vv. 1–4); chapter 4 contains another; and in the later chapters of Isaiah Jerusalem or "daughter of Zion" is addressed in a series of exquisite poems drawing on the same ideas and images.

With characteristic originality, the prophet combines two very different kinds of poem to make one well-rounded literary unit. First comes a lament (vv. 21–23), like the laments over the destruction of Jerusalem in the Book of Lamentations: compare it with Lam. 1 and 4 especially, ("How like a widow she has become"), although here it is the moral and spiritual decline and fall of the city that is being mourned, not its destruction. Bribery and corruption were the order of the day; the widows and orphans were neglected; the city that had once been a symbol of justice and righteousness, as in the Golden Age of David and Solomon (1 Kings 3–4), had fallen from grace; what had once been as pure and clear as silver was turned into dross.

The lament is then followed by a salvation oracle (vv. 24–26), in which the Lord of hosts, the Mighty One of Israel, promises to intervene. The city will pass through another difficult time, like the one described earlier in the chapter (vv. 7–9), but on this occasion the result will be a new, reformed Jerusalem, a "city of righteousness" as in the old days. Suffering can destroy, but it can also inspire devotion and obedience. The siege described in verses 7–9 left the city looking as if it had been destroyed by an earthquake; here the prophet visualizes another kind of catastrophe that brings out the best in her leaders. We are not to think of a disaster in which the corrupt rulers are ruthlessly removed and replaced by better ones, but of a situation in which those same rulers are inspired by new ideals of righteousness and faith (v. 26), and cease to be God's enemies (v. 24).

The poem is held together, not only by the logical sequence corruption-judgment-restoration, but by the striking use of two major Isaianic themes at the beginning and the end: "faith" and "righteousness". "Faithful city" is a beautiful phrase in Hebrew: both words require some comment. The word for "city" (*qirya*) is a poetic term that reminds us of other colourful descriptions like "city of chaos" (24:10), "Ariel, Ariel, the city where David encamped" (29:1) and "city of the great King"(Ps. 48:2). "Faithful" really means two things at once: on the one hand, it means "reliable, trustworthy" like witnesses (8:2), and on the other hand, it means "secure, established" like the Davidic dynasty (1 Sam. 2:35). So we have to understand the phrase "the faithful city" applied to Jerusalem as bringing together these two ideas: she is a symbol of God's faithfulness (cf. 49:7), and at the same time firmly established, able to survive enemy invasions, safe as houses. The connection is summed up in the famous saying in 7:9: "if you will not *believe*, surely you shall not be *established*", in which both italicized words are parts of the same Hebrew verb. "The faithful city" has nothing to fear, provided she trusts in God. Isaiah 28:16 also brings together the idea of a city's sure foundation and faith in God (cf. 30:15).

"City of righteousness" (v. 26) is if anything even more characteristic of Isaiah's language and thought. In the first place, it is
evident that the term *zedek* (pronounced *tsedek*), "righteousness", had very special associations with Jerusalem. Not only is
the term a favourite of Jerusalem-centred Isaiah, but there are
also many Jerusalemite names which contain that element *z-d-k*:
e.g. Melchi*zedek*, priest and king of Salem (= Jerusalem) (Gen.
14:18); *Zadok*, priest at Jerusalem (1 Kings 2:35) and his descen-
dant Jeho*zadak* (Haggai 1:1); Adoni*zedek*, king of Jerusalem
(Josh. 10); *Zedek*iah, king of Judah (2 Kings 24:18). So
Jerusalem was the "city of righteousness" par excellence.

But, in the second place, we have to recognize that the term
does not mean the same as "justice" or "piety" or "self-righteousness" or "goodness". It can have these meanings, but in
Isaianic tradition it also has a more concrete sense. It refers to
righteous acts carried out (by God or man) *on behalf of the
oppressed*, and thus has to be translated "victory" (41:2) or
"deliverance" (51:5) in many contexts. Actually it is this same
word that is translated "triumphs" in the ancient Song of
Deborah:

> To the sound of musicians at the watering places,
>   there they repeat the *triumphs* of the Lord,
> the *triumphs* of his peasantry in Israel.
>
> (Judg. 5:11; cf. 1 Sam. 12:7)

So the "city of righteousness" is the city that brings help to the
widow and the orphan, salvation to those in distress. The connection between the two terms, "righteousness" and "salvation",
recurs throughout Isaiah, especially in chapters 40–55: e.g.

> "Shower, O heavens, from above,
>   and let the skies rain down righteousness;
> let the earth open, that salvation may sprout forth,
>   and let it cause righteousness to spring up also." (45:8; cf. 51:5–6)

Verses 27–28 are a kind of gloss on the "faithful city" poem,
explaining in much less exalted style that the "city" in the poem is
Zion (as if we did not know this), and that justice and righteous-

ness are going to save her from destruction. "Redeemed" is a legal or financial term (Hebrew *padah*), and refers to a trans-action whereby Zion's rulers purchase their salvation from God, using for currency "justice" and "righteousness". In other words, they will give up their ill-gotten gains in exchange for honesty and justice. "Righteousness" here is no "saving act" or "triumph", as in the preceding poem, but synonymous with "virtue" or "good deeds". We are reminded of those stories where people are saved by their "righteous acts": e.g. the righteous few in Sodom (Gen. 18:22–33); Noah, Daniel and Job (Ezek. 14:14).

"Repentance" in verse 27 seems at first sight to be a new idea, not present in the poem. But in fact verse 26 has the same verb: "I will restore your judges" means "make them turn back" and is very near to the phrase "those in her who repent", i.e. those who "turn back" (from their evil ways). The little book of the prophet Jonah contains the most illuminating parallel to this: the same term is used both of God and the wicked citizens of Nineveh "repenting, turning back" (3:8, 9, 10).

To Isaiah those who do not "repent" are "rebels and sinners", and their fate will be destruction and elimination. This sounds like a conclusion, like the end of an earlier section of this chapter (v. 20) or the end of Psalm 1, for example. But there is a further addition, elaborating the theme of judgment and destruction. Verses 29–31 are once again in a different style and are addressed directly to the rebels and sinners: "you shall be ashamed . . . you shall blush". They are also about a different kind of dis-obedience. So far in this chapter we have heard of murder, dis-honesty and oppression, while here it is the worship of wooden idols or trees, elsewhere called "Asherim". This refers to the kind of worship we hear about in the days of the patriarchs: Abraham building altars at the oak of Moreh at Shechem (Gen. 12:6f.) and the oaks of Mamre at Hebron (13:18), for example. Later the practice was consistently condemned both in the Mosaic legislation (e.g. Deut. 12:3) and in some of the early Israelite legends: Gideon cut down the Asherah beside the altar of Baal in his home town, and built an altar to Yahweh in its place (Judg. 6:25–32).

Whether the present passage is to be interpreted literally, or should be taken as a colourful and emotive symbol of the disobedience and disloyalty portrayed earlier in the chapter, is hard to say. Perhaps it is best to understand it in both ways. In later chapters craftsmen who devote their labours to manufacturing idols are ridiculed and condemned (e.g. 44), and the condemnation is accompanied by emphatic declarations of monotheism: "besides me there is no God" (45:5). These are certainly calls to abandon idolatry, but they are surely also calls for single-minded devotion to God and commitment to the highest religious and moral ideals. So it is in this passage. A society that dedicates itself to self-indulgence, and neglects the poor and the needy and the stranger within its gates, is a corrupt and evil society and will eventually disintegrate under destructive pressures from within and without. It will wither like a garden without water, and then burn incessantly at the slightest spark until it is totally destroyed. The punishment fits the crime: the tree-worshippers will wither and die like trees in a forest fire (vv. 30f.).

OUT OF ZION SHALL GO FORTH THE LAW

Isaiah 2:1–5

[1]The word which Isaiah the son of Amoz saw concerning Judah and
     Jerusalem.
[2]It shall come to pass in the latter days
     that the mountain of the house of the Lord
   shall be established as the highest of the mountains,
     and shall be raised above the hills;
   and all the nations shall flow to it,
[3]   and many peoples shall come, and say:
   "Come, let us go up to the mountain of the Lord,
     to the house of the God of Jacob;
   that he may teach us his ways
     and that we may walk in his paths."
   For out of Zion shall go forth the law,
     and the word of the Lord from Jerusalem.

⁴He shall judge between the nations,
and shall decide for many peoples;
and they shall beat their swords into ploughshares,
and their spears into pruning hooks;
nation shall not lift up sword against nation,
neither shall they learn war any more.

⁵O house of Jacob,
come, let us walk
in the light of the Lord.

After the introduction in chapter 1, chapter 2 begins with another
title, shorter than 1:1, which conveniently introduces the first
main division of the book, a collection of prophecies of judgment
"concerning Judah and Jerusalem" (chapters 2–12). In addition
to the title in 2:1, there are other signs of editorial arrangement
which give structure and meaning to the collection. It begins
(2:2–5) and ends (12:1–6) with a Zion hymn of hope, an optimis-
tic framework in which to view the gloomy contents of Isaiah's
preaching. It also features three beautiful prophecies of hope,
built into its structure: "In that day the branch of the Lord shall be
beautiful and glorious" (4:2–6), "The people who walked in
darkness have seen a great light" (9:2–7), and "There shall come
forth a shoot from the stump of Jesse" (11:1–9). Whether or not
these and other hopeful words go back to Isaiah himself—and few
of them probably do—they have been arranged in such a way as
to transform Isaiah, the eighth-century prophet of doom, into the
prophet of hope who provided the background of so much New
Testament and early Christian thinking about salvation.

"The *word* of the Lord" which the prophet "*saw*" highlights
the distinctive meaning of the term "word of the Lord", and at
the same time draws our attention to the visionary experience of
the prophets. Similar expressions introduce the prophecies of
Micah and Habakkuk. Isaiah's vision in the Temple (chapter 6) is
probably not the only time he "saw the Lord". We might perhaps
translate the verse in modern terms: "The divine truth that was
revealed to the prophet . . ." Just how the process worked we can
never know, although chapter 6 gives us a clue. These expressions claim that the prophets' words are grounded in some
actual spiritual experience, and that therefore what they have to

say is divinely inspired and authoritative as no other teaching
—from priest, scribe or wise man (cf. Jer. 8:8–10, 18:18)—could
ever be.

Verses 2–5 are another poem on the "faithful city" (see 1:21–
26), and one of the most familiar passages in the Bible. They are
known best perhaps in the form of a paraphrase: "Behold, the
mountain of the Lord in latter days shall rise". They appear also
in another collection of eighth-century prophecies (Mic. 4:1–4).
The vision of a world without war, where people will "beat their
swords into ploughshares, and their spears into pruning hooks"
(v. 4), has naturally captured the imagination of many a political
and religious movement, pacifists, Quakers, nuclear disarmers
and others. Curiously enough, among the many Biblical passages
where the poem is alluded to or quoted, there is one where
Armageddon, the last battle, is described in a cruel parody of its
words:

> Beat your ploughshares into swords,
>   and your pruning hooks into spears;
> let the weak say, "I am a warrior." (Joel 3:10)

But the poem is more than a general vision: the prophecy focuses
on the city of Jerusalem, and exiles in all ages have looked to
these words for inspiration. One of the first Zionist organizations,
founded in Kharkov in Russia in 1882, with the aim of returning
to Jerusalem, took its name"BILU" from the initials of the
Hebrew of verse 5: "O house of Jacob, come let us walk . . ." (*Bet
Ya'akov Lekhu Wenelekha*). Political events since 1948 have
sadly left their hopes unfulfilled, since instead of "the word of the
Lord" going forth from Jerusalem (v. 3), Israel has become a
byword for superior military technology, a situation closer to
Joel's version of the prophecy than Isaiah's. The hopes expressed
in these verses are thus all the more poignant, among both Jews
and Christians, as they struggle to see beyond present failures to
the eventual establishment of justice and peace among the nations "in the latter days".

"In the latter days" means no more than "at some undefined
time in the future". It is one of the most frequent idioms in the

predictions of Israel's prophets: two of Jeremiah's frightening prophecies against the foreign nations conclude with it (48:47; 49:39); Ezekiel's famous prophecy against Gog of the land of Magog is another example (Ezek. 38:16). By New Testament times the formula had taken on a new meaning: "at the end of time", and for many Jews, including the New Testament writers and early Christians, prophecies containing it referred to the imminent coming of the kingdom of God. This is another example of how Old Testament prophecy was removed from its original context in ancient Israel and applied by the community of faith to their own experience.

"The house of the Lord" is the Temple at Jerusalem, built by Solomon, destroyed by Nebuchadnezzar, rebuilt in the days of Haggai and Zechariah, and finally destroyed by the Romans in A.D. 70. The hill on which it stood was known as Mount Moriah (2 Chron. 3:1) and according to Genesis 22 it was there that the "binding of Isaac" took place. "The highest of the mountains . . . raised above the hills" bears no resemblance to the actual lie of the land, as any who have visited Jerusalem will know. The Temple Mount is slightly higher than Mount Ophel, just south of it, on which the City of David was built (2 Chron. 27:3; 33:14), but is surrounded on all sides by a ring of hills (including the Mount of Olives) that are considerably higher than it. The prophecy is using words from an ancient myth about an exceedingly high mountain, like Mount Olympus in Greece or Mount Ida in Crete, or indeed Mount Sinai, which was a point of contact between heaven and earth. Psalm 48 contains another example of the connection between the myth and the Zion traditions.

In this passage Jerusalem is to rise to an enormous height, partly to make room for all the nations of the world, and partly to make sure that everyone on earth can see it. A similar idea appears in John 3:14: "As Moses lifted up the serpent in the wilderness, so must the Son of man be lifted up, that whoever believes in him may have eternal life."

The hope against hope that the nations will one day accept the word of the Lord surfaces in many Biblical passages. According to the Book of Daniel, even Nebuchadnezzar, destroyer of Jerusalem, repents and worships God (Dan. 4:34–37). Cyrus, king of Persia, acknowledges the authority of the Lord, the God of heaven (2 Chron. 36:23). Malachi 1:11 takes this idea as far as it can go: ". . . from the rising of the sun to its setting my name is great among the nations, and in every place incense is offered to my name".

What precisely "the law" and "the word of the Lord" in verse 3 refer to, and through what institution they are to be administered, is not specified: no king is mentioned, for example, as in 9:1–7, 11:1–5 and 42:1–4, no priest or prophet or judge. The idea is simply that, where now disputes are settled by the sword, "in the latter days" they will be settled by peaceful arbitration; and where now men spend time and energy on studying the art of war, there will come a time when instead they use all their intellectual resources, as Solomon did (1 Kings 3), to establish peace and justice in the world.

The call to the people of Israel in verse 5 to practise what they preach is an addition to the poem. The Micah version finishes differently:

> but they shall sit every man under his vine and under his fig tree,
>   and none shall make them afraid . . . (Mic. 4:4).

The Isaianic version, unlike Micah's, is clearly intended to lead the reader naturally into the next section which consists of a series of bitter criticisms of "the house of Jacob"—their greed, arrogance, idolatry, dishonesty and injustice. It is an appeal to the people of God to remember his ways (v. 3), and to live up to their mission to be "a light to the nations", an expression to which we shall return in chapter 42.

SO MAN IS HUMBLED

Isaiah 2:6–22

> 6For thou hast rejected thy people,
>   the house of Jacob,
> because they are full of diviners from the east
>   and of soothsayers like the Philistines,
>   and they strike hands with foreigners.

⁷Their land is filled with silver and gold,
and there is no end to their treasures;
their land is filled with horses,
and there is no end to their chariots.
⁸Their land is filled with idols;
they bow down to the work of their hands,
to what their own fingers have made.
⁹So man is humbled,
and men are brought low—
forgive them not!
¹⁰Enter into the rock,
and hide in the dust
from before the terror of the Lord,
and from the glory of his majesty.
¹¹The haughty looks of man shall be brought low,
and the pride of men shall be humbled;
and the Lord alone will be exalted in that day.

¹²For the Lord of hosts has a day
against all that is proud and lofty,
against all that is lifted up and high;
¹³against all the cedars of Lebanon,
lofty and lifted up;
and against all the oaks of Bashan;
¹⁴against all the high mountains,
and against all the lofty hills;
¹⁵against every high tower,
and against every fortified wall;
¹⁶against all the ships of Tarshish,
and against all the beautiful craft.
¹⁷And the haughtiness of man shall be humbled,
and the pride of men shall be brought low;
and the Lord alone will be exalted in that day.
¹⁸And the idols shall utterly pass away.
¹⁹And men shall enter the caves of the rocks
and the holes of the ground,
from before the terror of the Lord,
and from the glory of his majesty,
when he rises to terrify the earth.

²⁰In that day men will cast forth
their idols of silver and their idols of gold,

which they made for themselves to worship,
    to the moles and to the bats,
²¹to enter the caverns of the rocks
    and the clefts of the cliffs,
from before the terror of the Lord,
    and from the glory of his majesty,
    when he rises to terrify the earth.
²²Turn away from man
    in whose nostrils is breath,
    for of what account is he?

From the vision of hope by which the collection of Isaianic prophecies in chapters 2–12 is introduced (see 2:1), we move now into the first of three series of judgment prophecies (2:6–4:1; 5:1–30; 9:8–10:34). Like most of chapter 1 and, for example, Amos 3–6, these give us a clear view of the state of affairs in the eighth century B.C. We have to remember that this is a one-sided view, of course, much distorted by the prophets' rhetoric and by their stern moral and religious stance. It is thus very important that we should study these passages more for their moral and religious content than as source material for a social history of ancient Israel. However interesting some of the details may be, we have to try to keep a balance between ancient history and the timeless truths expressed in this exceedingly rich and colourful form.

The first section (2:6–4:1) consists of five separate units, the first four introduced by the Hebrew word *ki*, "for" (RSV), in 2:6, 2:12, 3:1 and 3:8, and the last by "the Lord said" (3:16). There is great variety in the form and content of these prophecies: for example, sometimes the prophet is addressing God directly (v. 6), sometimes he is speaking about the Lord (vv. 12–19), sometimes we hear the Lord himself speaking (3:4, 12, 14, 15). The subject matter ranges from idolatry and feminine coquetry to arrogance and injustice, all described in a wealth of colourful images and expressions.

The theme of the first description of the land of Judah (vv. 6–8) is that there is no room for God. So full of their own successes are they that they have forgotten that "the Lord alone will be exalted", a theme that runs throughout Isaiah's prophecies (e.g. 31:1). The attack is not on the professions listed in verse 6—the word "diviners" is actually not in the Hebrew text at all, and there is no other reference to Philistine soothsayers—but rather on foreign influences in general, which threaten the unique relationship between God and his people. "The east" suggests exotic ideas and foreign imports; and the uncircumcised Philistines represent all that Saul and David had fought to free Israel from.

"Striking hands with foreigners" would mean "entering into agreements with foreigners", but the Hebrew text actually means "and the children of foreigners are everywhere", as NEB translates it. The passage may have been influenced by events in the days of Nehemiah, leader of the threatened post-exilic community struggling to survive, when legislation on foreign marriages became a major issue (Neh. 13:23–27). As in the case of the silver and gold, and the horses and chariots of verse 7, there is nothing intrinsically wrong with having lots of foreigners around: this is not to be understood as racism. The danger is that in all the fascination of new ideas, new languages, new possessions and new inventions, God will be forgotten. This is spelt out in verse 8: it is possible to worship one's possessions instead of God, one's own achievements in place of God, and that is unforgivable (v. 9).

"Enter into the rock . . ." sounds like the original core of the prophecy, round which the rest of this passage has been built up. There is no escape; judgment is inevitable. There are some dramatic parallels in another eighth-century prophet's words:

"Though they dig into Sheol,
  from there shall my hand take them . . .' (Amos 9:2–4)

The "terror of the Lord" and the "glory of his majesty" are really self-explanatory, except that, at a time when the Assyrian armies were on the move and perhaps had already attacked Judah's northern neighbours, the "terror of the Lord" may have had peculiarly frightening associations.

Verse 11 reads like a proverb: Proverbs 16:5 and 18 are close parallels. But "in that day" sets the verses firmly within the "Day of the Lord" tradition. Amos 5:18 is our earliest example of this key concept:

Woe to you who desire the day of the Lord! . . .
It is darkness and not light . . .

It could be that Isaiah was familiar with Amos' words. He certainly draws upon the same tradition, and a very large number of Isaianic prophecies are set "in that day": 2:20; 3:7,18; 4:1,2; 5:30; 7:18,20,21,23, etc. Its origin is to be found probably in an ancient festival, at which the people's hopes were expressed in such formulae as "The Lord reigns" (as in Psalm 93), and God's victory over evil was celebrated. The eighth-century prophets, especially Amos, were struck by the hypocrisy of this celebration. Since the worshippers were themselves evil, "the Day of the Lord" would be a day when they, not their enemies, would be defeated. Later descriptions of the "Day of Judgment" draw on the same stock of tradition, but postpone the divine intervention until the end of time, a development we have already noted in connection with the phrase "in the latter days" (2:2).

In verses 12–16 we have a characteristically graphic description of the fate of the wicked, in this case the proud and the haughty. The picture of mighty trees, high mountains, huge fortified towers and tall ships is skilfully left in our minds, poised as it were for destruction "in that day". One is left to imagine an earthquake or a landslide or a siege or a tempest: whatever it is, these symbols of haughtiness have no chance of escape. Lebanon and Bashan, to the north of Israel, were famous for their forests. "Ships of Tarshish" means, as in the story of Jonah (1:3), large ships that could travel long distances, as far as distant Tarshish on the coast of Spain (see on 23:1). Some have sought to apply the geography of this description to approaching armies from the north, passing through Lebanon, Bashan, over the hills of Samaria, to the Red Sea and the port of Elath developed by King Uzziah earlier in the century (2 Kings 14:22). A passage in Zechariah 11:1–3 gives such a picture. But in the present context there is no need to look for detailed points of reference: the poem clearly intends us to take a serious look at all the beautiful and great "idols" that surround us, and to remember that they pass away and cannot compare with the glory and the majesty of the Lord of hosts.

The last part of this section adds various thoughtful comments on the nature and ambitions of men. In a pathetic act of repentance, too late to protect them from the terror of the Lord, they throw away their cherished "idols of silver and their idols of gold". Moles and bats live in darkness and in ruined buildings—"Is not the day of the Lord darkness and not light, and gloom with no brightness in it?" (Amos 5:20). "Turn away from man" (v. 22) might be better translated "Stop trusting in man": against a background of human arrogance, materialism and secularism, what good qualities can be discerned in man that one should trust in him or his achievements?

THE TOPSYTURVINESS OF SOCIETY—I

Isaiah 3:1–15

1For, behold, the Lord, the Lord of hosts,
    is taking away from Jerusalem and from Judah
  stay and staff,
    the whole stay of bread,
    and the whole stay of water;
2the mighty man and the soldier,
    the judge and the prophet,
    the diviner and the elder,
3the captain of fifty
    and the man of rank,
  the counsellor and the skilful magician
    and the expert in charms.
4And I will make boys their princes,
    and babes shall rule over them.
5And the people will oppress one another,
    every man his fellow
    and every man his neighbour;
  the youth will be insolent to the elder,
    and the base fellow to the honourable.

6When a man takes hold of his brother
    in the house of his father, saying:
  "You have a mantle;

you shall be our leader,
and this heap of ruins
    shall be under your rule";
7in that day he will speak out, saying:
"I will not be a healer;
    in my house there is neither bread nor mantle;
you shall not make me
    leader of the people."
8For Jerusalem has stumbled,
    and Judah has fallen;
because their speech and their deeds are against the Lord,
    defying his glorious presence.

9Their partiality witnesses against them;
    they proclaim their sin like Sodom,
    they do not hide it.
Woe to them!
    For they have brought evil upon themselves.
10Tell the righteous that it shall be well with them,
    for they shall eat the fruit of their deeds.
11Woe to the wicked! It shall be ill with him,
    for what his hands have done shall be done to him.
12My people—children are their oppressors,
    and women rule over them.
O my people, your leaders mislead you,
    and confuse the course of your paths.

13The Lord has taken his place to contend,
    he stands to judge his people.
14The Lord enters into judgment
    with the elders and princes of his people:
"It is you who have devoured the vineyard,
    the spoil of the poor is in your houses.
15What do you mean by crushing my people,
    by grinding the face of the poor?"

says the Lord God of hosts.

The third and fourth prophecies in this series turn from the
plight of man in general to the situation in Jerusalem in particular. The description of anarchy and the breakdown of law and
order in the city are set in the context of a famine (v. 1), and are

clearly interpreted as punishment brought upon the city by the sins and wickedness of her leaders (vv. 13–15). Like the lament on the "faithful city" in chapter 1, these poems stress the topsy-turviness of a society where insolence, greed, injustice and god-lessness prevail. The restoration of "the city of righteousness, the faithful city" (1:26), cleansed from its guilt, however, is delayed till chapter 4.

Verse 1 originally referred to the onslaught of anarchy: "stay and staff" are "pillars of state", sources of authority and stability, the leaders listed in verses 2 and 3, and if they are removed society breaks down. It was Assyrian policy to remove the military and political leaders from conquered territories with just this object in mind. Maybe the poem reflects a situation all too familiar to Isaiah and his contemporaries who had witnessed the invasions of northern Israel in the years leading up to the final conquest of Samaria in 722 B.C. The text as it stands, however, explains the "stay and staff" in a different way: according to the final words of verse 1, they refer to bread and water, and so in all probability to siege conditions such as those familiar to the citizens of Jerusalem in 701, towards the end of Isaiah's life (Isa. 36–37). It is often suggested that these words were added later still, probably with reference to the even more traumatic siege of Jerusalem in 588–6 B.C. (2 Kings 25). Although the Jerusalem Bible brackets the phrase, and the New English Bible misses it out altogether, it is not impossible to take the text at face value, and picture a scene of anarchy and famine at one and the same time—this is prophetic rhetoric after all, not ancient history.

The "pillars of state" are not listed in any special order, per-haps deliberately to echo the disorder in society. Military, politi-cal and religious leaders and officials are mixed up together as though no one is sure what his proper role in society is. There are some odd omissions too, like the priests. Ezekiel contains a more predictable list in an interesting parallel (7:26–27). Hosea 3:4 is another example. On the other hand, in more hopeful visions of the future, there will come one who can fill several of these roles in himself: "Wonderful Counsellor, Mighty God . . . Prince of Peace" (9:6), and judges and counsellors will be restored "as at the beginning" (1:26). But here the picture is one of anarchy and helplessness, in which people run to and fro desperately looking for support, for someone or something they can put their trust in. The soldiers, from heroic generals ("the mighty man") to junior officers ("the captain of fifty") have not returned from battle; the judges cannot be relied upon to preserve justice and peace; there is no wise statesman ("the counsellor"); the authority of the elders and "men of rank" has been undermined by insolent youth (v. 5). Even the skills and charms of prophets, diviners, soothsayers and magicians, often a last resort for the frightened and superstitious, have nothing to offer.

The topsyturviness of society is a frequent theme in the Wisdom literature of ancient Israel and elsewhere. The Preacher gives a good example:

Woe to you, O land, when your king is a child,
    and your princes feast in the morning! (Ecc. 10:16)

Job sadly contrasts his old way of life, when "men listened to him and kept silence for his counsel" (29:21), with his present degrading circumstances:

"But now they make sport of me,
    men who are younger than I . . ." (30:1)

Job, an elder statesman like those insulted by insolent youth in verse 5, could not understand why he had been singled out for this treatment: there is no mistaking Isaiah's view that the elder statesmen of Jerusalem, together with all the other "pillars of state", deserved it.

THE TOPSYTURVINESS OF SOCIETY—II

Isaiah 3:1-15 (cont'd)

The scene in verses 6 and 7 raises one or two interesting questions, some of which are easier to answer than others. Is it that times were so hard or dangerous that men stayed at home ("in the house of his father"), able only to make futile attempts at appointing new leaders? The "mantle"—"cloak" would be a better translation—then represents wealth and influence in a society where few people have any possessions at all. A more ingenious (but not necessarily more acceptable) interpretation finds in "the house of his father" a reference to an ancestral home and suggests that the request comes from one member of the aristocracy to another to "be our leader" as a serious attempt to set up some kind of an alternative government. Since the word for "leader" is conspicuous by its absence from the list in verses 2 and 3, and from passages describing the members of the Davidic dynasty, it has been suggested that it means no ordinary king or governor, but "dictator", an emergency measure. The scene ends, rather weakly, with the man at the centre of this planned coup denying that he has any advantage over the rest of the city, and rejecting the role offered to him. He says he is not a "healer", one who could bind up the nation's wounds; and the mantle he lacks is a physician's garb. Either way, the scene is a graphic device for rounding off the description of anarchy: 4:1 is another example of the same technique, and Amos 5:19 another.

"Jerusalem has stumbled" or "tottered" (v. 8) takes up the word translated "this heap of ruins" in verse 6, as a catchword, linking the two prophecies together. The second has a more critical, moralizing tone than the first, and explains the reasons why Jerusalem had sunk to such depths: "because their speech and their deeds are against the Lord". "Defying his glorious presence" is a rather strange phrase: NEB has "rebelling against the glance of his glorious eye" which is closer to the Hebrew text. The thought is clear enough, however, and is best interpreted as the opposite of "finding favour in the eyes of God" (e.g. Gen. 6:8; Prov. 3:4). It is as though they were deliberately rejecting the favour and protection of a benevolent king.

The rest of the poem enumerates the people's sins, and warns them of the inevitable consequences. It is in the form of a trial scene in which the evidence against the accused is first presented, and then the judge "stands to judge his people" (v. 13). "Partiality" is the first crime on the list (v. 9). It points forward to the way Judah's leaders have been treating the poor (vv. 12,

14–15) and is familiar from Deuteronomic law: "you shall not show partiality . . . Justice, and only justice, you shall follow, that you may live and inherit the land which the Lord your God gives you" (Deut. 16:19–20). Others suggest that the expression points back to the preceding phrase, and means "brazen impudence" or "shamelessness", defying God like the men of Sodom. NEB translates it "the look on their faces". "Woe to them!" means that the breakdown of society described in the previous verses is due to their criminal behaviour.

Verses 10 and 11 use Wisdom language like so much of Isaianic ethical teaching: the righteous shall be rewarded, the wicked punished. The observable fact that the whole of Judah suffers for the sins of its leaders, the righteous with the wicked, does not affect this brave statement of faith in the ultimate justice of God's world. Even in the blackest crisis, tell the righteous not to give up hope, because they will eventually be rewarded—somehow; and tell the wicked that they cannot escape from the inevitable consequences of their actions. The change of direction in these prophecies of judgment, towards comforting the innocent victims of injustice and oppression, is continued in the next verse with an affectionate "my people" (twice) and the statement that they at any rate are not responsible for the topsyturvy world in which they live. Their leaders are as immature and capricious as children, and as weak and untrained as women—another example of the scene we discussed earlier. In an age like the present, when both monarch and prime minister of Great Britain are women, one can only comment on how conventions have changed since these rhetorical verses were composed!

Some of the ancient versions, influenced perhaps by economic conditions in their day, suggest a quite different scene in verse 12; they are followed by NEB: "Money-lenders strip my people bare, and usurers lord it over them."

The judgment scene in verses 13–15 brings to a dramatic conclusion the series of four prophecies beginning with *ki*, "for" (2:6–3:15). The prophet envisages the heavenly court in which mortals are confronted with their sins. Psalm 82 is a good parallel:

God has taken his place in the divine council;
  in the midst of the gods he holds judgment . . .

Verse 13 actually reads "he stands to judge the peoples" (not "his people"), and sets the scene in a cosmic context, like Psalm 82, which ends:

Arise, O God, judge the earth;
  for to thee belong all the nations!

The "elders and princes" of Judah take their place in the dock alongside the leaders of all the other nations of the world. Their greed and inhumanity are no better than that of their gentile neighbours: the damage they have done to the vineyard of the Lord, that is to say Judah (see 5:1–7), is no less inexcusable. Is there any way they can justify their treatment of the poor? This direct confrontation between man and "the judge of all the earth", a frequent theme in Old Testament prophecy, is about man's ultimate social and moral responsibilities. Whether or not the scene is thought of as taking place in this life or on the Day of Judgment in the world to come, the religious experience it refers to is frightening and deadly serious. In the words of another eighth-century prophetic court scene:

The voice of the Lord cries to the city . . .
"Shall I acquit the man with wicked scales
  and with a bag of deceitful weights?" (Mic. 6:9–11)

THE FATE OF "THE DAUGHTERS OF ZION"

Isaiah 3:16–4:1

¹⁶The Lord said:
  Because the daughters of Zion are haughty
    and walk with outstretched necks,
    glancing wantonly with their eyes,
  mincing along as they go,
    tinkling with their feet;
¹⁷the Lord will smite with a scab
    the heads of the daughters of Zion,
    and the Lord will lay bare their secret parts.

¹⁸In that day the Lord will take away the finery of the anklets, the headbands, and the crescents; ¹⁹the pendants, the bracelets, and the scarfs; ²⁰the headdresses, the armlets, the sashes, the perfume boxes, and the amulets; ²¹the signet rings and nose rings; ²²the festal robes, the mantles, the cloaks, and the handbags; ²³the garments of gauze, the linen garments, the turbans, and the veils.
²⁴Instead of perfume there will be rottenness;
    and instead of a girdle, a rope;
  and instead of well-set hair, baldness;
    and instead of a rich robe, a girding of sackcloth;
    instead of beauty, shame.
²⁵Your men shall fall by the sword
    and your mighty men in battle.
²⁶And her gates shall lament and mourn;
    ravaged, she shall sit upon the ground.

¹And seven women shall take hold of one man in that day, saying, "We will eat our own bread and wear our own clothes, only let us be called by your name; take away our reproach."

In the fifth and last in this series of judgment prophecies (2:6–4:1), the prophet turns his blistering language in the direction of the women of Jerusalem. There are two good reasons for assuming that this is not merely an attack on "the monstrous regiment of women" themselves, but the masterly climax to a sequence of attacks on the arrogant, affluent leaders of Jerusalem as a whole. On the one hand, the sins of "the daughters of Zion" are not specified in a way that might suggest the prophet had a particular reason for attacking them: like the objects of his earlier prophecies, they are "haughty", but that is all. Coquettish behaviour and wearing finery and cosmetics do not in themselves constitute crimes, except for the most narrow-minded bigot, and we have no reason to suppose that Isaiah was such a person. Indeed, elsewhere he compares the new Jerusalem to a "bride adorned with jewels" (61:10), "clad in beautiful garments" (52:1). On the other hand, it does not require much imagination to recognize in these words a brilliant prophetic speech on the unspeakable horrors that are about to fall upon Jerusalem. What happens to the womenfolk in time of war is a familiar theme, and a graphic, heart-rending illustration of total disaster.

First of all, women symbolize the wealth and creaturely comforts of society. The wealthier the city, the longer the possible list of expensive luxury goods like that in verses 18–23. They represent, secondly, vulnerability: it requires so small a change of fortunes to reduce them from suave beauty, self-confidence and dignity to poverty, humiliation and bereavement. Such are the consequences of disease, rape, widowhood. Since it is the women who suffer the consequences of war perhaps more acutely than the men, this final, moving sequence of images has been introduced to sum it all up—in words from an earlier chapter: "How the faithful city has become a harlot!" Not until chapter 49 is the bereaved "daughter of Zion" restored, her sons returned to her (vv. 14–18). Proud Jerusalem in all her finery can be reduced to ruins in a moment; garments of gauze and veils cannot protect her from the judgment she deserves.

Four short sayings have been combined in this rich prophecy, two in verse, which probably go back to the eighth-century prophet himself (16–17; 24–26), and two in prose, both containing the formula "in that day" (18–23; 4:1), which may have a different origin. "The Lord said" introduces the first biting prophecy; it also serves to emphasize that this is the climax in which the themes of 2:6–4:1 are gathered together. The tall "daughters of Zion", in another context, might have provoked comments of approval, not to mention wolf-whistles; but here their haughty bearing, wanton glances and coquettish walk are merely a prelude to terrible tragedy. "Zion", a favourite term for Jerusalem in Isaianic tradition, here perhaps refers more specifically to "down-town" Jerusalem, that area of the city where the Temple stood, the wealthy had their residences, and the fashionable shops were. Verses 18–23 read like a shopkeeper's inventory.

The fate of these proud ladies is described in verse 17: they are to be smitten by some disfiguring disease and stripped naked. The word translated "secret parts" occurs only here in the Hebrew Bible, although well known in post-Biblical and modern Hebrew. A less imaginative suggestion, involving a minor change in the text and apparently found in the Vulgate, finds merely a parallel to the preceding half-verse: "strip the hair from the foreheads" (NEB). The "scab" suggests not only disfigurement, but also uncleanness and untouchability, since it is one of the symptoms of a defiling skin disease treated in priestly legislation (Lev. 13–14). The really frightening thing about both afflictions, skin disease and naked vulnerability, is that both come from God, both are divine afflictions, a view of suffering we find it hard to accept with our minds, but one which was intended by the prophet to high-light the enormity of Jerusalem's moral crimes. Moreover, if the lives of her prosperous, godless, arrogant citizens do end in disaster, his words will be proved right. Throughout his own lifetime Isaiah witnessed many such disasters, both in neighbour-ing cities and in Jerusalem itself.

Verse 18 is a kind of gloss, adding many details to the picture of "the daughters of Zion" described in verse 16. No less than twenty-one items of jewellery and clothing are listed, starting with "anklets", which actually takes up the word translated "tink-ling" (with their feet) in verse 16. The first part of the list consists mainly of jewellery and cosmetics (vv. 18–21), and the second mainly items of clothing (vv. 22–23), but beyond that there is no obvious pattern in the arrangement. Examples of many of the items have been discovered in ancient near-eastern tomb treasures, such as that of Tutankhamen, as well as among the womenfolk of modern bedouin tribes. Illustrations can be found in any of the standard works on Old Testament times. "Cres-cents" are metal ornaments in the shape of the crescent moon, worn incidentally by camels as well as women (Judg. 8:21,26). Their foreign provenance, with or without any explicit associ-ation with magic or pagan religion, adds extra point to the whole scene of exotic luxury in Jerusalem. The "boxes" in verse 20 may not have contained perfume, as our translation recommends: the word suggests rather something very personal, hence the NEB suggestion "lockets", that is, little caskets containing some memento of a person. Ancient evidence for this is so far lacking. "Amulets" or "charms" certainly does refer to some kind of superstitious bric-a-brac. Most of the garments mentioned are identifiable as of special beauty and grandeur, some of them worn by priests and kings. Zechariah 3:4–5 illustrates this in a reverse image of the present passage, where the humiliated priest puts off his filthy garments and is clothed in fine raiment.

Verse 24, like the previous "in that day" passage, is an explanatory comment, expanding the description of disease and degradation given in verse 17. The women will be stripped of their perfume and their fine clothes, struck by disease—baldness this time, not "a scab"—and reduced to shameful poverty. The scene then becomes more specific: these women have lost their menfolk in battle, and sit now at the deserted gates of the city, "ravaged" (NEB "stripped bare") and forlorn. In a beautiful image, reminiscent of parts of the Book of Lamentations, the city gates are pictured mourning the loss of their heroes; the gates where once crowds of people met regularly to exchange news and witness the dispensing of justice are now deserted:

> How lonely sits the city
> that was full of people!
> How like a widow she has become,
> she that was great among the nations! (Lam. 1:1)

The last scene in this rich passage returns to the women, desperate for male protection. They are willing to give up their rights to food and clothing, laid down in the law (Exod. 21:10), if only someone will marry them. The plight of widows is a frequent theme in the humanitarian legislation and teaching of the Old Testament (Exod. 22:22–24; Deut. 27:19); the story of Ruth is another case in point. Jerusalem, as represented by her proud womenfolk, has now become such a widow, as well as a harlot (1:21). This last sad verse brings us to the lowest ebb of Jerusalem's fortunes, and it is at that point that she finds hope.

JERUSALEM AFTER THE JUDGMENT

Isaiah 4:2–6

> ²In that day the branch of the Lord shall be beautiful and glorious, and the fruit of the land shall be the pride and glory of the survivors of

Israel. [3]And he who is left in Zion and remains in Jerusalem will be called holy, every one who has been recorded for life in Jerusalem, [4]when the Lord shall have washed away the filth of the daughters of Zion and cleansed the bloodstains of Jerusalem from its midst by a spirit of judgment and by a spirit of burning. [5]Then the Lord will create over the whole site of Mount Zion and over her assemblies a cloud by day, and smoke and the shining of a flaming fire by night; for over all the glory there will be a canopy and a pavilion. [6]It will be for a shade by day from the heat, and for a refuge and a shelter from the storm and rain.

This passage is an "in that day" prophecy like several preceding it, but it is not a judgment prophecy. Rather it balances the five judgment prophecies of 2:6–4:1 by returning to the supreme hope that centres on Jerusalem: in spite of everything, whatever befalls her, a new city will arise on Mount Zion, purified and protected by God. This was how the "faithful city" lament ended (1:24–26); and how the present section began (2:2–4). In a way, this last hope is stronger than the first, since now it has been hammered out of the experiences of failure and humiliation. A hope that can shine so brilliantly after total defeat is a hope to believe in—only after suffering and death is true resurrection possible. It seems likely that this prophecy comes from a time after Jerusalem had actually been destroyed, possibly as late as the fifth or fourth century B.C. As we shall see, the language and imagery belong more to the extraordinary world of Jewish apocalyptic—Joel, Daniel—than to the prophets. But, like the happy ending to the Book of Amos, and indeed the glorious salvation-oracles in the later chapters of this book (40–55), 4:2–6 is a superb illustration of how tragedy can be turned to hope. Even the blackest disasters are part of God's plan, and so now that they are over we can expect him to create a new world for us to live in. Without the horror and gloom of the preceding prophecies of judgment, this closing prophecy of salvation would be glib and unconvincing indeed.

Every word in the prophecy is heavy with associations: "the branch of the Lord" suggests an allusion to the Messiah, described as a "branch" in Jer. 23:5 and 33:15. Isaiah 11:1 contains similar language:

There shall come forth a shoot from the stump of Jesse,
  and a branch shall grow out of his roots.

But the actual term used (*tsemah*) does not appear in 11:1, and it can have the more general meaning of "plants, vegetation". The Lord will make things grow again: nature will come to life, imagery familiar to us from the Psalms (104:14; 147:8) and Isaianic passages about the desert blossoming like the rose (e.g. 35:1–2; 41:18–19; 51:3). There is a third layer of meaning which is perhaps worth considering. What springs out of the ground in several of the great Isaianic oracles is not just plants and trees but "salvation" and "righteousness":

'Shower, O heavens, from above,
  and let the skies rain down righteousness;
let the earth open, that salvation may sprout forth,
  and let it cause righteousness to spring up also;
I the Lord have created it." (45:8; cf. 61:11)

Against that background the present prophecy takes on a more profound meaning. The pictures of agricultural revival point to victory and religious renewal, which seem to be in the author's mind when he uses the words of the next few verses (glorious, holy, life, spirit, create). They can hardly refer to vegetation alone. Maybe the picture of a land flowing with milk and honey again contains all three aspects of restoration: victory and spiritual renewal; beautiful vegetation; and a new Davidic Messiah to lead the people.

Certainly "the survivors of Israel" will not be alone in a desolate landscape "like Sodom and Gomorrah" (1:9). They shall have something to be proud of. Perhaps these words about the survivors come from the fifth century B.C., the time when Nehemiah battled to get the city rebuilt and when the plight of "the remnant" is a frequent theme: read Ezra's prayer in Ezra chapter 9, for example. They were weak and vulnerable at the time, and the hopes of restored pride, dignity, holiness and divine protection expressed in the present prophecy would match that situation very closely.

"Everyone who has been recorded for life" is clearly derived from urban administration, in which citizens' names were listed for purposes of taxation as well as certain rights and privileges. In the present context the phrase "for life" ("enrolled in the book of life", NEB) adds another dimension to the registration metaphor, familiar to us from later apocalyptic writings such as the Book of Revelation chapters 5–8. This is the notion that the names of those who fear God and keep his commandments are recorded in a "Book of Life", while the names of those who do not are blotted out of that book. There are many references to this, the earliest of which is probably Exodus 32:32 in which Moses prays for forgiveness: ". . . and if not, blot me, I pray thee, out of thy book which thou hast written." Other examples are to be found in Dan. 12:1; Mal. 3:16; Luke 10:20. One of the standard greetings to this day on Jewish New Year cards is "May you be written in the book of life!", no doubt with the Day of Atonement (ten days after New Year's Day) in mind.

An essential component of this picture of the restored Jerusalem after the judgment is that she and her citizens be pronounced "holy". This key motif in Isaianic tradition, the connection between morality and holiness, points back to chapter 1 where it is achieved by *washing* away their sins, and forward to chapter 6 where the prophet's unclean lips are purified by the application of a *burning* coal. Again the "filth of the daughters of Zion" refers more to the corruption of the city as a whole than to her women in particular, whose immorality has nowhere been referred to; and the bloodstains of Jerusalem similarly no longer refer to the atrocities of Manasseh's reign alone (2 Kings 21:16), but to the sins and shortcomings of God's people as a whole.

The agent of divine intervention here, by which the people are to be cleansed, is described as "a spirit of judgment and a spirit of burning", images that point unmistakably to a representation of Judgment Day. Compare Isaiah 66:15–16:

"For behold, the Lord will come in fire,
  and his chariots like the stormwind,
To render his anger in fury,

and his rebuke with flames of fire.
For by fire will the Lord execute judgment..."

The final cleansing process will be painful: the "spirit of judgment" may be compared to the exterminating angel in Exodus 12 that went through the land destroying all the first-born of the Egyptians; and the "spirit of burning" may be explained as a blazing hot wind, sweeping through the land, biting into the flesh and removing scabs and deformities for ever.

The whole process amounts to a new creation: "Then the Lord will create..." (v.5). A similar view of forgiveness, in relation to a guilt-ridden individual, appears in Psalm 51:

Purge me with hyssop, and I shall be clean;
wash me and I shall be whiter than snow...
Create in me a clean heart, O God,
and put a new and a right spirit within me. (vv. 7,10)

It is also a New Exodus: led by a cloud by day and a pillar of smoke and a fire by night, the people will come once more into God's presence as they did in the wilderness (Exod. 13:21f.). The words for "site" and "assemblies" are rather unexpected: the first should perhaps mean simply "over every building on Mount Zion" (NEB) and the second recalls 1:13. In the new Jerusalem there will be a new kind of liturgy, in which everyone will take part and from which the hypocrisy that rendered it hateful to God in 1:13 will be finally removed. The resultant communion between God and his people is described as "glory", and like a bride and bridegroom, Jerusalem and her God rejoice beneath the bridal canopy (cf. 62:5). "It will be for a shade..." gives the canopy a different and more mundane function. A change of one letter in the Hebrew text, one that is supported by the ancient Greek translation of the Bible, would make God the subject and raise the verse to the level of Psalm 121:5–6: "And he will be a shade by day from the heat, and a refuge and a shelter from the storm and rain." The security of Jerusalem, forgiven and protected by her loving husband from all perils and dangers, is a moving climax to this glorious prophecy of salvation.

THE VINEYARD OF THE LORD OF HOSTS

Isaiah 5:1–7

[1]Let me sing for my beloved
    a love song concerning his vineyard:
My beloved had a vineyard
    on a very fertile hill.
[2]He digged it and cleared it of stones,
    and planted it with choice vines;
he built a watchtower in the midst of it,
    and hewed out a wine vat in it;
and he looked for it to yield grapes,
    but it yielded wild grapes.

[3]And now, O inhabitants of Jerusalem
    and men of Judah,
judge, I pray you, between me
    and my vineyard.
[4]What more was there to do for my vineyard,
    that I have not done in it?
When I looked for it to yield grapes,
    why did it yield wild grapes?

[5]And now I will tell you
    what I will do to my vineyard.
I will remove its hedge,
    and it shall be devoured;
I will break down its wall,
    and it shall be trampled down.
[6]I will make it a waste;
    it shall not be pruned or hoed,
    and briers and thorns shall grow up;
I will also command the clouds
    that they rain no rain upon it.

[7]For the vineyard of the Lord of hosts
    is the house of Israel,
and the men of Judah
    are his pleasant planting;
and he looked for justice,
    but behold, bloodshed;
for righteousness,
    but behold, a cry!

The celebrated parable of the vineyard introduces the next series of prophetic attacks on corrupt Jerusalem, comprising the whole of chapter 5. This, together with most of chapters 9 and 10, is taken up with judgment and warning: "Woe to those who..." (5:8,11,18; 10:1) and the refrain "For all this his anger is not turned away and his hand is outstretched still" (5:25; 9:12,17,21; 10:4). The autobiography in 6:1–9:7 places the whole sorry picture in the context of eighth-century political history, and makes it clear that divine judgment will come in the form of Assyrian invasions devastating the region in the last decades of that century.

Like other parts of the Book of Isaiah, however, the gloomy picture is alleviated by the insights and experiences of later generations: the fall of Assyria's capital Nineveh in 612 B.C., for instance, probably led to the addition of most of 10:12–34—"he will punish the arrogant boasting of the king of Assyria...". Still more powerful are the prophecies of a new age, when "the wolf shall dwell with the lamb..." (11:6), and a saviour of David's line will establish justice and peace to the ends of the earth. The seeds of such hope no doubt go back to Isaiah's own day and the ancient confidence in the power of Jerusalem and her God to survive; but much of it, like the picture of defeated Assyria, comes from a later age. Chapters 5–12, like 1–4, break away from their original eighth-century roots, and present a timeless blend of prophetic criticism on the one hand, and unforgettable hope for those in despair on the other: "With joy you will draw water from the wells of salvation" (12:3). Every age needs both.

The "love song" with which the parable begins is very short, being no more than a verse and a half (vv. 1b–2). It is not sung by the lover himself but by a friend of his, who comments on the whole course of events from the affection and passion of the beginning of the love affair to later disillusionment. The indignant lover himself then addresses the audience in his own vengeful words (vv. 3–6), and at the very end of the passage we are told that the lover is none other than the Lord of hosts, and his wayward mistress the people of Judah (v. 7). The rhetorical technique is the same as that used by the prophet Nathan when he confronted the guilty king David: there the punch line at the end of the parable is "Thou art the man" (2 Sam. 12:1–15). But there are two other parallels that help us to understand the force of Isaiah's poem. First, there is the love poetry of the Song of Solomon: there the bride is a garden (4:12), her neck like a watchtower (4:4; 7:4), her breasts like "clusters of grapes" (7:8) and her kisses sweeter than wine (7:9). The tender affectionate background of some of this language at the beginning of the passage makes the ending all the more cutting. Even more horrible is the implication of verses 5 and 6, which cannot but recall the poignant picture of humiliation at the end of chapter 3: the girl's fine clothes will be torn off her, she will be without protection and without dignity, raped and abandoned. The fate of Hosea's unfaithful wife, stripped, impoverished, starved and alone (Hosea 2) is another eighth-century B.C. example, although the allegorical double entendres in Isaiah's poem are subtler.

The other place to look for clues to the meaning of this passage is Isaiah 27:2–5 along with other examples of the application of the figure of the vineyard to Israel such as Jer. 2:21; 12:10–11; Ps. 80:8–18 and Matt. 21:33–41. The care and skill required over a very long period to build up a successful vineyard make it an excellent metaphor for God's care of Israel: "Thou didst bring a vine out of Egypt; thou didst drive out the nations and plant it" (Ps. 80:8). Constant hoeing, irrigation, pruning, building and repairing walls to keep out sheep, not to mention the whole process of building a wine vat and harvesting and pressing the grapes, all add up to a lot of work. Failure, whether due to the poor quality of the grapes produced (v. 2) or to destruction (v. 5) or neglect (v. 6a), or drought (v. 6b), was a major disaster which could not be put right for many years. "Briers and thorns" figure in many Isaianic descriptions of the destruction of Israel: e.g. "In that day every place where there used to be a thousand vines, worth a thousand shekels of silver, will become briers and thorns" (7:23; cf. v. 25; 32:13). In addition to their hostile presence, choking the vines, they are highly inflammable and also figure in pictures of colossal conflagrations (9:18; 10:17; 27:4).

If we were to look for detailed points of comparison in the allegory, as some of the ancient commentators did, then the "fertile hill" would of course be Mount Zion and the "watchtower" the Temple. According to v. 7 the vines are "the men of Judah", which prompts us to recognize in v. 2 the fruits by which they are known. The word translated "wild grapes" occurs only here and probably refers to bitterness. Perhaps the idea is that the authority of the "men of Judah", which should have brought peace and hope to the country, instead turned "justice to wormwood [the bitterest of all herbs] and cast down righteousness to the earth" (Amos 5:7). Finally, it is not hard to recognize the symptoms of enemy invasion in verse 5–6: first the destruction of the surrounding countryside, then the breaching of the walls of Jerusalem herself. The scene of devastation, neglect and barrenness is rounded off with the ever-present natural threat of drought.

We seem to have come a long way from the scene with which we began this section, with love songs and allegories. The last verse reminds us that we are still moving in the same circles. Verse 7 first explains the meaning of the preceding allegory, as we saw, and then sums up the theme of the whole passage in two word plays:

> . . . he looked for justice [*mishpat*],
>   but behold, bloodshed [*mishpak*];
> for righteousness [*tsedaka*],
>   but behold, a cry for help [*tse'aka*]!

Word plays, allegories, artificial love songs and the like, these are the stock-in-trade of the prophets, and remind us once more that we are dealing with literary craftsmen of the highest order, familiar with a whole variety of rhetorical techniques, trained in the art of getting their message across in such a way as to make it clear, convincing, arresting and memorable.

As well as the love song style and the allegory of Israel as "the vineyard of the Lord of hosts", there is also an argument going on here, almost as though set in a court of law: "And now . . . judge, I pray you, between me and my vineyard" (v. 3). There is nothing flippant or frivolous about the choice of literary techniques here;

the audience stand condemned, accused of injustice and oppression. They have no excuse; they have had every privilege; judgment is now inevitable. In the words of Jesus, "the true vine": "If a man does not abide in me, he is cast forth as a branch and withers; and the branches are gathered, thrown into the fire and burned" (John 15:6).

THE SEVEN WOES—I

Isaiah 5:8–25

8Woe to those who join house to house,
  who add field to field,
until there is no more room,
  and you are made to dwell alone
  in the midst of the land.
9The Lord of hosts has sworn in my hearing:
  "Surely many houses shall be desolate,
  large and beautiful houses, without inhabitant.
10For ten acres of vineyard shall yield but one bath,
  and a homer of seed shall yield but an ephah."

11Woe to those who rise early in the morning,
  that they may run after strong drink,
who tarry late into the evening
  till wine inflames them!
12They have lyre and harp,
  timbrel and flute and wine at their feasts;
but they do not regard the deeds of the Lord,
  or see the work of his hands.

13Therefore my people go into exile
  for want of knowledge;
their honoured men are dying of hunger,
  and their multitude is parched with thirst.
14Therefore Sheol has enlarged its appetite
  and opened its mouth beyond measure,
and the nobility of Jerusalem and her multitude go down,
  her throng and he who exults in her.
15Man is bowed down, and men are brought low,

and the eyes of the haughty are humbled.
¹⁶But the Lord of hosts is exalted in justice,
    and the Holy God shows himself holy in righteousness.
¹⁷Then shall the lambs graze as in their pasture,
    fatlings and kids shall feed among the ruins.

¹⁸Woe to those who draw iniquity with cords of falsehood,
    who draw sin as with cart ropes,
¹⁹who say: "Let him make haste,
    let him speed his work
    that we may see it;
  let the purpose of the Holy One of Israel draw near,
    and let it come, that we may know it!"
²⁰Woe to those who call evil good
    and good evil,
  who put darkness for light
    and light for darkness,
  who put bitter for sweet
    and sweet for bitter!
²¹Woe to those who are wise in their own eyes,
    and shrewd in their own sight!
²²Woe to those who are heroes at drinking wine,
    and valiant men in mixing strong drink,
²³who acquit the guilty for a bribe,
    and deprive the innocent of his right!

²⁴Therefore, as the tongue of fire devours the stubble,
    and as dry grass sinks down in the flame,
  so their root will be as rottenness,
    and their blossom go up like dust;
  for they have rejected the law of the Lord of hosts,
    and have despised the word of the Holy One of Israel.
²⁵Therefore the anger of the Lord was kindled against his people,
    and he stretched out his hand against them and smote them,
    and the mountains quaked;
  and their corpses were as refuse
    in the midst of the streets.
  For all this his anger is not turned away
    and his hand is stretched out still.

Following on from the biting words of the prologue (vv. 1–7), Isaiah begins a series of seven "Woe-sayings" in which the sins of "the men of Judah" are itemized. The series is, however, divided by the insertion of the autobiography in chapters 6–9 (v. 7) and some other prophecies of doom in 9:8ff., so that the first six sayings are in the present chapter, while the seventh, clearly linked to the others by its refrain, does not appear until chapter 10:1–4.

The shape of these "Woe-sayings" is straightforward enough: they begin "Woe to those who . . ." or "Woe to you who . . ." (Amos 5:18), and end with a description of judgment. Some examples consist of only the first part (vv. 18–21), while others contain some form of expansion like the additional judgment section in verses 14–17. But there is some controversy about their origin. According to some they come from the context of funeral laments: the "Woe" is a cry of mourners as they lament the passing of the deceased. In other words, the villains listed in these passages are as good as dead, like Jerusalem in the "faithful city" lament (1:21ff.), and the prophet's words have sinister undertones designed to make maximum impact on their audience. "Woe" is not a regular element in funeral laments, however, and a more likely explanation of its origin is to be found in some kind of primitive incantation or curse. We must remember that prophets, however sophisticated their literary skill and however profound their theological insight, were at the same time visionaries and soothsayers, claiming supernatural powers of all kinds, and if that is so, then it would be natural to find in their legacy to us evidence for the skill of those "whose magic binds even the monster of the deep, who are ready to tame Leviathan himself with spells" (Job 3:8, NEB).

Before we look at the first "Woe" in detail, there is another general remark that applies to them all. Whatever their origin, at funerals or in incantation rites, their content suggests some connection with the Wisdom literature. Prophetic attacks on excessive drinking, for example here (vv. 11–12) and in Amos (6:1–7), have close parallels only in Proverbs (23:19–21) and Ecclesiastes (10:16–17). Acquiring land and property, whether by moving a

neighbour's landmark (Prov. 22:28; 23:10f.) or by manipulating
the legal system (Isa. 10:1) is another example, as is the sin of
relying wholly upon human wisdom and resourcefulness (v. 21),
when true wisdom is to be found in "fearing God and keeping his
commandments" (cf. Prov. 1:7; 9:10; Ecc. 12:13; Job 1:1; 28:28;
Ecclesiasticus 1:1–30). Perhaps "Woe to ... " is the negative
form of "Happy is the man who ... ", so familiar from the "beati-
tudes" in both the Old Testament and the New (e.g. Job 5:17;
Pss. 1:1; 32:1–2; 119:1,2;128:1; Prov. 3:13; 8:32,34; Ecc. 10:17;
Ecclesiasticus 14:1–2; Matt. 5:3–11). Luke 6:20–26 certainly
puts the two side by side. It looks very much as if the intellectual
background of the prophets was not so very different from that of
the authors of the Wisdom literature—indeed, in all probability
prophets went to the same schools as the "wise men".

The first "Woe" (vv. 8–10) deals with land possession, a subject of enormous importance in ancient Israel, both socially and
theologically. "Joining house to house" refers to building pro-
jects whereby wealthy landowners expand their property with the
inevitable consequence that the poor are squeezed out. "Adding
field to field" refers to the acquisition of more and more land,
whether by legal or illegal means. The story of Naboth's vineyard
(1 Kings 21) provides a telling illustration of the kind of development attacked here. King Ahab tried first to acquire his neighbour's vineyard by honest means, but when that failed, he
resorted to violence to get it. He had the wretched Naboth stoned
to death on a trumped-up charge of *lèse-majesté*, and simply took
possession of the deceased's vineyard. The key issue in that story,
and in many other Biblical passages about land possession, is that
the land was Naboth's by ancestral right: "The Lord forbid that I
should give you the inheritance of my fathers" (21:13). The same
applies to the two passages from Proverbs already alluded to
(22:28; 23:10–11): "Remove not the ancient landmark which
your fathers have set." Laws in the Pentateuch trace the basis of
land ownership back to an even more fundamental principle:
God himself is the real owner of the land. He gave it to Israel,
allocating it to each of the tribes (Josh. 13–19), in accordance with
the promise to Abraham and his seed for ever (Gen. 15:18–21;

Exod. 6:8; Deut. 1:8). So the preceding parable of the vineyard is very much in mind here. This is God's land, given into your safe keeping: so woe to those who misuse it!

The other point to remember in this first "Woe" is that land, and by analogy all other property, is shared, and if it finds its way into the hands of one individual or one social class, there is something very wrong with society. Biblical legislation insists that landowners must honour certain obligations to the poor, "the widow and the orphan and the stranger that is within your gates". For example, the land at the edge of their fields was to be left unreaped or unharvested for the poor to enjoy (Lev. 19:9–10; 23:22; cf. Deut. 24:19–21). "Joining field to field" can be taken to mean cutting the edges down to a minimum, thus leaving as little as possible for the poor. The result of this acquisitive behaviour on the part of the rich in Isaiah's day is that "there is no more room", and the only people living in the land are wealthy land-owners. The precious land of Israel, the promised land, has to be shared. It belongs as much to the poor as to the rich, because in the last analysis it belongs not to man, but to God: "the land is mine; for you are strangers and sojourners with me" (Lev. 25:23).

Verses 9–10 contain the second part of the "Woe-saying" in which the imminent fate of the accused is described. Verse 9 alludes to the prophet's experience of divine revelation: he has heard "with his own ears", like Paul (2 Cor. 12:1–4) or Elijah (1 Kings 19:13), the voice of the Lord of hosts. What he heard him say was that he promises that those magnificent new houses will not flourish, and the newly-acquired land will yield very little. The measurements in the first half of verse 10 simply mean that a huge vineyard will produce only a small amount of wine (a bath is one tenth of a homer, and roughly equivalent to five gallons). The point about the quantities in the second half of the verse is that, while normally, in the nature of things, seed yields far more than its own bulk, here the yield is far less, since an ephah (like a bath) is one tenth of a homer. Without taking the figures too literally, the verses make it clear that there is no chance that the greedy property-owners will enjoy their ill-gotten gains.

THE SEVEN WOES—II

Isaiah 5:8–25 (cont'd)

The second "Woe-saying" is the longest: two verses describe the crimes of the accused (vv. 11–12), and the judgment that awaits them takes up the next five verses (vv. 13–17). Like the first "Woe", this one attacks people's misuse of the "Lord's vineyard", harking back once more to the opening parable of the chapter. In this case it is the misuse of the fruit of the vine that is attacked, as it is in a number of passages in the Wisdom literature: e.g.

Who has woe? Who has sorrow?
  Who has strife? Who has complaining?
Who has wounds without cause?
  Who has redness of the eyes?
Those who tarry long over wine...
At the last it bites like a serpent,
  and stings like an adder.
Your eyes will see strange things... (Prov. 23:29–35)

Instead of wine being innocently used to "gladden the heart of man" (Ps. 104:15), or as a source of income which could improve the lot of all Jerusalem's citizens, not just the privileged few, it was interfering with the running of the country.

If greed is the first deadly sin in this list (v. 8), then the second is sloth. Ecclesiastes ends his attack on drunkenness with the proverb:

Through sloth the roof sinks in,
  and through indolence the house leaks. (10:18)

For the prophets, drunkenness came to be associated with the affluent aristocracy, a symbol of decadence and the misuse of public funds. This is no teetotaller's abhorrence of alcohol in general, but yet another assault on the corruption of Judah's leaders.

Their crimes are summed up in the second half of verse 12:

.. they do not regard the deeds of the Lord,
  or see the work of his hands.

Some commentators assume that this refers to those mighty acts of divine intervention by which God punishes the wicked. But the words used here do not have such a meaning, and in any case, how could the wicked "regard the deeds of the Lord" if they had not yet happened? Judgment is still in the future. It is more likely that these expressions refer to the acts of God, creator of all things in heaven and earth—including the vineyard they are ruining and the wine they are squandering. The age-old Jewish blessing over wine points in this direction: "Blessed art thou O Lord, our God, King of the Universe, who created the fruit of the vine!"

There is another point here: God is also the creator of the poor and needy, not just the rich. As Job, the Bible's wealthiest aristocrat, puts it: "Did not he who made me in the womb make him [his servant]?" (Job. 31:15). There is a proverb that links this idea with one's obligations towards the poor: "He who mocks the poor insults his Maker" (Prov. 17:5). So in 5:12 Isaiah seems to be condemning his rich audience for their arrogant disregard of human rights. They do not understand that, in misusing the fruit of the land and oppressing the poor, they are "insulting the creator" and will have to pay the penalty.

Verses 13–17 describe the judgment that awaits them. The land is still at the centre of the picture which is presented in two parts, the second (vv. 14–17) probably an expansion and explanation of the first. The people will be thrown out of their land, deprived of its rich produce. In place of feasting and drunkenness, there will be starvation and death; in place of proud affluence and prosperity, there will be degradation and ruin. Finally, cleared of corruption and oppression, the land will be filled with justice and holiness, and God's people will live in peace and security like lambs grazing in their pasture, a lovely scene alluded to again in chapter 40:

> He will feed his flock like a shepherd,
>   he will gather the lambs in his arms . . .
>   and gently lead those that are with young. (40:11)

"My people" in verse 13, like "my vineyard" in verses 3–5,

expresses the pathos of a situation in which God punishes the one he loves, as well as the scandal that God's own people should behave in such a way. Their "want of knowledge" comes straight out of the same proverbial context as much as the rest of this chapter, for "the fear of the Lord is the beginning of knowledge" (Prov. 1:7). The details of enemy invasion—siege conditions, devastation of the land, deportation of the leaders—are familiar from all the eighth-century prophets, whether pointing to what has happened already in neighbouring cities, or interpreting, in retrospect, what had happened in Judah as an awful act of divine intervention. "Honoured men ... multitude" nicely sums up the two aspects of Judah's affluence the citizens were most proud of, their rich splendour and dignity on the one hand, their strength in numbers on the other—both swept away in a moment by the Lord of history.

"Sheol" is the Hebrew word for the abode of the dead, a place where the dead continue to exist in a shadowy, colourless state, cut off from God. Two Isaianic passages will fill in some of the details: chapter 14 describes the arrival of the deceased king of Babylon in Sheol, taunted by the shades; and Hezekiah gratefully contrasts his escape from death with the fate of "those who go down to the pit" (38:17–18): "For Sheol cannot thank thee, death cannot praise thee". Here Sheol, or "hell" as the older English versions usually translated it, is personified as a giant or a monster with an insatiable appetite. Again this is proverbial as Habakkuk 2:5 shows:

> the arrogant man shall not abide.
> His greed is as wide as Sheol;
> like death he never has enough. (cf. Prov. 30:16)

There is a graphic parallel in the ancient Canaanite myths from Ras Shamra (Ugarit) too: "As Death has jaws touching earth, lips reaching to the sky and a tongue touching the stars, Baal will enter his stomach, going down through his mouth, as one swallows an olive ... "

Verse 15 takes up a theme elaborately developed in 2:6–22. Verse 16 is a majestic example of that leap of faith whereby the destruction of Jerusalem and the devastation of the promised land by enemy invasion is not seen as a defeat for Israel's God, but on the contrary a mighty act of divine intervention, in which the justice and holiness of the Holy One of Israel are displayed for all to see. What inspired this leap of faith, and when it took place in the heart of precisely whom—Isaiah himself or a later, even exilic writer—we cannot always know for sure. But the texts are filled to the brim with it, and as readers we are called to share in it today.

"The Lord of hosts" is the creator of heaven and earth; and justice is what he demands of his people, a just society, a just world. Holiness refers to moral and spiritual purity, not only ritual. "Righteousness", as we have seen already, is no abstraction: it means a "righteous act" and is one of many "righteous acts" or "triumphs" (Judg. 5:11), in which "the Holy One of Israel" transforms history into a means of divine revelation for "those who have eyes to see and ears to hear". Surely in such a context verse 17 does not refer to depopulated ruins as in Lamentations 5:17–18, where the subject is jackals, not lambs, but to a scene of restored peace and justice, where the underprivileged and vulnerable members of society are freed from oppression and live, for the first time, as in their own land.

The second half of the verse is difficult: the word rendered "fatlings" occurs only here and in Psalm 66:15; while "kids" are not mentioned in the Hebrew text at all. All we can say for sure is that somebody "shall feed among the ruins", and it is not hard to see here a continuation of the picture of restored righteousness, in which innocent victims of oppression can once more move freely about their own land. Chapter 32:16–20 is an illuminating variation on the same theme:

> Then justice will dwell in the wilderness,
>   and righteousness abide in the fruitful field.

THE SEVEN WOES—III

Isaiah 5:8–25 (*cont'd*)

There then follow four short "Woe-sayings" followed by a single judgment (vv. 24–25), intended as a warning to all four categories of sinner. Verses 18–19 (the third in the series of seven) are addressed to inveterate criminals, recidivists, who cannot escape from their evil habits, just as though they were harnessed to their crimes as a beast of burden is to its load. "Iniquity" (Hebrew *avon*) can include the consequence of sin, as well as sin itself, and thus the prophet may be referring to the inevitability of punishment as well. "Cords of falsehood" has sparked off some discussion and it has become quite common to emend the word "falsehood" (*shaw*) to "sheep" (*seh*) or the like (cf. NEB, Jerusalem Bible), and with it "cart ropes" to "a heifer on a rope" (NEB). The meaning of the text as it stands, however, is subtler: "cords of falsehood" means "deceptively thin cords", like a spider's web, and refers to the first stage in a progression. "I'll do it just this once", says the sinner—and that is how it starts. Soon he cannot stop himself, and the slender thread that tempted him into sin initially has become a "cart rope" binding him inextricably to his wicked habits and their consequences.

Verse 19 is about tempting providence. The "work" and the "purpose of the Holy One of Israel" are speeding towards their fulfilment, but they do not believe it. Another prophet, confronted by people saying, "The days grow long, and every vision comes to naught", tells them, "In your days, O rebellious house, I will speak the word and perform it, says the Lord God" (Ezek. 12:21–28). This was exactly what Isaiah meant: "Woe to those who continue to doubt God's word!" Their mocking tone, taunting the Holy One of Israel, challenging him to act, has a hollow ring to it in the present context, between the scenes of humiliation in the preceding verses, and the judgment of fire and earthquake at the end of this group of "Woes".

The fourth "Woe" (v. 20) is about the topsyturviness of society: the wicked prosper at the expense of the innocent, and the legal processes are used to smother victims of oppression instead of helping them. In the words of another eighth-century prophet:

Grace Church Library
Pottstown, Pennsylvania

But you have turned justice into poison
    and the fruit of righteousness into wormwood ... (Amos 6:12)

Blatant dishonesty and deceit bring prosperity and contentment
to the ruling class, but dark despair and bitter suffering to everyone else. The sufferings of the Hebrews in Egypt were no harsher
(Exod. 1:13–14).

The fifth "Woe" (v. 21) attacks "those who are wise in their
own eyes". True "wisdom", as we have had occasion to point out
more than once, must include "fearing God and keeping his
commandments" (see on 5:8). Of course it includes practical
wisdom, sagacity, prudence and resourcefulness as well, but
these must be leavened with "the fear of God". Proverbs 1:1–7
makes this clear and sets the tone of the whole book; the apocryphal book of Ecclesiasticus begins in the same way (chapter 1).
The opposition between the prophetic "word of the Lord" and
the politicians' "wisdom" (2 Sam. 16:23; 1 Kings 3–4) hinges on
this. To quote another proverb, this time from the Psalms: "Except the Lord build the house, they labour in vain that build it"
(127:1, AV). Elsewhere Isaiah criticizes the politicians for giving
the king wrong advice on negotiations with Egypt (31) and Assyria (7; cf. 2 Kings 16), for example, but here the subject is once
more arrogance, the refusal to "regard the deeds of the Lord" (v.
12) together with mocking disbelief (v. 19). The positive corollary
of this "Woe" is to be found in Prov. 3:5–8.

The sixth "Woe" (vv. 22–23) turns to corruption in the law-
court. The first half takes up the vineyard theme again in order to
represent the judges as weak-minded, undisciplined creatures
whose strengths and virtues go no further than holding their
liquor and mixing cocktails. In situations where real strength of
character is needed, to refuse bribes or to defend human rights,
they are miserable and culpable failures.

The judgment is again, as in verses 13–17, divided into two
parts, each introduced by a conventional "Therefore ... " The
first part (v. 24) describes the fate of the wicked in two images,
burning like stubble or a hayfield, and decaying like the root or
the blossom of a plant. This keeps up the imagery of the vineyard

of the Lord of hosts and his "pleasant planting" with which the section began. If chapters 1–4 centre on the city of Jerusalem, chapter 5 is about the land of Judah, the corruption within it and the fate that awaits it. The somewhat prosaic explanation inserted after these colourful pictures, referring to the rejection of "the law of the Lord of hosts" and "the word of the Holy One of Israel", adds little to what has been said already in the chapter, except perhaps to sum up the catalogue of vices—greed, sloth, pride and the rest—by pointing out that they are all forbidden in the law of the Lord of hosts, and by his servants the prophets. This will be the fate of all who reject the teaching of the prophets. Indeed, if we can take the next verse into account at the same time, the anger of the Lord of hosts has already struck.

It is usually assumed that a new image makes its appearance in verse 25, perhaps inspired by the writer's own experience: an earthquake, leaving a scene of death and destruction in its wake, hardly dissimilar to the aftermath of a devastating enemy invasion, the more usual manifestation of God's wrath in eighth-century prophecy. True, there is a reference to an earthquake in Amos 4:11 (cf. 1:1). But "quaking mountains" can have quite a different meaning as we saw in chapter 2; there the cedars of Lebanon, high mountains, lofty towers and stately ships stand for the proud and haughty leaders of Jerusalem. Is the present verse not another example of the same? It is people that are being struck by the hand of God, not mountains: he "smote them [his people], and the mountains quaked; and their corpses were as refuse in the midst of the streets." Is there room for an earthquake there? Surely the verse is about the downfall of Judah's leaders, a moment ago as safe as mountains, suddenly reduced to quivering wrecks, and then ruthlessly slaughtered.

The mention of "streets" in verse 25 is an indication that this verse belongs more to the Jerusalem-centred prophecies of chapters 2–4 than the present chapter which focuses on the land, from the vineyard at the beginning to the darkened land at the end (vv. 26–30).

Verse 25 ends with a refrain ("For all this . . . ") that also links this prophecy with a series of four prophecies (9:8–12, 13–17,

18–21; 10: 1–4) that come immediately after the autobiographical section 6:1–9:7. One of these (10:1–4) is the last of the seven "Woes" we have been considering. The purpose of these four prophecies is to point to recent military and political disasters in neighbouring states, notably Syria and Ephraim (the Northern Kingdom of Israel), and warn the people of Jerusalem and Judah that the same fate awaits them if they persist in their evil ways. The very next passage in chapter 5 (vv. 26–30) introduces the invading force which is (under Israel's God) the cause of these disasters.

THE LAND DARKENED BY INVADING ARMIES

Isaiah 5:26–30

> [26]He will raise a signal for a nation afar off,
>   and whistle for it from the ends of the earth;
>   and lo, swiftly, speedily it comes!
> [27]None is weary, none stumbles,
>   none slumbers or sleeps,
>   not a waistcloth is loose,
>   not a sandal-thong broken;
> [28]their arrows are sharp,
>   all their bows bent,
>   their horses' hoofs seem like flint,
>   and their wheels like the whirlwind.
> [29]Their roaring is like a lion,
>   like young lions they roar;
>   they growl and seize their prey,
>   they carry it off, and none can rescue.
> [30]They will growl over it on that day,
>   like the roaring of the sea.
>   And if one look to the land,
>   behold, darkness and distress;
>   and the light is darkened by its clouds.

Verses 26–30 contain the first of several graphic, urgent descriptions of an approaching enemy army: 7:18–25 and 10:27b–32 are two more examples. The little Book of Habakkuk begins with another (1:5–11), and descriptions of the fall of Nineveh in the

Book of Nahum contain several more. This one has two functions in its present context. On the one hand, it concludes the prophecies about the land. As we have seen, chapter 5 begins with the parable of the vineyard, and then, in the "Woe-sayings", various examples of the misuse of the land are picked upon, while a number of agricultural and pastoral images keep up the metaphor. Thus enemy invasion, together with the images of young lions seizing their prey and dark clouds gathering overhead, provides a fitting and awe-inspiring climax. On the other hand, the invasion passage clearly also points forward to the historical narrative in 6:1–9:7. It is in effect a powerful preface to the sequence of events described in the next three and a half chapters, beginning "In the year that King Uzziah died" (6:1) and ending with allusions to the invasions of Tiglath-Pileser III, king of Assyria (9:1), and perhaps the coronation of Hezekiah in 725 B.C. (9:2–7).

It is likely, but not by any means certain, that the author was originally thinking of the Assyrian armies, perhaps even drawing on eye-witness reports from the north. But in this particular passage there are no details that tie the description specifically to the Assyrians, and indeed it would be wrong to restrict it to them. The texts as we have them come from a later period, and summon us to interpret them in a wider context. Jeremiah's descriptions of an approaching army (see chs. 4–6) have some very similar details in them, and they originally referred to the Babylonians; while a later Isaianic prophecy uses similar imagery to describe the approach of the chariots of the Lord:

"For behold, the Lord will come in fire,
    and his chariots like the storm-wind..." (66:15)

In each case the point is the same: God is going to intervene in Israel's history, either by manipulating the armies of the world's great imperial powers, or by appearing himself in some miraculous, apocalyptic event. Whatever the original meaning of such passages, in their present context they speak of confrontation between man and God and of man's ultimate responsibility before his Maker.

The invasion starts with a signal from God. Just as "by the word of the Lord the heavens were created" (Ps. 33:6), so military leaders like Tiglath-Pileser III, Nebuchadnezzar, king of the Chaldeans (2 Chron. 36:17) and Cyrus, king of the Medes and Persians (Ezra 1:1; cf. Isaiah 45:1ff.), act on his command. Whatever happens, throughout all creation, is under God's control—a theme to which we shall return:

> I make the light, I create darkness,
>   author alike of prosperity and trouble.
> I, the Lord, do all these things. (Isa. 45:7, NEB)

"Raising a signal" refers to some kind of flag: the word is used of a pole raised high for all to see (Num. 21:8) as well as of a sail or a pennant on the mast of a ship (Isa. 33:23).

"A nation afar off" (RSV) is not what the Hebrew text has. The Hebrew word is plural—"the nations from far" (AV)—and suggests the kind of apocalyptic battle envisaged by Ezekiel (chs. 38–39). Perhaps the original text had a singular word, referring to Assyria alone, and a later scribe, influenced by ideas discussed above, opened the prophecy out by making it plural. Others have suggested that the plural is original, but referred to the many nations that joined forces under the Assyrian flag, as in 14:26, 29:7 and elsewhere. "Whistling" compares God's authority over the massed armies of Assyria to a man's effortless control of his dog, or, if we take into account 7:18, his bees.

Verses 27–28 depict the army under God's command as strong, well-disciplined and devastatingly efficient: they are all physically fit, no one ever falls asleep on guard-duty, their dress and equipment are in immaculate condition. Like "the nations" in verse 26, the horses' hooves and whirring chariot wheels in verse 28 stretch historical realism to its limits and remind us we are reading a description of divine intervention, not just military history. Isaiah 66:15–16 is thus a more illuminating parallel than 2 Kings 15:29.

Three vivid images round off the picture of impending doom: the roaring of lions, the thunder of waves, and a darkened sky. It is not difficult to connect these images with scenes of war: the sounds of a huge army on the move, blood-curdling war-cries, brutality, looting, pillaging, wave upon wave of irresistible forces pounding the walls of a city, the sky blackened with the dark smoke from burning fields and houses. The Assyrian armies in particular had a name for ruthlessness and deadly efficiency. But in the Old Testament prophetic tradition, these images suggest a still more terrifying reality, transcending human power. In Amos, for example, the image of a roaring lion occurs more than once. Again it can apply to enemy invasion (3:12), but 1:2 makes clear what is really at stake: "The Lord roars from Zion, and utters his voice from Jerusalem". It is the Lord who is the real subject of the passage. The mighty waves of the sea are also at his beck and call to punish and to destroy. Whether he chooses to use an invading army or a storm at sea or an earthquake, it is the same God who confronts the wicked.

Darkness over the land points to the fate of the Egyptians in the Exodus (Exod. 10:21–23; cf. Wisdom of Solomon 17:14–21) and to the ultimate confrontation between God and man on Calvary (Luke 23:44–45)—not only to military invasions (8:22). Although for the eighth-century prophets, terror, defeat and darkness were manifested in the relentless advance of the Assyrian armies, their language transcends those historical circumstances and points to principalities and powers, subdued by God's creative word in Genesis, but released from time to time to remind us of the depths to which human nature can descend and the power of a just God to intervene on behalf of the oppressed.

A VISION OF GOD'S HEAVENLY COURT—I

Isaiah 6:1–8

[1]In the year that King Uzziah died I saw the Lord sitting upon a throne, high and lifted up; and his train filled the temple. [2]Above him stood the seraphim; each had six wings: with two he covered his face, and with two he covered his feet, and with two he flew.
[3]And one called to another and said:
  "Holy, holy, holy is the Lord of hosts;
  the whole earth is full of his glory."

⁴And the foundations of the thresholds shook at the voice of him who called, and the house was filled with smoke. ⁵And I said: "Woe is me! For I am lost; for I am a man of unclean lips, and I dwell in the midst of a people of unclean lips; for my eyes have seen the King, the Lord of hosts!"

⁶Then flew one of the seraphim to me, having in his hand a burning coal which he had taken with tongs from the altar. ⁷And he touched my mouth, and said: "Behold, this has touched your lips; your guilt is taken away, and your sin forgiven." ⁸And I heard the voice of the Lord saying, "Whom shall I send, and who will go for us?" Then I said, "Here am I! Send me."

In chapter 6 we have the earliest dated incident in the prophet's life and it is usually assumed that it refers to his call. But the question immediately arises as to why the account does not appear, as is the case with Jeremiah and Ezekiel, at the beginning of the book. One explanation is that it is an integral part of the historical narrative 6:1–9:7 which, for reasons already discussed, has been inserted into the series of "Woe-sayings" and other prophecies that run from 5:8 to 10:4. The theme of this narrative is confrontation between prophet and king, the tension between faith in God and political expediency that characterized the first period of Assyrian advance into Israel, and expands on the judgment motif of enemy invasion implied throughout the five preceding chapters. Another explanation might be that the first five chapters are intended to provide background for the vision in chapter 6, to give us an idea of what is meant by "a people of unclean lips" in verse 5. It was in a land corrupted by greed, arrogance, drunkenness, injustice, oppression and murder that Isaiah was to preach, to a people whose "speech and deeds are against the Lord, defying his glorious presence" (3:8).

But there is another point worth noting on the arrangement of the material in these chapters. According to the heading in 1:1, the prophet's visions began before the death of King Uzziah. In other words, if we take the text at face value, then chapters 1–5 come from the days of Uzziah (787–736 B.C.)—hence the many parallels with Amos and Hosea; chapter 6 begins a section of material from the reign of his successor Ahaz (736–725 B.C.); and other chapters again (see 36:1) come from the reign of his successor Hezekiah (725–697 B.C.). The apparent inconsistency between 1:1 and 6:1 can be very simply resolved if we accept that Isaiah's vision of the heavenly court is not his first experience of God, but one of many "which he saw concerning Judah and Jerusalem in the days of Uzziah, Jotham, Ahaz, and Hezekiah, kings of Judah" (1:1).

It is natural to assume that "the year that King Uzziah died", probably 736 B.C., was a turning point in the life and experience of the prophet, since it represents a turning point in the history of Israel. In the first place, it marks the end of a long and prosperous reign, associated with military successes, impressive building operations, agricultural advances—"for he loved the soil" (2 Chron. 26:6–15). The year of Uzziah's death also marked the beginning of the Assyrian threat, which hung over Israel and Judah for the rest of the century (2 Kings 15:17–31—Uzziah is sometimes called Azariah). As early as 738 we hear of the first campaigns of Tiglath-Pileser III (744–727 B.C.) into Syria and Lebanon, and by 736 he had annexed Gilead and Galilee (2 Kings 15:29). For the prophet, of course, Uzziah's long reign represented a time of decadence, and Tiglath-Pileser was the stick with which the Lord of hosts was going to punish them (10:5). News of the approaching threat of Assyrian invasion was thus one of the frightening factors in the situation that sparked off his visionary experience described in chapter 6. Maybe another factor in the prophet's terror in the Temple "in the year that King Uzziah died" was the familiar story of how Uzziah became a leper; for it was in the Temple, before that same altar of incense, that "leprosy broke out on his forehead" (2 Chron. 26:16–21). The holiness that made Uzziah a leper can kill and maim; Isaiah discovered it could also cleanse and forgive (6:7).

In the first two verses of the chapter, however, there is no specific mention of the Temple: the word translated "temple" in most English versions (*hekal*) often means "palace", and the scene, wherever it is set, is one of royal majesty. Psalm 11:4 is an illuminating parallel: "The Lord is in his holy temple, the Lord's throne is in heaven". Later verses suggest that the prophet was in the Temple at the time of this vision, but what he saw was the majesty and holiness of a heavenly palace. This is one of many such descriptions in which a visionary gets a glimpse "behind the scenes", as it were, where he sees God administering the affairs of men, instructing his angelic attendants, discussing individual cases like Job (Job 1:6–12; 2:1–6) or Ahab (1 Kings 22:19–23). In this case he overhears the singing of the seraphim, and a snatch of dialogue, and is moved to interrupt them (v. 8). It all sounds very much like the experience of Paul: "a man in Christ . . . was caught up to the third heaven—whether in the body or out of the body I do not know . . . and he heard things that cannot be told, which man may not utter" (2 Cor. 12:1–4). The Apocalypse of John of Patmos is a prophecy of the same type (Rev. 1:3; 22:19). Isaiah 40 is another example, based on chapter 6, which we shall examine later. Here the prophet's feet were in the Temple at Jerusalem, but in his spirit he was lifted, like Ezekiel, Enoch, Muhammad and many other visionaries into "the council of the Lord" (Jer. 23:18–22), where he "saw the Lord, seated upon a throne, high and lifted up".

His attendants are described as "seraphim", flying above him. How many there were and what they looked like is not stated. The name *seraph* suggests in Hebrew some association with "burning", and fire is a common motif in such descriptions, not only here (vv. 6–7), but elsewhere as in Ezekiel 1 (vv. 4, 13, 27) and 2 Kings 6:17. There does not seem any need to suppose that the fiery serpents in Numbers 21 and Isaiah 14:29, which are instruments of destruction and without any human characteristics, have anything to do with the seraphim here. What are being described are winged attendants in a vision of "things that cannot be told". Perhaps, like the cherubim guarding the entrance to the garden of Eden (Gen. 3:24), some of them carried in their hands flaming swords, or, perhaps more likely, their six wings were made of flames. That is how they are often represented in art. Apart from their wings they have faces, which have to be shielded from the dazzling brightness of God's glory, loins modestly covered by a second pair of wings ("feet" is a euphemism in Hebrew: as in Judg. 3:24 which reads literally "covers his feet"; see AV), hands with which one of them lifts the burning coal from the altar (v. 6), and voices that sing God's praises and speak the words of forgiveness to the prophet (v. 7). We shall hear their voices again at the beginning of chapter 40, and four six-winged creatures appear round the heavenly throne in Revelation 4. But apart from a few references in apocryphal writings, the seraphim are nowhere else mentioned by name in Biblical tradition.

A VISION OF GOD'S HEAVENLY COURT—II

Isaiah 6:1–8 (*cont'd*)

The short hymn sung by the seraphim is one of the most familiar in both Jewish and Christian liturgical tradition: "Holy, holy, holy is the Lord of hosts . . ." It is sung daily as part of the Jewish Morning Service, and in Christian worship it appears, with variations, at the heart of the Prayer of Consecration at Holy Communion. It is known as the "Sanctus" (Latin for "holy"), or "Trisagion" (Greek for "thrice holy") in Christian parlance, and "Kedushah" (Hebrew for "holy") in Jewish. Its liturgical role goes right back to its first appearances in the Bible, both here in Isaiah 6 where the seraphim are singing it antiphonally ("one called to another"), and in Revelation 4 where it is being sung ceaselessly by various creatures who "fall down before him who is seated on the throne . . ." (4:10).

It was natural for Christians to recognize in this solemn hymn a reference to the Trinity. Bishop Heber's famous Trinity Sunday hymn is a good example:

> Holy, holy, holy, Lord God Almighty!
>> All thy works shall praise thy Name, in earth and sky and sea;
> Holy, holy, holy, merciful and mighty,
>> God in Three Persons, blessèd Trinity!

Jewish commentators explain the threefold repetition of the word "holy" as a reference to the manifestation of God's holiness (1) in heaven, (2) in this world and (3) in the world to come—an idea partially present in the form of the Sanctus most commonly used in church:

Holy, holy, holy, Lord God of hosts,
heaven and earth are full of thy glory;
glory be to thee, O Lord most high.

The fact is that such a threefold structure is not uncommon in liturgical language, as the "Blessing of Aaron" illustrates (Num. 6:24–26), and lends itself to inventive interpretation on the part of those who sing it or ponder upon it regularly.

What the prophet is saying to us, in the context of his terrifying vision, is that holiness is at the heart of his message: the holiness of God, the holiness of men, the holiness that can kill, the holiness that can also forgive. Throughout the sixty-six chapters of the Book of Isaiah, this moment of revelation is alluded to in the continually repeated title "Holy One of Israel". Perhaps it was the eighth-century prophets, especially Isaiah, who discovered the true nature of holiness. A vision of God's perfect holiness, high and lifted up, surrounded by perfect attendants, served to highlight the imperfection and inadequacy of human efforts to achieve holiness, in the Temple and elsewhere. We have heard of the hypocrisy of Judah's leaders, carrying out all the ritual regulations with impeccable devotion, but leading lives of immorality and corruption: "Even though you make many prayers, I will not listen" (1:15), says the Holy One of Israel. Holiness and justice are inseparably connected: you cannot have one without the other.

In ancient legend people were struck dead for disobeying ritual rules and regulations like the two sons of Aaron (Lev. 10:1–3) or poor innocent Uzzah (2 Sam. 6:6–7), or indeed King Uzziah himself, although in Uzziah's case ritual disobedience is coupled with arrogance and bad temper (2 Chron. 26:16–21). But, for Isaiah, holiness is an ethical matter, and uncleanness is not ritual uncleanness, like that of the various forbidden meats (Lev. 11), or of a leper (Lev. 13–14), but moral uncleanness—as the preceding five chapters make very clear. The sin for which the prophet is forgiven is his involvement with and contamination by an unclean people, that is to say, arrogant, decadent, dishonest, greedy drunkards and the like, not people who had either accidentally or deliberately offered the wrong sacrifice or missed a solemn assembly.

The other theme in the hymn of the seraphim is the glory of the Lord of hosts. This is creation language, reminiscent of Psalm 8 or Psalm 19 or Isaiah 40 (a chapter which has many connections with chapter 6), and this too has ethical implications as we saw. Before the vast beauty and order of creation, how can people dare to behave with such highhandedness? What is more, this is God's world: let no one forget that, when lands or people are under their care and protection. As we have seen, many of the vices criticized by the prophet can be understood as the misuse of property for selfish ends, and the neglect or exploitation of people in need. The whole earth is God's; if you harm it in any way, you are insulting its Maker (see on 5:12).

Verse 4 describes the effect of the vision on the prophet and on the Temple. It seemed to him as if the whole building shook, like Mount Sinai when the Lord descended onto it in fire (Exod. 19:18); and it was filled with smoke, again like Mount Sinai (Exod. 19:18). Like Moses, the prophet was close to God, and the experience was shattering. He uses a rare word probably meaning "I am doomed" and again the emphasis is on morality. Such a terrifying visionary experience is fairly common in the prophetic literature. Jeremiah describes it as a "burning fire shut up in my bones" (20:9) and Isaiah speaks elsewhere of "pangs like the pangs of a woman in travail" (21:3). Often the first words spoken by God (or his angels) are therefore "Fear not!" (e.g. Exod. 20:20; Judg. 6:23; Luke 1:13, 30; 2:10). Isaiah, however, can only answer: "I am a man of unclean lips, and I dwell in the midst of a people of unclean lips" (v. 5).

But unlike the sons of Aaron or poor Uzzah or King Uzziah, Isaiah's experience ends with cleansing and forgiveness, not death. The use of a burning coal for the purposes of ritual cleansing is not found anywhere else in the Bible. The idea of cleansing by fire does occur in Malachi (Mal. 3:2–3) and, by implication, in those comparisons of judgment to a furnace in which people are refined (e.g. Isa. 1:25). But these passages describe something very different from Isaiah's experience in chapter 6. More to the point may be the idea of punishing "lying lips" and "a deceitful tongue" with "red-hot charcoal" which appears in Psalm 120 (see v. 4). If this was a traditional way of thinking about slander in ancient Israel (James 3:5–6 may be relevant too), then the prophet's vision could be standing it on its head: for Isaiah holiness was an ethical quality, not cultic, and fire on the lips brought him forgiveness and hope, instead of "staining the whole body, setting on fire the cycle of nature..." (James 3:6). Or maybe this was the moment when the fire that later burned in Jeremiah's bones (20:9) entered into Isaiah: Jer. 1:9 suggests a connection, as do the verses which follow here.

When the prophet has been forgiven, he overhears a dialogue between God and his heavenly court (just as in 40:1–8), which he is immediately inspired to interrupt and answer by offering himself. He then finds himself, like Moses (Exod. 3:10–11), and indeed Jeremiah (1:4–8), faced with an impossible task as a prophet of the Lord.

THE PROPHET'S MISSION TO A SINFUL PEOPLE

Isaiah 6:9–13

⁹And he said, "Go, and say to this people:
  'Hear and hear, but do not understand;
  see and see, but do not perceive.'
¹⁰Make the heart of this people fat,
    and their ears heavy,
    and shut their eyes;
  lest they see with their eyes,
    and hear with their ears,
  and understand with their hearts,
    and turn and be healed."
¹¹Then I said, "How long, O Lord?" And he said:
  "Until cities lie waste
    without inhabitant,
  and houses without men,
    and the land is utterly desolate,
¹²and the Lord removes men far away,
    and the forsaken places are many in the midst of the land.

13 And though a tenth remain in it,
   it will be burned again,
like a terebinth or an oak,
   whose stump remains standing
   when it is felled."
The holy seed is its stump.

The bitter content of the prophet's message is then spelt out to
him in two prophecies of judgment: the first declares that it is too
late for repentance (vv. 9–10), the second foretells destruction
(vv. 11–13). The two are linked by the prophet's pathetic attempt
to intercede for his people—"How long, O Lord?"—a cry from
the heart that belongs to the language of lamentation. A look at
some familiar Psalms will give an idea of what it means:

How long, O Lord? Wilt thou forget me for ever?...
How long must I bear pain in my soul,
   and have sorrow in my heart all the day?
                                        (13:1–2; cf. 74:10; 90:13)

Like Christ's "cry of dereliction" on the cross (Ps. 22:1; cf. Mark
15:34), it is not really a question, expecting an answer, but a cry
for help: "Do not let this go on for ever! Do not forsake us!"
Amos pleaded for his people when he learnt of the fate that
awaited them (Amos 7:2, 5), and Moses offered his life for them
(Exod. 32:33). In Isaianic tradition this theme is taken up
supremely in chapter 53, where the Servant of the Lord is
represented as one who "bore the sin of many, and made
intercession for the transgressors" (v. 12).

   This little "How long, O Lord?" in chapter 6 reveals Isaiah's
love for his city, his land and his people, and how hard a task lay
before him. But like Jeremiah (7:16) he is not to pray for his
people: they are doomed. First he is to tell them to "hear but not
understand, to see but not recognize". He is to give them ignor-
ance, make them blind and unreceptive; to do all he can to
prevent them from seeing the error of their ways and repenting.
The irony is unmistakable: whereas, in the normal course of
events, a prophet might be expected to teach wisdom and impart
knowledge to his audience, and to arouse in their hearts the

stirrings of spiritual renewal, Isaiah is instructed to condemn them. In other words they are beyond redemption. This is surely a perfectly understandable view for an eighth-century prophet to come to, and one which was borne out by the tragic events of the latter part of that century. Later writers sought to identify the seeds of hope in many passages (even this one: see below), and there were often other prophets who stood for the exact opposite. Think of Jonah, for example, who protested at the idea of offering the opportunity to repent and the possibility of forgiveness to the Assyrians, or indeed of the author of chapter 40 of the present book. There is no need to agonize over the morality of a God who does not allow repentance. The stern justice of this passage matches the moral horrors of the preceding five chapters, and must surely be contained within the nature of God. Nor need we explain the passage as retrospective, influenced by the prophet's failure to get through to his people. It is the bitter irony of a just God addressing people who mock him (5:19).

Notice how the sarcastic "this people" is repeated twice rather than the more affectionate "my people".

Verse 10 describes the fatal disease with which the prophet is instructed to afflict the people. Three organs are affected: the mind (Hebrew *leb*, "heart", is the seat of the intellect, not the passions), the eyes and the ears, and according to the last words of the verse, there is no cure. The distinction between the prophet who has "eyes to see and ears to hear" and his blind insensitive people reappears in the New Testament where these verses are quoted to explain the purpose of the parables: "To you has been given the secret of the kingdom of God, but for those outside everything is in parables; so that they may indeed see but not perceive . . ." (Mark 4:11–12).

The description of judgment in verses 11–13 contains several familiar images and ideas, but also some unusual features. Verse 12 seems to refer to deportation and may not go back to the earliest form of the prophecy. This is also suggested by the fact that "the Lord" is referred to in the third person, while in the rest of the passage he is the speaker. The picture of a deserted land is a familiar one in later parts of the book where for example Zion is triumphantly told:

You shall no more be termed Forsaken,
  and your land shall no more be termed Desolate,
But you shall be called My delight is in her,
  and your land Married . . . (62:4)

The rest of the description carries on where chapter 5 left off. The whole land—cities, people, houses—will be devastated. It will be like a forest fire destroying everything in its path, even the mightiest and most ancient trees. This is what "terebinth" and "oak" are intended to suggest: the one (often also translated "oak") is specially mentioned in connection with ancient sanctuaries (Josh. 24:26; Judg. 6:11, 19), and the other occurs more than once as a symbol of proud strength (e.g. Isa. 2:13; Zech. 11:2). Even they will fall before the fire of God's judgment.

The next part of verse 13 is very hard to understand, as you will see if you compare the various English versions:

"whose substance is in them, when they cast their leaves" (AV)
"whose stump remains standing when it is felled" (RSV)
"a sacred pole thrown out from its place in a hill-shrine" (NEB)

Obviously the key word is the one translated "substance/stump/ sacred pole", because it is the remnant, it stands for what is left after the disaster. Whatever it means it is identified with the "holy seed" in the final words of the prophecy, and that is the important thing. However total the devastation, something—be it a mere stump or stick—would survive, and from it would grow "the noble stem of Jesse" (cf. 11:1), the "righteous Branch" (Isa. 4:2; Jer. 23:5; 33:15) of David's family tree which would produce, in the fullness of time, "a Saviour, who is Christ the Lord" (Luke 2:11).

Now it is most unlikely that the explanatory note at the end of the chapter, the ray of hope in the midst of judgment, goes back to the original prophecy. As we have seen, Isaiah held out no hope at all to his people. But, building upon the pleading in verse 11—"How long, O Lord?"—which shows the prophet still had some sympathy for them, it transforms total gloom into a prophecy of hope. The fire will purify Israel, and in place of former corruption a new king will arise to bring justice and peace, wisdom and understanding into the land (11:1–9). Such was the faith of later Judeans in their Davidic messiah, that a mere "stump", symbol of total destruction, could be transformed into a sign of hope. The dissident sect, whose writings are nowadays known as the Dead Sea Scrolls, ridiculed this Judean interpretation: their text reads: "How could this stump be the holy seed?" But for Jews and Christians, ancient and modern, in the context of a book that foretells the coming of a son of David who shall be called "Wonderful Counsellor, Mighty God, Everlasting Father, Prince of Peace" (9:6), the meaning is clear enough.

THE SIGN OF SHEARJASHUB

Isaiah 7:1–9

[1]In the days of Ahaz the son of Jotham, son of Uzziah, king of Judah, Rezin the king of Syria and Pekah the son of Remaliah the king of Israel came up to Jerusalem to wage war against it, but they could not conquer it. [2]When the house of David was told, "Syria is in league with Ephraim," his heart and the heart of his people shook as the trees of the forest shake before the wind.

[3]And the Lord said to Isaiah, "Go forth to meet Ahaz, you and Shearjashub your son, at the end of the conduit of the upper pool on the highway to the Fuller's Field, [4]and say to him, 'Take heed, be quiet, do not fear, and do not let your heart be faint because of these two smouldering stumps of firebrands, at the fierce anger of Rezin and Syria and the son of Remaliah. [5]Because Syria, with Ephraim and the son of Remaliah, has devised evil against you, saying, [6]"Let us go up against Judah and terrify it, and let us conquer it for ourselves, and set up the son of Tabe-el as king in the midst of it," [7]thus says the Lord God:

It shall not stand,
    and it shall not come to pass.
[8]For the head of Syria is Damascus,
    and the head of Damascus is Rezin.

(Within sixty-five years Ephraim will be broken to pieces so that it will no longer be a people.)

⁹And the head of Ephraim is Samaria,
　and the head of Samaria is the son of Remaliah.
If you will not believe,
　surely you shall not be established.'"

The next two chapters contain a sequence of signs based on the names of three children: Shearjashub (7:1–9), Immanuel (7:10–17) and Mahershalalhashbaz (8:1–4). It seems natural to assume that, as in the case of another eighth-century prophet (Hosea 1:2–9), all three were sons of Isaiah, although the text only makes this plain in the case of the first and third. However that may be, it is the meaning of the names as prophetic signs that is important, not who they were. They are addressed to the rulers of Judah, in particular King Ahaz (736–725 B.C.), during what is called the Syro-Ephraimite crisis, and make three points: (1) there is hope, even in the present crisis ("A-remnant-will-return"); (2) this hope will be fulfilled sooner than you expected ("God-is-with-us") and (3) Syria and Ephraim will be conquered ("Speed-booty-hurry-plunder"). The narrative makes the additional point that the prophet was not believed, following on from the prophecies in chapter 6, and comes to us as a plea for faith in God, a theme familiar to us already from the "faithful city" poem in chapter 1, and one that will recur again in Isaianic tradition more than once (e.g. 30:15).

"In the days of Ahaz" refers to the years 736–725 B.C., that is to say, the years immediately following Uzziah's death (6:1). Jotham and Ahaz had acted as regents since 756, when Uzziah was smitten with leprosy (2 Chron. 26:16–21), until his death in 736, when Ahaz became sole ruler. Verse 1 comes from the history of the reign of Ahaz as described in 2 Kings 16, and introduces the relevant political background. According to his own account, known to us from clay tablets and pieces of stone monument, Tiglath-Pileser III (744–727 B.C.) had already invaded Syria in 738 to quell an uprising. In 735 Rezin, king of Syria and Pekah, king of Ephraim (= the Northern Kingdom of Israel) (735–732 B.C.) tried to involve Jerusalem under King Ahaz in a similar anti-Assyrian revolt. Judging by the list of states men-

tioned by Tiglath-Pileser in his account, it would appear that
Ahaz was the only one to keep out of the coalition. Judah was
thus isolated, threatened by Syria and Ephraim to the north, and
by Edom to the south (2 Kings 16:6). Probably Philistia and other
neighbouring states joined in Rezin's campaign to force Judah
into joining them (9:12). But Ahaz, spurred on no doubt by that
sense of superiority and national pride from which the Zion
traditions—in the Psalms and the Book of Isaiah—drew their
inspiration, stood aloof from his neighbours' courageous enter-
prise, and sent messengers to Tiglath-Pileser, with presents of
silver and gold, to ask for military aid against them. In 733 B.C. the
Assyrians captured Galilee and in the following year they conquered Damascus, capital of Syria, and killed Rezin, its king.
Ahaz survived: he even journeyed to Damascus to meet the
Assyrian king in person (2 Kings 16:10). Sporadic revolts and
Assyrian reprisals continued to the end of the century, culminating in the destruction of Samaria in 722 and—when Judah too
finally made a bid for freedom—in the surrender of Jerusalem in
701.

The present incident took place in 733, during a siege of
Jerusalem by the Syro-Ephraimite allies (v. 1). They hoped to
replace the obstinate King Ahaz with a puppet king named ben
Tabeel, whose name suggests he was a Syrian. Verse 2 describes
the terror of the citizens of Jerusalem, including the king, in terms
of trees shaking in the wind. The formula "house of David"
simply means the king, and was chosen here by the author to
highlight the fact that the underlying theme of these chapters is
the survival of the Davidic dynasty, from which was to come a
saviour (9:6-7; 11:1-5).

Into this situation the Lord sent the prophet with his son to
confront King Ahaz. The scene is set somewhere near a conduit,
or man-made water channel. There were presumably several
such conduits running from the "upper pool", and this is the one
that ran in the direction of the "Fuller's Field", an open space for
drying and bleaching laundry, probably on the outskirts of the
city. This was also the place from which Hezekiah addressed the
Assyrians during the siege of Jerusalem in 701 (36:1-3). In the

present context the detail suggests that Ahaz was anxiously inspecting the city's water supply in preparation for a siege—when he should have been turning to God for help.

The name Shearjashub clearly incorporates part of the prophet's "word" to the king: Shear (pronounced with two syllables) means "remnant" and can refer to the survivors of some catastrophe (10:20) as well as to a surviving son and heir (14:22)—both relevant here. In prophetic language Jashub (pronounced *yashuv*) usually means "will (re)turn" (from exile) or "will turn, repent" (as in 6:10). In some contexts it might mean "return safely from battle" or even "return from the dead". Probably different sparks of hope were intended to be lit by the many-faceted name.

Verses 4–9 contain the words of Isaiah's prophecy beginning and ending with a call to faith. A later verse perhaps explains the link (merely implied here) with Shearjashub:

> "In returning and rest you shall be saved;
> in quietness and trust shall be your strength." (30:15)

The angry assault of the two kings is no more to be feared than the tail-end of a smouldering torch. They can easily be handled as the Assyrian hosts are about to demonstrate: they are but human powers. Stripped of its international status, what is the Syro-Ephraimite alliance? It is no more than two mere mortals, Rezin and the son of Remaliah.

Verse 8b is bracketed in the RSV, presumably on the grounds that it is too accurate a prophecy for Isaiah actually to have made, and must be a later interpolation. It seems to refer to the year 670 B.C. or thereabouts when Esarhaddon, king of Assyria (680–669), conducted damaging campaigns into the region of Samaria (which lost its independence in 722), resulting in further depopulation. Certainly it is likely that this is a later interpolation, written after the event, but it is nonetheless part of Isaianic prophecy in the texts as we have them, and reminds us that Isaiah is consistently represented as a prophet whose words, visions and ideals transcend his eighth-century environment.

The first of the three "Sign" passages ends with a pun: "If you will not believe [ta'aminu], you shall not be established [te'-amenu]." The words for "believe" and "established" look alike in Hebrew, sound alike and contain the same root; and the prophet uses this fact to point to a connection between faith and security. The Jerusalem Bible tries to keep the word play in English: "If you do not stand by me, you will not stand at all." To "stand by" something is "to trust in it, believe in it". The two ideas come together very often in the word ne'eman, translated "sure, established" in connection with a house or a dynasty (e.g. 1 Sam. 25:28; 1 Kings 11:38), but "faithful, reliable" as applied to a person (e.g Deut. 7:9 (God); Isa. 8:2). It even occurs with both meanings in one verse (1 Sam. 2:35). The word "Amen", from the same root, is both an expression of faith ("I believe") and a statement about reliability ("verily, truly . . .", Matt. 5:26; 6:5, 16). So the "faithful city" (1:21–26) will stand firm in the midst of the present crisis and the "house of David" will survive. What is needed is faith in God's power to achieve this, whatever happens.

THE SIGN OF IMMANUEL

Isaiah 7:10–17

¹⁰Again the Lord spoke to Ahaz, ¹¹"Ask a sign of the Lord your God; let it be deep as Sheol or high as heaven." ¹²But Ahaz said, "I will not ask, and I will not put the Lord to the test." ¹³And he said, "Hear then, O house of David! Is it too little for you to weary men, that you weary my God also? ¹⁴Therefore the Lord himself will give you a sign. Behold, a young woman shall conceive and bear a son, and shall call his name Immanuel. ¹⁵He shall eat curds and honey when he knows how to refuse the evil and choose the good. ¹⁶For before the child knows how to refuse the evil and choose the good, the land before whose two kings you are in dread will be deserted. ¹⁷The Lord will bring upon you and upon your people and upon your father's house such days as have not come since the day that Ephraim departed from Judah—the king of Assyria."

"Again the Lord spoke to Ahaz"—because the first sign had had no effect. No indication is given of the time and place of the "Immanuel" sign, although the recurrence of the formula "house of David", referring to King Ahaz, probably shows that the two signs come from pretty much the same context, that is to say, before the king's delegation to Assyria set out. The name means "God is with us", and implies that there is no need to join forces either with Assyria or with the Syro-Ephraimite alliance—because God is on our side, a stronger ally than any human power. But there is much more to this passage than that.

"Ask a sign . . ." gives continuity with the preceding passage, implying "If you don't believe me, then ask me to prove it." The word "sign" (*'ot*) is used of all kinds of proofs of God's power, from a rainbow (Gen. 9:12, 17) to the Plagues of Egypt (Exod. 7:3; Num. 14:22). Isaiah's oddly-named sons are described collectively as "signs and portents" in 8:18. The Immanuel sign may thus be an unusually significant personal name borne by a son of Isaiah, like the two other names, and no more (none of these names has yet been discovered in ancient sources). On the other hand, it could refer to some miraculous happening like the "sign" given to Hezekiah later in the book (38:7). The immediate context suggests the former, as there is nothing miraculous about the other two "signs", but, in the wider context of Jewish and Christian tradition, attention has focused on the event—not on a special name but on the birth of a special child. There is then the problem of who the child is, who his mother is, and, if he is a special child, what the following two verses (15–16) mean.

Verse 11 introduces the passage by suggesting that, whether Ahaz likes it or not, he is going to be given something spectacular by way of a sign. Nothing is impossible for God's prophets: they can bring back the dead from Sheol (like Elijah in 1 Kings 17:17–24), and they can make the sun go backwards in the sky (Isa 38:7–8). Ahaz's response in verse 12 also implies that the sign was going to be something miraculous: with sham piety he argues that it is wrong to "put the Lord to the test" (cf. Deut. 6:16). Of course his real reason for refusing a sign is that he does not want to listen to Isaiah's advice.

Verse 13, in which the prophet angrily criticizes the king, informs us that Ahaz has been "wearying men": either a general comment on the oppression of the poor by the rich, or a more specific comment on his handling of the present crisis. Either way, his rejection of the advice of God's prophet is tantamount to blasphemy, treating God in the same high-handed manner as he treats his subjects. With such a build-up (vv. 10–13), unlike the other two signs, we are surely being led to expect a sign consisting of something more than the significant name of a child. Maybe in the original form of the prophecy "Immanuel" was the sum total of the message: God is with us, who can threaten us? But the text as it now stands, both the build-up to 7:14 and the development in verses 15–17, must be about something more.

Both Jewish and Christian interpreters naturally ask the question, Who is the child (and his mother)? as well as, What does the name mean? One traditional Jewish explanation is that the child is Hezekiah, and that his conception and birth, miraculously foretold by the prophet in the days of King Ahaz, heralds the dawn of a new age of hope for beleaguered Jerusalem. In spite of historical problems such as Hezekiah's date of birth (he was twenty-five in 725 B.C. according to 2 Kings 18:2), this has the merit of recognizing in the verse a Davidic oracle like those in 9:6–7 and 11:1–5. It becomes a declaration that there will always be a king in Jerusalem on the throne of David. The other main Jewish interpretation, traceable like the first to the Middle Ages, maintains that the "young woman" is the prophet's wife, as in 8:3–4, and "Immanuel" the name of Isaiah's second son. The point of the prophecy is then very similar to 8:1–4: very soon the Syro-Ephraimite crisis will be past—only trust in God's presence. The merit of this interpretation, its link with the prophecies before it and after it, has already been noticed.

Christian tradition, also influenced by the build-up in the preceding verses and the parallels in chapters 9 and 11, identified the child with Jesus, another "Son of David", and the young woman with Mary his mother. The word for "young woman" (*almah*) does not tell us whether she was a virgin, married or single. The specific word for "virgin" (*betulah*) is not used. Yet virginity is not ruled out by the text as it stands, and an interpretation that laid emphasis on the miraculous nature of the sign might legitimately maintain both that the prophet was able to foretell correctly the conception and birth of a male child, and that the young mother would be a virgin. This is apparently what the Greek translators of the passage did in the second century B.C., in rendering *almah* as "virgin" (Greek *parthenos*). The Gospels carried on this tradition (Matt. 1:23; Luke 1:26–27) and thus provided a Biblical basis for the doctrine of the Virgin Birth. Isaiah 7:14 therefore became one of the many Isaianic verses applied to the life, death and resurrection of Jesus Christ, verses that continually remind us of the timeless dimension of Old Testament prophecy. It was not regarded as exclusively concerned with what actually happened in 733–732 B.C. or what Isaiah actually said. With the first of the Jewish interpretations mentioned above, this Christian interpretation saw the text as more open-ended and theologically far richer than that.

Having looked at traditional Jewish and Christian interpretations of Isaiah 7:14, it now remains for us to mention some modern attempts to get back to what Isaiah originally meant. Ignoring the literary build-up and messianic parallels, it has become fashionable to see here a prophecy of judgment, not hope. The verse describes a sense of false security in Judah, inspired by the total collapse of the Syro-Ephraimite alliance: a time when mothers will be calling their children "Immanuel" to celebrate their escape. Within a generation, before the children are properly grown up, they would be eating curds and honey, that is to say, the produce of uncultivated land, deprived of the vineyards, orchards, cornfields and cattle they had become accustomed to enjoying. Finally, total disaster would come upon them in the form of a cataclysmic Assyrian invasion. It would be a disaster comparable only to the break-up of the kingdom of Solomon (1 Kings 12) into two separate kingdoms, Judah in the south and Ephraim (or Israel) in the north. Such an interpretation undoubtedly agrees with 6:9–13*a*, although not with verse 13*b* (see p. 75).

As a final example of how these prophecies can be applied to later situations, the "Damascus Rule" from Qumran understands 7:17 to refer to that liberating moment in the history of the sect when it, as the new Israel (=Ephraim), departed from the corrupt hierarchy at Jerusalem (=Judah), and was free to establish the community of the New Covenant on the shores of the Dead Sea (G. Vermes, *Dead Sea Scrolls in English* (Penguin), p. 104). One man's food is, it appears, another man's poison. It is not impossible that the Immanuel prophecy, when first uttered, spoke of judgment and doom (the next oracle is certainly of that kind); but like the Qumran community, both Jews and Christians have adapted it in different ways and turned it into a prophecy of salvation. It would certainly be a retrograde step if we were to cut through all the many-splendoured layers of later tradition and focus exclusively on the original doom. Not only would this be spiritually unenlightening: it would also be a betrayal of the spirit of the texts as we now have them.

THE RAPE OF THE LAND

Isaiah 7:18–25

[18]In that day the Lord will whistle for the fly which is at the sources of the streams of Egypt, and for the bee which is in the land of Assyria. [19]And they will all come and settle in the steep ravines, and in the clefts of the rocks, and on all the thornbushes, and on all the pastures.

[20]In that day the Lord will shave with a razor which is hired beyond the River—with the king of Assyria—the head and the hair of the feet, and it will sweep away the beard also.

[21]In that day a man will keep alive a young cow and two sheep; [22]and because of the abundance of milk which they give, he will eat curds; for every one that is left in the land will eat curds and honey.

[23]In that day every place where there used to be a thousand vines, worth a thousand shekels of silver, will become briers and thorns. [24]With bow and arrows men will come there, for all the land will be briers and thorns; [25]and as for all the hills which used to be hoed with a hoe, you will not come there for fear of briers and thorns; but they will become a place where cattle are let loose and where sheep tread.

The formula "In that day" (see chs. 2 and 3) introduces four graphic descriptions of how things will be when the king of Assyria invades the land. The first two are typical Isaianic prophecies of doom, with the Lord as prime mover and Assyria as his agent of destruction. The other two mention neither God nor Assyria, and describe rather the aftermath of an invasion. They contain no datable references, but together they make up a frightening warning that a minor crisis, like the Syro-Ephraimite War, is nothing compared with the divine judgment that will inevitably fall upon "a people of unclean lips" (6:5). The "house of David" and his people, trembling with fear and fussing over the city's water system, have got their priorities completely wrong.

In the first image the invasion is compared to a plague of insects, summoned, like the gnats in Exodus, by a signal from God to swarm all over the land. Elsewhere the ferocious sting of the bee is alluded to, e.g.:

They surrounded me like bees,
    they blazed like a fire of thorns ... (Ps. 118:12; cf. Deut. 1:44)

But here it is the sheer number and noisomeness of the insects, flies and bees. Natural historians, ancient and modern, tell us that beekeepers can persuade their bees to come out of the hive or return from the fields by whistling. The reference to Egypt does not fit too readily into an eighth-century B.C. context. Not until the seventh century did Egyptian campaigns into Palestine become significant (e.g. 2 Kings 23:29), even although we hear of attempts on the part of Judah to involve them at an earlier period (e.g. Isa. 31:1). More likely the reference was added to heighten the effect later, possibly even as late as the Ptolemaic period (third century B.C.) when apocalyptic visions refer to forces massing on Judah's southern frontiers as well as her northern (e.g. Dan. 11).

The second image represents God as using Assyria like a razor on wretched Judah, just as in 10:5 he uses Assyria as a stick to beat him. It may be that we are intended to recognize here three distinct acts: mourners had their heads shaved (Isa. 15:2);

David's envoys had their beards half shaved off as an insult by the king of the Ammonites (2 Sam. 10:4); and shaving the private parts ("feet" can be a euphemism: 3:17) would then be another obscene assault on human dignity. It is more likely, however, that the shaving alludes to denuding the land, stripping it bare of all vegetation: "the head and the hair of the feet" simply means "totally" ("from head to toe"), and the reference to the beard, which in Israel was a mark of distinction, singles out the flowers, trees and shrubs that add beauty to the land. The verse then means that the king of Assyria is going to burn up all the vegetation in the land of Judah. All that makes the land so lovely to look upon will be ruthlessly cut away.

Verse 21 describes the scene after all the cities, vineyards, olive groves, orchards and cornfields have been devastated, and the people living there reduced to a nomadic level of civilization. The reference to "curds and honey" follows on from verse 15: these constitute the only produce possible in such a land. This is therefore a picture of bare survival after the catastrophe. The view that there would be any survivors at all, however weak and vulnerable, sparked off in the hearts of later readers the hope that, after total conflagration, a new age would dawn. This is the explanation of the reference in verse 22 to "the abundance of milk", which cannot be an original part of the prophecy, but which has the effect of transforming the image from one of bare survival in a barren wilderness to one of life and prosperity in a land "flowing with milk and honey"—almost! This is another example of the kind of reinterpretation that is such an integral part of our texts (cf. 6:13).

The last of the four "In that day" prophecies harks back to the parable of the vineyard in 5:1–7, and consists of three variations on the "briers and thorns" theme (5:6). Verse 23 alludes to the commercial implications of the catastrophe: vines worth a shekel each will turn into worthless "briers and thorns". The enormous value of a well-cared for vineyard as an investment, producing abundant grapes every season for many years (cf. Song of S. 8:11), becomes clear when one realizes that the cost of a single vine, at this price (which is probably a hyperbole) is equivalent to half the cost of a ram.

In the second variation (vv. 21–22) "briers and thorns" stand for hostile enemy forces infesting the land, like the flies and bees in verse 19. It will not be safe to wander about the country unarmed. They might also include petty thieves and murderers thriving on the breakdown of law and order. Although it is not mentioned here, the informed reader will know that "briers and thorns" also burn very easily (9:18), which means that the days of Judah's ugly invaders are numbered (10:17; 27:4).

Finally (v. 25) "briers and thorns" will make it impossible to cultivate the open land where once vines grew in abundance (5:2, 6). Only animals will be seen there, not grazing, but "let loose", hedges and walls having been broken down (5:5), and "trampling" destructively all over the land (cf. Dan. 8:7, 13; Isa. 16:4; Ezek. 34:18–19). The last scene contains no glimmer of hope: even the cattle and sheep are hostile and destructive. There is no trace of peaceful grazing or rich dairy produce here as in verse 22 (cf. 5:17).

THE SIGN OF MAHER-SHALAL-HASH-BAZ

Isaiah 8:1–10

¹Then the Lord said to me, "Take a large tablet and write upon it in common characters, 'Belonging to Maher-shalal-hash-baz.' " ²And I got reliable witnesses, Uriah the priest and Zechariah the son of Jeberechiah, to attest for me. ³And I went to the prophetess, and she conceived and bore a son. Then the Lord said to me, "Call his name Maher-shalal-hash-baz; ⁴for before the child knows how to cry 'My father' or 'My mother,' the wealth of Damascus and the spoil of Samaria will be carried away before the king of Assyria."

⁵The Lord spoke to me again: ⁶"Because this people have refused the waters of Shiloah that flow gently, and melt in fear before Rezin and the son of Remaliah; ⁷therefore, behold, the Lord is bringing up against them the waters of the River, mighty and many, the king of Assyria and all his glory; and it will rise over all its channels and go over all its banks; ⁸and it will sweep on into Judah, it will overflow and pass on, reaching even to the neck; and its outspread wings will fill the breadth of your land, O Immanuel."

⁹Be broken, you peoples, and be dismayed;
    give ear, all you far countries;
  gird yourselves and be dismayed;
    gird yourselves and be dismayed.
¹⁰Take counsel together, but it will come to naught;
    speak a word, but it will not stand,
    for God is with us.

This passage concludes the series of prophecies based on the
three boys' names, dealing first with Mahershalalhashbaz,
Isaiah's remaining son, then finishing with further references to
the name Immanuel (vv. 8, 10). The original historical context is
established as 733–32 B.C. by specific references to Syria and
Ephraim (vv. 4–6) and the Assyrian menace (vv. 7–8).

"Then the Lord said to me", together with verse 5, indicates
that as in chapters 6 and 7 we are again dealing with Isaiah's
personal memoirs. He first tells of the prophetic experience in
which the extraordinary name Mahershalalhashbaz was revealed
to him. The idea of first writing the name down before witnesses,
then giving it to his son and explaining it as a sign of things to
come, came from God. The word for "tablet" is not the usual
one, familiar from Exodus 32 and elsewhere (e.g. Isa. 30:8); it
occurs only once in the Hebrew Bible and normally means a
"sheet (of papyrus or paper)" in post-Biblical Hebrew. The important thing here is that it is "large" (clay tablets were not often
large), and that it is legally valid.

"Common characters" has also caused some discussion: a
minor emendation of the text to give "indelible characters" is not
convincing (the word proposed really means "incurable"). Probably it simply means "characters that anybody can read easily".
This is probably also the meaning of a celebrated parallel: "Write
down the vision; inscribe it on tablets so that a man may read it
easily" (Hab. 2:2, NEB margin). The Hebrew script was much
simpler than the immensely complicated system of most of
Israel's ancient neighbours (e.g. Egyptian hieroglyphics, Assyrian cuneiform), and literacy was probably more widespread
among ordinary people in Israel than elsewhere in the ancient
Near East.

The document is addressed "to Mahershalalhashbaz", and that is all we are told about its contents. The RSV translation suggests that the heading is an ownership stamp or seal, like the hundreds of jar-handle stamps inscribed "*la-melek*", "belonging to the king", that have been discovered in excavations in Palestine.

The witnesses named include a prominent priest, referred to in the account of Ahaz's expedition to Tiglath-Pileser (2 Kings 16:10–16). Isaiah clearly had access to the royal court, and was able to enlist the support of the most influential people. His purpose here (as in 7:14) was to prove his ability to foretell the future, and convince an insensitive and unreceptive audience (6:9–10) of his power and authority. In verse 3 he stresses that his wife had not yet conceived: how could he have known that she was going to have another child, and that it would be a boy? There is no need to remove this supernatural element from the account as many modern scholars have done by rendering the Hebrew "I *had* gone to the prophetess . . ." Surely the prophet's powers are an integral part of these stories. We can assume that about a year passed between the writing of the name before witnesses and the birth of the child, all within the period of the Syro-Ephraimite crisis.

More significant than the prophet's ability to foretell the birth of a son, is the meaning of his name and its relevance to contemporary history. The four component parts of the name are clear enough: two are verbs meaning "to hurry" (*maher, hash*) and two are nouns meaning "spoil" (*shalal, baz*). But the grammar of the name is difficult. If it is a real name (and there is no evidence that it is), then we might expect some religious or militaristic meaning, such as the war cry attested in ancient Egypt, "Let the spoil hasten . . . !" Otherwise we should probably understand it as embodying a general impression, heightened by the very sound of the word, of bloodthirsty, loot-hungry soldiers rushing in for the kill. Its application to the Assyrian conquest of Israel's northern neighbours needs no further comment (cf. 5:26–30).

Verses 5–8 have the standard form of a prophecy of judgment, beginning with an account of the crimes of the accused ("Because this people . . .") and then pronouncing judgment upon them ("therefore, behold, the Lord . . ."). But the two parts are linked by a new image for the terrifying might of Assyria: the people, accused of despising the gently flowing waters of Shiloah, will be overwhelmed by the mighty waters of a far greater river, which is going to burst its banks and flood the whole land "reaching even to the neck". The great river is of course the Euphrates, which together with its vast system of irrigation canals made the "Land of Two Rivers" (=Mesopotamia) so rich and fertile; and the "waters of Shiloah" refers to the modest canal that carried water round the eastern slope of David's City (Mount Ophel) from the spring of Gihon (1 Kings 1:33, 38, 45) to the Pool of Siloam (the Greek form of Shiloah: John 9:7). Later in Isaiah's lifetime this canal was rendered superfluous by the magnificent "Siloam Tunnel" (or "Hezekiah's Tunnel"), hewn out of the living rock (2 Chron. 32:30), and functional to this day. Both Shiloah and the great River are of course symbols here, the one for Jerusalem, the faithful city, with nothing to fear from Rezin and the son of Remaliah, the other for the mighty "king of Assyria and all his glory". It was not a bigger and better water supply that Ahaz needed—if he wanted that, he could have had it and it would "sweep on into Judah . . ." What was needed was faith in God. But Ahaz was not convinced, and went to Assyria for help (2 Kings 16:7).

The prophecy of judgment has a double sting in its tail. At the end of verse 8 a new image is introduced, that of a huge bird of prey hovering over Judah (Hos. 8:1; Jer. 48:40) and the sinister suggestion that "Immanuel" means confrontation with a God of relentless judgment, and not "God is on our side" after all. Or at least that is one possibility. It is also possible that this last sentence contains a note of hope: the outstretched wings suggest protection (Pss. 17:8; 91:4) and "Immanuel" has the same meaning as it had in 7:14.

The translation "your land, O Immanuel" (AV, RSV, Jerusalem Bible) assumes that these words of hope are addressed to Immanuel, that is to say, the child whose birth is foretold in 7:14, and who, according to traditional interpretations of that verse, is a son of the royal house of David. Recent interpreters (represented by NEB) rule this out, but the wider context of chapters 7, 9 and 11, as we have seen, make the "messianic" interpretation of such passages possible—and theologically important.

Verses 9–10 consist of a short hymn, reminiscent of several Psalms celebrating the impregnability of Jerusalem, especially Psalm 46:

> God is in the midst of her, she shall not be moved ...
> The nations rage, the kingdoms totter ...
> "Be still, and know that I am God ..."
> The Lord of hosts is with us ...

The repeated imperatives give the hymn a stylistic affinity with later chapters of Isaiah (e.g. chapters 51 and 52), although there is more salvation than judgment there. The triumphalist, vindictive language addressed to foreign nations, instead of the men of Judah, confirms our impression that the hymn has little to do with the original message of Isaiah as spoken to Ahaz and his court during the Syro-Ephraimite crisis. Half way through verse 8 we move as it were out of the eighth century B.C. into a prophetic vision of hope beyond disaster, centring on a saviour called Immanuel who would overcome the world. The associations of the name Immanuel have not allowed either this passage or the one in 7:10 ff. to remain tied to their time.

I WILL WAIT FOR THE LORD

Isaiah 8:11–22

[11]For the Lord spoke thus to me with his strong hand upon me, and warned me not to walk in the way of this people, saying: [12]"Do not call conspiracy all that this people call conspiracy, and do not fear what they fear, nor be in dread. [13]But the Lord of hosts, him you shall regard as holy; let him be your fear, and let him be your dread. [14]And he will become a sanctuary, and a stone of offence, and a rock of stumbling to both houses of Israel, a trap and a snare to the inhabitants of Jerusalem. [15]And many shall stumble thereon; they shall fall and be broken; they shall be snared and taken."

16Bind up the testimony, seal the teaching among my disciples. 17I will wait for the Lord, who is hiding his face from the house of Jacob, and I will hope in him. 18Behold, I and the children whom the Lord has given me are signs and portents in Israel from the Lord of hosts, who dwells on Mount Zion. 19And when they say to you, "Consult the mediums and the wizards who chirp and mutter," should not a people consult their God? Should they consult the dead on behalf of the living? 20To the teaching and to the testimony! Surely for this word which they speak there is no dawn. 21They will pass through the land, greatly distressed and hungry; and when they are hungry, they will be enraged and will curse their king and their God, and turn their faces upward; 22and they will look to the earth, but behold, distress and darkness, the gloom of anguish; and they will be thrust into thick darkness.

Isaiah's memoirs conclude, as they began, with an account of the prophet's experience of God and the attitude he must adopt towards "a people of unclean lips" (6:5). First comes a warning (vv. 11–15) to hold fast to the truth as it has been revealed to him, and not to "walk in the way of this people". The "strong hand of the Lord" (cf. Ezek. 8:1; 37:1), like the fire burning in the bones of another prophet (Jer. 20:9), is not just a way of emphasizing the importance of what is said, but a reference to the overpowering trance-like experience or ecstasy of the prophet, especially one who believes he has to stand out against his own people. Chapter 6 fills out the picture of such an experience; but we can assume that every time such a formula as this is used—even the phrase "thus said the Lord"—an actual prophetic experience is envisaged by the author.

In effect this prophecy consists of a confession on the part of the prophet that he has been tempted to "walk in the way of this people", and a threat of divine judgment on "both houses of Israel". In particular, the people's fear of the Syro-Ephraimite "conspiracy" is criticized: they have more regard for "two smouldering stumps of firebrands" (7:4) than for the Lord of hosts. Verses 12 and 13 stand in exact parallel except that conspiracy (v. 12) does not correspond with "holy" in verse 13. Two emendations have been proposed. According to one, "regard as holy" (*taqdishu*) is emended to "make your conspirator" (*taqshiru*)—the only conspiracy to enter into is one with the Lord of hosts. The other emends both "conspiracy" (*qesher*) and "holy" (*qadosh*) to "difficult, hard" (*qasheh*): "You shall not say 'too hard' of everything that this people calls hard . . . It is the Lord of hosts whom you must count 'hard'. . . " (so NEB). Both make good sense, but so does the text as it stands. "Holiness" is a particular concern of this prophet, especially, as we saw in chapter 6, where its awesome ethical dimensions are emphasized. Fear of the Holy One of Israel is what the prophet demands, in place of unfounded dread of human powers.

Verse 14 lists no less than five definitions of God, corresponding roughly to five descriptions of the people's fate in verse 15. First he will "become a sanctuary" (*miqdash*). Certainly "a snare" (*moqesh*) or a "hardship" (*miqsheh*, NEB) would provide a better parallel between the two verses, but "a sanctuary", something sacred and something that can kill (cf. 2 Sam 6:7) also makes good sense, and requires no emendation. In favour of the text as it stands is the fact that the next two definitions of God as a "stone" and a "rock" can also have a positive meaning in theological language (1 Sam. 7:12; Pss. 18:2; 19:14; 28:1; 92:15), but are here used as instruments of judgment: "stone of offence" and "rock of stumbling". The last two "definitions" of God as a "trap" and a "snare" anticipate a vivid picture of the Day of Judgment later in the book:

Terror and the pit, and the snare
are upon you, O inhabitant of the earth! (24:17)

Verse 15 sums up the section by representing the wrong-headed and stubborn people as, on the one hand, stumbling, falling and breaking their limbs like people groping about in the dark, and as, on the other hand, like silly birds, flying into snares and traps.

Verses 16–18 remind us that the prophet is not alone any more: he is accompanied by "disciples" and by "the children whom the Lord has given me". In fact the previous prophecy was addressed to more than one person as the plural verbs in verses 12 and 13 prove (in Hebrew, that is). The children we know about, but the "disciples" are problematical. Are they anything more than the two witnesses, Uriah and Zechariah, mentioned at the beginning of the chapter? Or does it refer to some genuine converts among the people? The word occurs only here and at 50:4 and 54:13 where it is translated "taught". None of the ancient translations into Greek or Aramaic recognize a reference to disciples here. It is not the word for "disciple" in later Hebrew, and can certainly not be used as Biblical evidence for the existence of an Isaianic "school". The most we can say is that the prophet here takes comfort in their existence, along with his children, at a time when God "is hiding his face from the house of Jacob". This is the language of a lament sung at a time of failure and doubt, when the determination to "wait for the Lord . . . and hope in him" may not come very easily: Psalm 13, which we had occasion to quote in connection with 6:11, is a beautiful parallel. There are many others (e.g. Pss. 22, 27, 69, 88, etc.).

It remains for us to consider the meaning of verse 16. What are the "testimony" and the "teaching", and what exactly is to be done with them? It is possible that they refer to the Mahershalalhashbaz document: "testimony" (*te'udah*) occurs only here and in Ruth 4:7, and could be a fairly accurate description of it, although "teaching" (*torah*) normally has a more general meaning. The difficulty is to establish continuity between verses 1–4 and 16–18. More likely these verses constitute a fourth, originally independent utterance of the prophet, built into the present autobiographical series. In that case we should expect the two terms to refer to "the word which Isaiah the son of Amoz saw . . . " (2.1) in general, and the binding and sealing no more than figurative expressions for "driving his message home". "Among" is a most irregular translation of the Hebrew preposition: it would normally mean "in, into". "In the heart of my disciples" (Jerusalem Bible) makes good sense (cf. Jer. 31:33), and agrees with the point made above that Isaiah, lonely and rejected, takes comfort in the fact that at least some of his people are receptive.

Taken out of context, verse 16 has been cited in two important areas of discussion. Some have used the verse to prove that it was normal for prophets in ancient Israel to have circles of disciples around them who recorded their words. This would then be the only verse in the Old Testament that specifically refers to such a phenomenon, apart from Jeremiah's solitary amanuensis Baruch (Jer. 45:1). However the words of the prophets were transmitted, it seems unlikely that there were "disciples" in any technical sense: a phrase wrongly translated "among my disciples" certainly cannot be used as evidence!

The other, more interesting, use to which the verse has been put is in apocalyptic traditions. The other prophets that "seal" their prophecies are Daniel (9:24; 12:4, 9) and John (Rev. 10:4), where the purpose is clearly eschatological: "But you, Daniel, shut up the words, and seal the book, until the time of the end ... Blessed is he who waits..." (Dan. 12:4, 12). There are eschatological elements in the Book of Isaiah, especially in chapters 24–27, and this semi-technical sense of "seal" must be taken along with them.

After these few verses on the exception—people who listen— the section ends where it began (6:9) with the norm—people who mock him and are doomed. "And when they say..." (RSV) is better rendered "But people will go on saying..." (v. 19). "Mediums and wizards" are of course condemned in Biblical law (Lev. 19:31; Deut. 18:10f.) and in the cautionary tale of Saul and the Witch of Endor (1 Sam. 28). Trying to contact the inhabitants of Sheol ("the dead on behalf of the living"), however, continued in ancient Israel, as it does in our own day. "Their God" (RSV) should be "their gods", that is to say pagan gods, probably with ancestral gods ("teraphim") in mind (e.g. Gen. 31:19, 34, 35), or the spirits of the dead (referred to as "gods" in 1 Sam. 28:13). Verse 20 contrasts these feeble and ineffectual sources of hope with "the law" and "the testimony". Turn to it, hear the word of God, cries the prophet, or else you will never emerge from the darkness of present danger and suffering into the light of day. With that the prophecy ends in a short poetic description of distress, famine, anger, despair ("they look up ... they look down to the ground"—that is to say, desperately trying to find help), gloom, anguish and finally exile (vv. 21–22). The bewildering conglomeration of words and images could fit a national crisis, ancient or modern; they can be applied with equal poignancy to the personal crisis, spiritual, or otherwise, of an individual. In every crisis, says the prophet, true hope comes from the "Lord of hosts, who dwells on mount Zion" (v. 18) . . . and this is exactly what the next prophecy is all about.

FOR TO US A CHILD IS BORN

Isaiah 9:1–7

> [1]But there will be no gloom for her that was in anguish. In the former time he brought into contempt the land of Zebulun and the land of Naphtali, but in the latter time he will make glorious the way of the sea, the land beyond the Jordan, Galilee of the nations.
> [2]The people who walked in darkness
> have seen a great light;
> those who dwelt in a land of deep darkness,
> on them has light shined.
> [3]Thou hast multiplied the nation,
> thou hast increased its joy;
> they rejoice before thee
> as with joy at the harvest,
> as men rejoice when they divide the spoil.
> [4]For the yoke of his burden,
> and the staff for his shoulder,
> the rod of his oppressor,
> thou hast broken as on the day of Midian.
> [5]For every boot of the tramping warrior in battle tumult
> and every garment rolled in blood
> will be burned as fuel for the fire.
> [6]For to us a child is born,
> to us a son is given;
> and the government will be upon his shoulder,
> and his name will be called
> "Wonderful Counsellor, Mighty God,
> Everlasting Father, Prince of Peace."
> [7]Of the increase of his government and of peace
> there will be no end,

upon the throne of David, and over his kingdom,
  to establish it, and to uphold it
with justice and with righteousness
  from this time forth and for evermore.
The zeal of the Lord of hosts will do this.

This is one of the best known messianic prophecies in the Old
Testament and, in its present context, it stands as the impressive
climax to Isaiah's memoirs (6:1–9:7). Just as the first series of
judgment prophecies (chs. 2–4) ended with a glorious prophecy
of hope (4:2–6), so now after the prophet's terrifying vision of the
heavenly court (ch. 6), his failure to convince the house of David
that "God is with us" (ch. 7) and his final predictions of "distress
and darkness" (ch. 8), there comes this superb dynastic poem
picturing the birth of a royal saviour who will establish a kingdom
of justice and righteousness.

The continuity of the poem with what goes before is unmistak·
able. Chapter 8 ended with a picture of darkness that has no dawn
and then, with that leap of faith that characterizes so much of this
book, the text goes on: "But there will be no gloom for her that
was in anguish . . . the people who walked in darkness have seen a
great light". Whether or not the poem was originally composed
by Isaiah, and how early it was placed in its present context—we
shall look at these questions in a moment—it certainly fits, as
Matt. 4:13–16 illustrates.

Verse 1, however, is not as straightforward as it seems; a glance
at two or three English versions of the passage will make that very
plain. In the Hebrew text it comes at the end of the previous
chapter, and the messianic poem begins in chapter 9 with the
words "The people who walked . . . " The meaning of the verse is
then completely reversed. Instead of a change from gloom to
hope in the middle of the verse, the darkness continues to the
end. The verse begins with a rhetorical question, not a statement:
"Is it not all gloom for her that is in anguish?" (Jerusalem Bible).
The main part of the verse describes two acts of oppression, not
one: in the first, the lands of Zebulun and Naphtali are attacked,
and in the second, "the way of the sea, the land beyond the

Jordan, Galilee of the nations". The word translated in RSV
"will make glorious" only once has this meaning in the Hebrew
Bible (Jer. 30:19; RSV "make honoured"), and elsewhere means
"to make heavy, deal heavily with"; so NEB here, and hence
the traditional (AV): "and afterwards did more grievously
afflict . . . "

This understanding of the verse suggests an interesting historical background for it. It seems to refer to two of the Assyrian
invasions. In 738 B.C. Tiglath-Pileser III invaded Syria and northern Palestine, the latter being where the two tribal regions of
Zebulun and Naphtali were. Then in 733 he again invaded the
area and set up three Assyrian administrative provinces that
correspond very closely to the other names mentioned in the
verse: *Du'ru*, called after its capital Dor, a city on the "way of the
sea" south of Haifa; *Gal'azu* with its capital at Ramoth Gilead
"beyond the Jordan"; and *Magidu*, which included Galilee and
the northern plains and had its capital at Megiddo, to this day one
of Israel's most impressive Biblical sites. We can be fairly confident, then, that originally this verse goes back to the early days
of Isaiah's life, before the next Assyrian invasion which resulted
in the annexation of Samaria in 722, and before the leap of faith
by which it was transformed from judgment to hope, from past
gloom to future light. The Isaiah Scroll from Qumran and Matt.
4:13-15 prove that this transformation took place at an early
stage; and as it now stands, it is a messianic prophecy in which the
dawning of light in verse 2 is set in the north of Palestine, in the
region of Galilee, Nazareth and Capernaum (Matt. 4:12-13).

As our English versions usually indicate, the messianic poem in
verses 2-7 has a structure and style that prove it was originally an
independent poem, whatever its present connection with verse 1.
It is obviously written in royal dynastic language and was probably composed for a coronation in Jerusalem. Isaiah himself must
have been in Jerusalem for three coronations, those of Jotham
(741 B.C.), Ahaz (736) and Hezekiah (725), and it would make
good sense in the light of our discussion of verse 1 to date it to the
last of these celebrations. Not only was this the start of a new
reign in Jerusalem; in the previous year the long and oppressive

reign of Tiglath-Pileser, whose punishing campaigns into the north have left their mark on Isaianic tradition as we saw, also came to an end. So there were at least two new beginnings to celebrate, and every reason to sing of victory and the end of oppression.

On the other hand, the language and imagery of the poem—the legendary "day of Midian", the transcendent names of the new king, the picture of everlasting peace and justice—might equally suggest that the poem has no connection with any historical period, but envisages a messianic age far beyond the present, and such a poem might have been composed in Jerusalem at any time from the reign of David onwards. However that may be, no poem could fit more perfectly into the context of Isaianic tradition: light for those in darkness, military imagery, the Son of David, and the picture of justice and righteousness in his kingdom are all typically Isaianic themes.

"The people" are not named and therefore can be applied to the victims of Tiglath-Pileser, in "Galilee of the nations" for example, or to Ahaz's ill-fated subjects, or to anyone else who can visualize the coming of a Saviour. The word translated "deep darkness" (RSV) or "shadow of death" (AV) occurs only here in Isaiah. It is commonest in the more mythological language of the Psalms and the Book of Job, and may originally have been a place-name meaning "Death's shelter or domain". Since "shadow" in Hebrew suggests protection and safety (e.g. Isa. 4:6; 25:4; Ps. 121:5), it need not denote anything sinister or frightening. When Psalm 23:4 is sung at funerals, however, it refers literally to bereavement and death:

Even though I walk through the valley of the shadow of death,
  I will fear no evil;
for thou art with me.

In the context of Matt. 4 it refers to a land of unrepentant sinners, where John the Baptist had just been arrested. Here it is a land where people have been suffering from injustice and oppression at the hands of a foreign power, not to mention their own villainous leaders. Now they have something to celebrate like a successful harvest or a victory (v. 3). Many modern scholars recommend emending "the nation" to "the gladness", thereby doubling the joy of this verse. But there is no ancient evidence to support this.

The recent death of Tiglath-Pileser may have given rise to the belief that oppression, symbolized by yoke, staff and rod, was finally over (v. 4). It seemed as if God had stopped beating Israel with the rod of his anger (10:5). "The day of Midan" is an allusion to the sensational victory of Gideon and his three hundred men over 120,000 Midianites (Judg. 6–8). No doubt in 612 B.C., when Assyria's capital Nineveh finally fell and her empire came to an end, verses 4–5 became even more meaningful (cf. Nahum 3). It might also be significant that Gideon's victory was one in which light, suddenly and decisively, shone in the darkness (Judg. 7:20).

Verse 6 is rich in royal protocol, probably derived ultimately from Egypt. The formula "For to us a child is born" was probably not sung at the birth of a royal heir, but at his succession to the throne. The same applies to another royal hymn:

> He said to me, "You are my son,
> today I have begotten you" (Ps. 2:7)

He became a new person, as it were, as God's adopted son, and to represent this change in status the king was given "throne-names": "Wonderful Counsellor" refers to the hope that he is to possess, more than anyone else in the government, the political skills to govern (Prov. 8:14–16); "Mighty God" or rather "Divine Warrior" represents him as invincible champion of the oppressed; "Everlasting Father" sees in him an unfailing source of protection and love (63:15f.); and "Prince of Peace" means controller of the people's well-being and prosperity. In Egypt royal titles consisted of five names, and it may be that two mysterious letters at the beginning of verse 7 in the Hebrew text are relics of a fifth here too: "Eternal Judge" is one suggestion. But the origins of the verse in ancient near-eastern protocol were soon forgotten: Jewish scholars understood it as one long name, "Pelejo'ezelgibborabi'adsarshalom" (like Mahershalalhashbaz);

while Christian commentators, applying them to Jesus Christ, divided them into five: "Wonderful, Counsellor, The Mighty God, The Everlasting Father, The Prince of Peace" (AV). In the title "Mighty God" they also found a rare proof text for the divinity of Christ, their Messiah.

"The zeal of the Lord of hosts" refers to decisive action, especially in battle, as the five Isaianic examples illustrate: this one; 37:32; 42:13 ("fury"); 59:17 ("fury"); 63:15. The translation "fury" shows that within the word's meaning is the idea of a "jealous God" (as in the Second Commandment: Exod. 20:5), impatient with any opposition and a fierce champion of those he loves. The stronger the love, the stronger the jealousy, as anybody who has ever been in love can testify!

FOR ALL THIS HIS ANGER IS NOT TURNED AWAY

Isaiah 9:8–21

> ⁸The Lord has sent a word against Jacob,
>   and it will light upon Israel;
> ⁹and all the people will know,
>   Ephraim and the inhabitants of Samaria,
>   who say in pride and in arrogance of heart:
> ¹⁰"The bricks have fallen,
>   but we will build with dressed stones;
>   the sycamores have been cut down,
>   but we will put cedars in their place."
> ¹¹So the Lord raises adversaries against them,
>   and stirs up their enemies.
> ¹²The Syrians on the east and the Philistines on the west
>   devour Israel with open mouth.
>   For all this his anger is not turned away
>   and his hand is stretched out still.
>
> ¹³The people did not turn to him who smote them,
>   nor seek the Lord of hosts.
> ¹⁴So the Lord cut off from Israel head and tail,
>   palm branch and reed in one day—
> ¹⁵the elder and honoured man is the head,

and the prophet who teaches lies is the tail;
¹⁶for those who lead this people lead them astray,
and those who are led by them are swallowed up.
¹⁷Therefore the Lord does not rejoice over their young men,
and has no compassion on their fatherless and widows;
for every one is godless and an evildoer,
and every mouth speaks folly.
For all this his anger is not turned away
and his hand is stretched out still.

¹⁸For wickedness burns like a fire,
it consumes briers and thorns;
it kindles the thickets of the forest,
and they roll upward in a column of smoke.
¹⁹Through the wrath of the Lord of hosts
the land is burned,
and the people are like fuel for the fire;
no man spares his brother.
²⁰They snatch on the right, but are still hungry,
and they devour on the left, but are not satisfied;
each devours his neighbour's flesh,
²¹Manasseh Ephraim, and Ephraim Manasseh,
and together they are against Judah.
For all this his anger is not turned away
and his hand is stretched out still.

After the long, mainly autobiographical section known as Isaiah's memoirs (6:1–9:7), we return to prophecies of doom and "Woe-sayings" as in chapter 5. It can be persuasively argued that originally these three stanzas on the anger of God belonged to the same period as 5:25–30 (see p. 62). From their heading ("against Jacob") they seem to have been addressed to the Northern Kingdom some time after the Syro-Ephraimite disaster but before the fall of its capital Samaria in 722 B.C. As they are arranged now, however, they present a rather different picture. Addressed to Jerusalem, like the rest of the book, they do not so much attack Ephraim and Manasseh as relate their crimes and punishments as a warning: however devastating God's treatment of the Northern Kingdom, his anger has still not abated and "his hand is stretched out still"—against Judah. Hence the stanza which follows them and which carries on where the blistering attacks on Judah in chapter 5 left off: "Woe to those who decree iniquitous decrees ...!" (10:1–4). Only then when judgment is complete can the prophet move on to picture the fall of Assyria (10:5–34).

The rhetoric of Amos contains two similar passages. In one he recounts all the disasters that have befallen Israel, with the refrain, "Yet you did not return to me, says the Lord" (4:6–11). In the other, he systematically condemns all Israel's neighbours for their crimes against humanity, and then dramatically turns on Israel herself: "For three transgressions of Israel, and for four ..." (1:3–2:6). Isaiah 9:8–10:4 is built up in the same way to condemn Jerusalem by pointing to the fate of her neighbours. We should understand all the verbs in each stanza to refer to past time, except the refrain, which draws from the experience of Ephraim and Samaria the frightening lesson that it is Jerusalem's turn next if they go on as they are.

The first stanza (vv. 8–12) tells how the inhabitants of Samaria would not listen to the word of the Lord as spoken by the prophets, and were punished. In a later chapter the inexorable working out of God's purpose becomes a frequent theme:

> For as the rain and the snow come down from heaven,
>   and return not thither but water the earth,
> making it bring forth and sprout,
>   giving seed to the sower and bread to the eater,
> so shall my word be that goes forth from my mouth;
>   it shall not return to me empty,
> but it shall accomplish that which I purpose,
>   and prosper in the thing for which I sent it. (55:10–11)

Ephraim and Manasseh (v. 21), the two sons of Jacob's favourite son Joseph, gave their names to the largest and richest regions of the Northern Kingdom. Later anti-Samaritan feeling in Jerusalem picked on verse 9 and ones like it (e.g. Amos 3:12; Ecclesiasticus 50:26). But of course their arrogance was no worse than that of the citizens of Jerusalem (chapter 5), and that is exactly the point of this section.

"The bricks have fallen . . . the sycamores have been cut down" (v. 10) refers to some set-back, either literally to the destruction of buildings, or, like the quaking mountains in 5:25, metaphorically to Samaria's leaders. Either way, the set-back does not convince the people they are in real danger: brick and cheap wood can be replaced by dressed stone and cedarwood, symbols of stateliness and outward strength (1 Kings 10:27).

All the verbs in verses 11–12*a* are clearly past tenses in Hebrew, and refer to what happened to those arrogant "inhabitants of Samaria", as a cautionary tale for the prophet's audience in Jerusalem: look what happened to them! The Hebrew text has "the adversaries of Rezin" in verse 11, that is to say, the Assyrians under Tiglath-Pileser, who "marched up against Damascus and took it, carrying its people captive to Kir, and he killed Rezin" (2 Kings 16:9). It was not until 722 that the Assyrians destroyed Samaria, and, while that is clearly what the text as it stands refers to, probably the original allusions were to smaller scale hostilities between Israel and her neighbours, Syria and the Philistines (v. 12), as well as to internecine civil war between Manasseh and Ephraim (v. 21).

In spite of all these painful warnings, the people still did not mend their ways, and the refrain, first encountered in 5:25, draws together the themes of divine displeasure with human sin and the threat of divine intervention as a form of punishment. "His hand is stretched out" to smite and to destroy, as in the Exodus traditions where it is aimed at the Egyptians (Exod. 9:15) or the David stories where it is directed at Israel (2 Sam. 24:16). "The hand of God" is an exception to the prohibition of images of God, and figures prominently in Jewish and Christian representations of Biblical scenes.

The second stanza (vv. 13–17), in a unique attack on the whole of Israelite society, describes how unrepentant and godless people are punished, whatever their status: young and old, leaders and led, false prophets, even the widow and the orphan. Once more "seeking the Lord of hosts" is called for, that is to say, listening to his prophet, accepting his interpretation of contemporary history, and admitting that suffering and defeat are deserved. The two idioms in verse 14, one zoological and the other botanical, require little comment, except to note that the word translated "palm branch" also means "dome, vault, hat" and therefore refers to the "crown" of a high palm tree; while the "reed" or "bullrush" is a more mundane material from which ropes are made (Job 41:2). Verse 15 interprets the "head and tail" of verse 14, and by implication "palm branch and reed", rather unexpectedly, as representing two sources of authority: the elder statesman, who like Ahaz rejected the word of God—"those who are wise in their own eyes" (5:21)—and the false prophet "who teaches lies". The verse is thus concerned with apportioning blame for Israel's fate, perhaps inserted here in the days of Jeremiah (read Jer. 23), whereas originally "head and tail, palm branch and reed" meant simply everyone, high and low, the whole spectrum of society, as the rest of the stanza makes clear. Even widows and orphans are godless fools (v. 17) and can expect no compassion. This is the only passage in the Old Testament where their suffering is included in a picture of judgment.

The third stanza (vv. 18–21) adds internal strife to the picture of anarchy and desperation: "no man spares his brother" (v. 19). Fire has a double meaning here: on the one hand the burning "briers and thorns" make the point that wickedness is self-destructive. The highly inflammable "briers and thorns" that infest the vineyard of the Lord (5:6; 7:23–25) will catch fire, and in that conflagration the whole country will be destroyed (v. 18). On the other hand, "the wrath of the Lord of hosts" is also a consuming fire and it will burn up the land and its inhabitants (v. 19)—people will be "fuel for the fire" like the bloodstained equipment of a defeated army (9:5).

The two short sentences at the end of verses 19 and 20 should probably be taken together: in Hebrew they have a similar structure and are parallel in meaning. The Hebrew text of the second has a still more desperate image than the RSV translation: "each man devours the flesh of his own arm", like the Ancient Mariner. Ephraim and Manasseh are mentioned by name, not only because they were the most closely related of all the northern tribes, being sons of Joseph, but also because they were the largest and strongest regions in the Northern Kingdom.

The reference to Judah in verse 21, like the gloss in verse 15, looks like a comment by someone in Jerusalem; and the worst of it all, he says, was that these bloodthirsty, desperate criminals were against Judah. He may have had in mind the Syro-Ephraimite war, or more likely, it is an anti-Samaritan comment from a much later period (see above on 9:9). At all events he conveniently misses the point of this section, which was to draw a lesson from the fate of the Northern Kingdom, and apply it to Judah.

WOE TO JUDAH ... WOE TO ASSYRIA

Isaiah 10:1–6

> [1]Woe to those who decree iniquitous decrees,
>   and the writers who keep writing oppression,
> [2]to turn aside the needy from justice
>   and to rob the poor of my people of their right,
> that widows may be their spoil,
>   and that they may make the fatherless their prey!
> [3]What will you do on the day of punishment,
>   in the storm which will come from afar?
> To whom will you flee for help,
>   and where will you leave your wealth?
> [4]Nothing remains but to crouch among the prisoners
>   or fall among the slain.
> For all this his anger is not turned away
>   and his hand is stretched out still.
>
> [5]Ah, Assyria, the rod of my anger,
>   the staff of my fury!
> [6]Against a godless nation I send him,
>   and against the people of my wrath I command him,
> to take spoil and seize plunder,
>   and to tread them down like the mire of the streets.

The last of the stanzas ending with the refrain "For all this his anger ..." is different in many ways from the preceding ones. Indeed so different is 10:1–4 from the other stanzas that its relationship to what precedes it has often been missed. In the first place, it is addressed to the people it attacks: "To whom will you flee for help?" (v. 3). The previous stanzas have all been about Ephraim, Manasseh and Samaria, that is to say, the Northern Kingdom, in the third person. The prophet describes their crimes and the depths of anarchy and desperation to which they have been reduced by the intervention of an angry God. Then he turns to his audience in Jerusalem, as he did at the end of the Parable of the Vineyard, and says in effect: "You are no better. Your turn will come!" We can immediately recognize another attack on injustice and oppression, just like the bitter prophecies of doom in chapters 1–5, all of them addressed to Judah, and six of them starting with the heavily loaded term "Woe to . . .". These six and the present passage in fact make up a little collection of "Woes" (see on 5:8–25).

The effect of this rhetorical device is heightened in a number of ways. "My people" in verse 2 contrasts the crimes of Judah with those of the Northern Kingdom that precede it, and in addition makes them seem all the more serious since they are crimes against God's own beloved people. The mention of "widows" and "the fatherless" similarly contrasts with the pitiless scene in 9:17: he is in in effect saying, "Their plight, O men of Judah, is your fault!" Finally the concluding words of the stanza, before the refrain, depict Judah's leaders as trapped in those very scenes of humiliation and carnage that they thought were reserved for Ephraim and Samaria. Certainly 10:1–4 may originally have been the seventh in a series of "Woe-sayings" preserved in chapter 5; but that is no reason to neglect its present literary context (as most modern commentators do). Its added refrain and its position make it clear that it is intended as a biting climax to the poem that begins in 9:8. It alters the whole meaning and purpose of the poem: the refrain now applies to the impending fate of Jerusalem, and there is no doubt that the word "Israel", in the very first verse of the poem, included Judah after all:

> The Lord has sent a word against Jacob,
>   and it will light upon Israel.

Verse 2 explains what is meant by "those who decree iniquitous decrees" and the "writers who keep writing oppression" in verse 1. Those in positions of authority in Judah were manipulating the legal system in such a way as to favour their own interests, particularly in matters of land and property ownership. In a society where the poor were not represented on the legislative body, their rights had to be protected by the law of the land. If the laws were unjust, then they were at the mercy of the ruling classes. Exod. 22:21–24 illustrates the kind of legislation they ought to have been following, a legislation devised to protect the underprivileged in ancient Israel, and how such legislation was sanctioned: "If you do afflict them and they cry out to me, I will surely hear their cry, and my wrath will burn ..."

Verse 3 assumes that a "day of punishment" is inevitable, and describes it as a terrible catastrophe. The word translated "storm" means much more than any meteorological phenomenon can suggest. "Ruin" (NEB), "destruction" (Jerusalem Bible) and "desolation" (AV) are nearer the mark. In Modern Hebrew it is the word used to describe the extermination of six million Jews in Nazi concentration camps, corresponding to the English word "holocaust".

The following verses, also a "Woe-saying" of a kind, are about Assyria, and their position, immediately after the final stanza of the poem of God's anger, is interesting. Just as the addition of 10:1–4 transformed the poem in 9:8ff. from a description of the Northern Kingdom to an attack on Jerusalem, so verses 5ff. take us beyond judgment and destruction to hope and the possibility of a new start. Assyria, the means of judgment, is also arrogant and haughty and must be punished too (v. 12). Thereafter the announcement of the fall of Assyria makes way for another messianic prophecy (11:1–9) and the hymn of thanksgiving in chapter 12, which concludes the first main division of the book.

Continuity between verses 4 and 5, that is, from the one "Woe-saying" to the other, is further established by the anger-motif. The refrain at the end of verse 4 states, for the last time, that God's "anger is not turned away, and his hand is stretched out still": and verse 5 tells us what kind of big stick he holds in that outstretched hand, and what he uses it for. To make the point even more emphatically, God himself is speaking now: "the rod of my anger . . . against a godless nation I send him . . ." What he has to say is this: all the defeats and disasters brought upon Israel by the Assyrians are part of his plan—the mighty army of Assyria is but a tool in his hand.

The belief that national disaster can be God's will seems to have been hammered out of Israel's experiences in the eighth century B.C. The idea that God uses suffering to educate or discipline his people is universal: e.g.

> Behold, happy is the man whom God reproves;
>> therefore despise not the chastening of the Almighty. (Job 5:17)

But the application of this notion systematically to national history was new. The whole "Deuteronomistic History" (Josh.–Kings) is built around this pattern as, for example, 2 Kings 17 and 24 illustrate. When Jerusalem fell in 586 B.C. this too was under-stood to be God's work, and that meant that there was hope for his people, since now they had "received from the Lord's hand double for all their sins" (40:2) and could start again in newness of life. This stems from a faith so strong that, whatever happens, it can see God's hand at work in it.

The "rod" in God's hand stands for something painful but life-giving. Without it Israel would have died out like the Canaanites, the Amorites, the Babylonians and all the other ancient peoples that survive only in ancient texts. In the words of a Biblical disciplinarian:

> Do not withhold discipline from a child;
>> if you beat him with a rod, he will not die.
> If you beat him with a rod
>> you will save his life from Sheol. (Prov. 23:13–14)

The second part of verse 5 could mean "my fury is in their hand", a graphic way to describe the Assyrian invasions. Verse 6 picks up a number of familiar themes from earlier judgment prophecies: "godless" from 9:17; "spoil" and "plunder" from the name Mahershalalhashbaz (8:1–4); "tread them down" from 7:25;

"in the streets" from 5:25. The present context, however, is not a judgment prophecy directed against Jerusalem, but against Assyria, and the point of repeating all these examples of defeat and humiliation is that they too are demonstrations of God's justice, and that Assyria is a mere instrument in the out-stretched hand of an ultimately loving God.

THE ARROGANCE OF ASSYRIA

Isaiah 10:7–19

> 7But he does not so intend,
>   and his mind does not so think;
>   but it is in his mind to destroy,
>   and to cut off nations not a few;
> 8for he says:
>   "Are not my commanders all kings?
> 9Is not Calno like Carchemish?
>   Is not Hamath like Arpad?
>   Is not Samaria like Damascus?
> 10As my hand has reached to the kingdoms of the idols
>   whose graven images were greater than those of Jerusalem and
>   Samaria,
> 11shall I not do to Jerusalem and her idols
>   as I have done to Samaria and her images?"

12When the Lord has finished all his work on Mount Zion and on Jerusalem he will punish the arrogant boasting of the king of Assyria and his haughty pride. 13For he says:

> "By the strength of my hand I have done it,
>   and by my wisdom, for I have understanding;
>   I have removed the boundaries of peoples,
>   and have plundered their treasures;
>   like a bull I have brought down those who sat on thrones.
> 14My hand has found like a nest
>   the wealth of the peoples;
>   and as men gather eggs that have been forsaken
>   so I have gathered all the earth;
>   and there was none that moved a wing,
>   or opened the mouth, or chirped."

¹⁵Shall the axe vaunt itself over him who hews with it,
    or the saw magnify itself against him who wields it?
As if a rod should wield him who lifts it,
    or as if a staff should lift him who is not wood!
¹⁶Therefore the Lord, the Lord of hosts,
    will send wasting sickness among his stout warriors,
and under his glory a burning will be kindled,
    like the burning of fire.
¹⁷The light of Israel will become a fire,
    and his Holy One a flame;
and it will burn and devour
    his thorns and briers in one day.
¹⁸The glory of his forest and of his fruitful land
    the Lord will destroy, both soul and body,
    and it will be as when a sick man wastes away.
¹⁹The remnant of the trees of his forest will be so few
    that a child can write them down.

The judgment prophecy continues with two arrogant speeches from the mouth of the king of Assyria (vv. 8–11 and 13–14), and a prophecy that his army and his land will be completely destroyed (16–19). His crime, the crime of one who was supposed to be a mere tool in God's hand, is encapsulated in the proverbial language of verse 15: "Shall the axe vaunt itself over him who hews with it . . .?" From an outside observer's view of history, verse 7 takes us into the mind of one of the participants. Instead of obedience to God's will, instead of merely doing his duty, the king of Assyria begins to enjoy his ugly commission and to follow his own imperialistic lust for power. His first speech opens by claiming that his commanders are equal in military might and prestige to the rulers of whole countries, in particular the countries which he has conquered and whose kings he has in fact replaced. The ominous list of cities agrees quite closely with what we know of Assyrian successes during Isaiah's lifetime: Calno and Arpad in northern Syria were conquered in 738 B.C.; Hamath on the Orontes in 720; and the Hittite city Carchemish on the northern frontier of Syria in 717. Damascus fell to Tiglath-Pileser III in 734 (2 Kings 16:19), and Samaria in 722 (2 Kings 17).

Verses 10 and 11 go on to compare idolatrous kingdoms, like Syria, with Samaria and Jerusalem, and Samaria with Jerusalem. The point of the first comparison is that, even in the eyes of a pagan outsider like the king of Assyria, there was supposed to be a distinction between Israel's religion and that of her neighbours. Yet Jerusalem and Samaria were both idolatrous, and fair game for him. The comparison between Jerusalem and Samaria, on the other hand, looks like more anti-Samaritan propaganda, since, although the king of Assyria saw no distinction between them and planned to destroy both without discrimination, we know that while he was correct about the idolatry of Samaria and had every right to destroy it (2 Kings 17:7–18), he failed to conquer Jerusalem (Isa. 36–37):

> He shall not come into this city, says the Lord. For I will defend this city to save it, for my own sake and for the sake of my servant David. (Isa. 37:34–35)

The fact that the king who destroyed Samaria in 722 B.C (Shalmaneser V) was not the same as the one who besieged Jerusalem in 701 (Sennacherib), merely serves to illustrate once again that these texts are not historical but prophetic. Their intention is to teach, interpret and inspire, not to record what happened in ancient Israel. The king of Assyria is a composite character in the present chapter, a prophet's symbol for divine intervention in the history of his people.

Verse 12 pictures a time when the sufferings of Mount Zion and Jerusalem are over, and the Lord turns his attention to the "arrogant boasting of the king of Assyria". The comment may have been added in the light of the catastrophe of 586 B.C., and should be compared with chapter 40. Again the historical vagueness—Assyria had been destroyed forever in 612—must not blind us to the religious and poetic value of the verse. "The king of Assyria", here and throughout the Book of Isaiah, has much more than a purely historical meaning.

The second of his haughty speeches (vv. 13–14) contains the vocabulary of blasphemy. More than once Israel is rebuked for saying, "My power and the might of my hand have gotten me this wealth" (Deut. 8:17). Judg. 7:2 is another example. Elsewhere "those who are wise in their own eyes" are condemned (5:21), because wisdom comes from God; or to put this another way, "The fear of the Lord is the beginning of wisdom" (Prov. 1:7; 9:10; Job 28:28). Moving boundaries and landmarks is likewise condemned in many passages as a challenge to the sovereignty of God: the Song of Moses puts it this way:

> When the Most High gave to the nations their inheritance,
>> when he separated the sons of men,
> he fixed the bounds of the peoples
>> according to the number of the sons of God. (Deut. 32:8)

Finally the phrase "like a bull" or possibly "like the Mighty One" claims equality with the "Mighty One of Israel", that is with God himself (Isa 1:24), although the Hebrew text of this last phrase is not certain. All these blasphemous boasts and actions are not only attributed to the king of Assyria, but proudly placarded before us by the king himself. He then goes on haughtily to claim that his victories were easily won: the peoples of the world were more vulnerable than the eggs in a bird's nest. The eggs would have been defended by a courageous hen, flapping her wings, pecking at the intruders and squawking frantically; but before the advance of the king of Assyria in all his might and splendour, the nations of the world, paralysed with fright, could do nothing.

Such boasting on the part of one who is a mere tool in the hand of the Lord of hosts is absurd: as if an axe could tell the woodman what to chop down, or a stick the teacher which pupil to punish. It is not only absurd to talk like that: it is blasphemous. The woodman is the one who decides which trees to chop down, and in this case the trees are Assyrian trees. After the Lord of hosts has finished with them, "the remnant of the trees of the forest will be so few that a child can write them down" (v. 19). There will also be a plague which will reduce fit warriors to cadavers (v. 16). Probably the "burning" in the second half of verse 16 is a fever that attacks them as well, like "the burning of a fire", and replaces their glory with disfigurement and degradation. The campaign against Israel will destroy him, because the Holy One of Israel is a consuming fire; if he so much as touches Israel, he will be burnt alive (v. 17).

This picture of the fate of Assyria may have been influenced by the legend of what happened in 701 B.C. as recounted in chapter 37. The boasts of the king of Assyria there (37:24–25) are not dissimilar to those we have been considering in chapter 10, and, in addition to colourful prophecies describing crashing cities, their citizens withering like tender grass, there is the cryptic reference to a sudden catastrophe that sent the Assyrians back to Nineveh: "And the angel of the Lord went forth and slew a hundred and eighty-five thousand in the camp of the Assyrians ..." (37:36). Is this the plague predicted in 10:16? All the massed forces of Assyria would be devoured "in one day" (10:17). Or else the poet has simply gathered together a variety of images from other poems and combined them into a particularly gruesome prophecy, appropriate to the haughty subject, without having any actual event in mind.

No attempt is made to discover the seeds of hope in "the remnant of the trees" as was done in 6:13. Hope in this passage rests in the totality of destruction. Once the king of Assyria has completed his task of punishing Israel, he will be destroyed, and the people of God will be able to start again. That is the theme of the next passage.

BE NOT AFRAID OF ASSYRIA, MY PEOPLE

Isaiah 10:20–34

20In that day the remnant of Israel and the survivors of the house of Jacob will no more lean upon him that smote them, but will lean upon the Lord, the Holy One of Israel, in truth. 21A remnant will return, the remnant of Jacob, to the mighty God. 22For though your people Israel be as the sand of the sea, only a remnant of them will return. Destruction is decreed, overflowing with righteousness. 23For the Lord, the Lord of hosts, will make a full end, as decreed, in the midst of all the earth.

²⁴Therefore thus says the Lord, the Lord of hosts: "O my people, who dwell in Zion, be not afraid of the Assyrians when they smite with the rod and lift up their staff against you as the Egyptians did. ²⁵For in a very little while my indignation will come to an end, and my anger will be directed to their destruction. ²⁶And the Lord of hosts will wield against them a scourge, as when he smote Midian at the rock of Oreb; and his rod will be over the sea, and he will lift it as he did in Egypt. ²⁷And in that day his burden will depart from your shoulder, and his yoke will be destroyed from your neck."

He has gone up from Rimmon,
²⁸   he has come to Aiath;
    he has passed through Migron,
        at Michmash he stores his baggage;
²⁹they have crossed over the pass,
        at Geba they lodge for the night;
    Ramah trembles,
        Gibeah of Saul has fled.
³⁰Cry aloud, O daughter of Gallim!
        Hearken, O Laishah!
        Answer her, O Anathoth!
³¹Madmenah is in flight,
        the inhabitants of Gebim flee for safety.
³²This very day he will halt at Nob,
        he will shake his fist
        at the mount of the daughter of Zion,
        the hill of Jerusalem.

³³Behold, the Lord, the Lord of hosts
        will lop the boughs with terrifying power;
    the great in height will be hewn down,
        and the lofty will be brought low.
³³He will cut down the thickets of the forest with an axe,
        and Lebanon with its majestic trees will fall.

Four shorter passages on the fate of Assyria follow: anyone who relies on Assyria for help will be totally destroyed (vv. 20–23); Jerusalem has nothing to fear from Assyria (vv. 24–26); Jerusalem alone will survive the Assyrian invasion (vv. 27–32); the Lord of hosts will cut them down with an axe (vv. 33–34). There are many echoes of earlier ideas and images: Shearjashub, Mighty God, the anger of God, the day of Midian, the burden and the yoke on Israel's back. Probably, like other anti-Assyrian passages, they come from the reign of Josiah (640–609 B.C.) when the decline of Assyrian power sparked off in Jerusalem renewed national confidence which could ideally be expressed in Isaianic idiom. We should not therefore expect to find accurate history reflected here.

The first passage (vv. 20–23) contains several ambiguities: the remnant can be a sign of hope or a symbol of almost total destruction; "Israel" and "the house of Jacob" can refer to the whole people of Israel or just the Northern Kingdom; and who or what exactly is destroyed, "as decreed in the midst of the whole earth", is not certain. It seems probable that, like the following prophecy (vv. 24–26), this one is about Israel as a whole. Certainly in the phrase "the Holy One of Israel" it cannot have any other meaning, and "your people Israel" points in the same direction. Furthermore it was Judah, under King Ahaz, that "leant upon him that smote them" (i.e. turned to Assyria for help: 2 Kings 16; Isaiah 7–8), not the Northern Kingdom. The passage thus alludes to the "overflowing" destruction, "reaching even to the neck" (8:5–8), that resulted from Ahaz's faithlessness and disobedience (chapter 7 fills in the details). Such is the fate of those who rely on Assyria.

Here however the prophet looks beyond that catastrophe to a time when Israel "will lean upon the Lord", and that puts a different complexion on things. In the first place, "in truth" (v. 20) picks up the theme of believing, and therefore being established, from chapter 7 (see especially v. 9). Then there is the remnant motif: verse 21 begins with the words Shearjashub, the name of Isaiah's first son (chapter 7), and that spells hope for the people. Thirdly, "overflowing" is given a new meaning. In 8:8 it suggests an irresistible flood sweeping over the land, destroying everything in its path: here the flood is an act of righteous intervention, totally under God's control, "overflowing with righteousness" (v. 22). Finally the enemy will be totally destroyed; no part of the earth will ever again be overrun or oppressed by the king of Assyria (v. 23).

In verses 24–26 the Lord of hosts addresses his "people who dwell in Zion" and tells them, as he told Ahaz in chapters 7–8, not to fear the Assyrian oppressors. Assyria is acting under his orders and soon, when his anger passes, they will be the ones to suffer. Their defeat will be no less spectacular than Gideon's victory over the Midianites (Judg. 6–8), or the Exodus itself. There God's rod had a very different function—miracle-working on behalf of instead of chastizing his people (e.g. Exod. 7–9). But now those who were once dutifully serving God as "the rod of his anger" (10:5) have provoked him to anger and will themselves be punished with the scourge. And having witnessed the humiliation of God's people through nine chapters of mainly doom-laden invective, we are approaching the saving climax of Isaiah 1–12, which picks up the fragments of hope scattered among the earlier chapters and out of them constructs a prophecy of victory and salvation.

"And in that day" in verse 27 surely introduces another prophecy, as it did in verse 20. The second part of the verse is admittedly difficult, as you will see from the various English translations, but however we understand it, it does not seem necessary or desirable to split the verse in two (RSV). The thought of verses 27–32 seems to be that the threat of defeat and oppression will approach the very hills around Jerusalem, but at the last moment will depart. Verse 27 predicts this in general terms, and the next five verses picture in vivid detail how it happens. The account of an approaching army has usually been understood to refer to the invasion of Sennacherib in 701 B.C., and in view of its importance in Isaianic tradition and the legendary aura that it acquired (chapters 36–37), it hardly seems necessary to question this traditional interpretation, even if the geography does not fit perfectly. The route described may not have actually been that of Sennacherib in 701, but in its present context surely that is what the passage is about.

The last phrase in verse 27 as it stands means something like "and the yoke will be destroyed because of fatness". Ancient commentators assumed this referred to Sennacherib's retreat from Judah (37:36–38): "the yoke" stands for Sennacherib, and "fatness" for the rich land of Judah during Hezekiah's long and prosperous reign (2 Chron. 32:27–31). This makes sense, but the wording is nonetheless awkward and many emendations have been proposed. Almost without exception they try to identify another place-name to add to the start of the invaders' route: e.g. "Rimmon" (RSV, Jerusalem Bible, NEB), a few miles north of Michmash (v. 28); or "Samaria", 25 miles north of that. Rimmon is perhaps the most in line with the rest of the list, but Samaria would have polemical relevance as well.

The action words in the thrilling description of an approaching enemy army are as significant as the place-names: the enemy "falls upon (better than 'comes to') . . . passes through, crosses over . . . (and finally) halts . . . and shakes his fist . . ."; the victims 'tremble . . . flee . . . cry aloud . . . flee for safety". Perhaps the place-names were also selected for their meaning rather than for strict geographical reasons: Aiath, "a ruin"; Migron, "hurled to the ground" (?); Ramah and Gibeah, "mountains" or "heights" that tremble (v. 29); Gallim, "waves" (8:7–8); Laishah, "lioness"; Madmenah, "dung-heap"; and Gebim, "pits". The last place, Nob, is certainly one of the hills round Jerusalem, perhaps the Mount of Olives or Mount Scopus. The effect is cumulative: according to the account in Isaiah 36–37, "in the fourteenth year of King Hezekiah, Sennacherib king of Assyria came up against all the fortified cities of Judah and took them" (36:1). But Jerusalem survived:

As the mountains are round about Jerusalem,
so the Lord is round about his people. (Ps. 125:2)

Finally (vv. 33–34) the awesome fate of Assyria is described as the destruction of a great forest of majestic trees. The Lord of hosts will take an axe and cut down the powerful, well-established leaders of an empire that had survived for centuries and had spread all over the world. Even her most magnificent and precious achievements, her "cedars of Lebanon", will be destroyed. As in verses 16–19, there will be no remnant; not even a stump will survive from that proud and evil forest.

THE NOBLE STEM OF JESSE

Isaiah 11:1–9

> [1]There shall come forth a shoot from the stump of Jesse,
>   and a branch shall grow out of his roots.
> [2]And the Spirit of the Lord shall rest upon him,
>   the spirit of wisdom and understanding,
>   the spirit of counsel and might,
>   the spirit of knowledge and the fear of the Lord.
> [3]And his delight shall be in the fear of the Lord.
>
> He shall not judge by what his eyes see,
>   or decide by what his ears hear;
> [4]but with righteousness he shall judge the poor,
>   and decide with equity for the meek of the earth;
> and he shall smite the earth with the rod of his mouth,
>   and with the breath of his lips he shall slay the wicked.
> [5]Righteousness shall be the girdle of his waist,
>   and faithfulness the girdle of his loins.
>
> [6]The wolf shall dwell with the lamb,
>   and the leopard shall lie down with the kid,
> and the calf and the lion and the fatling together,
>   and a little child shall lead them.
> [7]The cow and the bear shall feed;
>   their young shall lie down together;
>   and the lion shall eat straw like the ox.
> [8]The sucking child shall play over the hole of the asp,
>   and the weaned child shall put his hand on the adder's den.
> [9]They shall not hurt or destroy
>   in all my holy mountain;
> for the earth shall be full of the knowledge of the Lord
>   as the waters cover the sea.

Following on from chapter 10, we must see a contrast between the cutting down of the Assyrian forest in 10:33–34 and the appearance in the midst of the devastation of "a shoot from the stump of Jesse". The one sign of life in what was left of Judah, the one city that survived the world-wide destruction, the one tree still standing, was Jerusalem—

... out of Zion shall go forth the law,
   and the word of the Lord from Jerusalem. (2:3; 37:32)

Other commentators, wishing to emphasize the link between chapters 10 and 11 still more, remove the last two verses of 10 from their context in a series of anti-Assyrian prophecies and, assuming a new beginning at 10:33, apply them to the destruction of David's kingdom, as background to 11:1-9. We had a similar problem at the beginning of chapter 9; and the ending of chapter 6 shows how the Davidic hope can be added by later believers to a description of judgment and despair. But whether the description in 10:33-34 refers to the downfall of the whole Assyrian Empire, including Judah, or just to Judah, the miraculous appearance in Jerusalem, the one city not destroyed by the Assyrians, of a live tree bringing hope into the world again, is true to the Isaianic vision.

The style and content of this second of the book's "messianic" prophecies suggest comparison with exilic literature like Jer. 33:14-16, Ezek. 37:24-25 and the later parts of Isaiah (e.g. 32:1-8; 42:1-4), rather than with the first one in 9:1-7.

The image in verse 1 is of a noble, healthy tree, with strong roots and fruitful branches, putting forth new shoots. Job 14:7-9 is a more detailed description of the same scene, using much of the same language. The word translated "stump" (RSV) has nothing to do with the "stump" in 6:13, and really means "trunk, stem" (AV) or, in genealogical terms, "stock (NEB, Jerusalem Bible), race". The word translated "grow" has the sense of "be fruitful". A "shoot" is a tough new growth on a healthy tree, the material that wicker-baskets are made of, for example, and schoolmasters' canes (Prov. 14:3).

The mention of Jesse, David's father (1 Sam. 16:1-13), shows that we are dealing with genealogical imagery: the "stock" is David's dynasty and the new "shoot" or "branch" is a new king or "Messiah", a "son of David", who will "come forth" and "bear fruit" in Jerusalem. Verse 2 lists some of these "fruits" (wisdom, understanding, etc.), and later we hear of righteousness, justice, faithfulness and "the knowledge of the Lord". The gifts of this new king come from God as they did in ancient legend, where the spirit of the Lord "rested" on the seventy elders (Num. 11:25–26), "took possession of" Gideon (Judg. 6:34), and "came mightily" upon Samson (Judg. 14:19; 15:14) and upon David (1 Sam. 16:13). The seventy leaders provide the closest parallel, because they shared with Moses the prophetic leadership of Israel. The new king is going to be characterized by all the skills and strengths prescribed in Proverbs (e.g. 1:2–7; 8:4–11; 24:3–7) and Solomonic legend (e.g. 1 Kings 3:3–28). Wisdom, understanding, counsel and knowledge refer to the ancient pragmatic skills, common to all cultures—"be wise as serpents" is how Jesus put it (Matt. 10:16). "Might", that is, strength of character, is part of the same picture, summed up by Wisdom herself in Prov. 8:

> I have counsel and sound wisdom,
>   I have insight, I have strength.
> By me kings reign,
>   and rulers decree what is just. (vv. 14–15)

But "the fear of the Lord" is distinctively Israelite. It is not enough that Israel's king should be like the kings in all the other nations. In the language of Proverbs, "the fear of the Lord is the beginning of wisdom" (1:7; 9:10). Deuteronomy puts it this way:

> When he sits on the throne of his kingdom, he shall write for himself in a book a copy of this law ... and he shall read in it all the days of his life, that he may learn to fear the Lord his God, by keeping all the words of this law ... that his heart may not be lifted up. (Deut. 17:18–20).

The Isaianic vision sees a king who will live up to all these requirements. Verse 3b declares that he will be scrupulously fair in the administration of justice, putting right the injustices of his predecessors (e.g. 5:18–23). Verses 4–5 add a more religious emphasis on "righteousness" and "faithfulness" recalling the "faithful city" in chapter 1. The vision of an ideal king whose strength lies, not in physical or military force, but in persuasive rhetoric and wise decisions also comes from traditional Wisdom teaching:

A wise man is mightier than a strong man ...
for by wise guidance you can wage your war,
    and in abundance of counsellors there is victory. (Prov. 24:5–6)

Proverbs 15 has a whole collection of variations on the theme of verse 4. This king will succeed, where others have failed, in protecting the interests of the poor and vulnerable members of society. In modern parlance he will exercise "positive discrimination" in favour of those who need help.

The three Hebrew words at the beginning of verse 3, translated "And his delight shall be in the fear of the Lord", may be due to a scribal error: they look in Hebrew very like a variant of the last part of verse 2. They do make sense, however, emphasizing the centrality of "the fear of the Lord" in the description of the ideal king and perhaps adding another image. The word translated "his delight" comes from a verb normally meaning "to smell", and so the meaning would be that the king will be clothed in righteousness and faithfulness (v. 5) and wearing "the fear of God" as perfume. A royal Psalm contains similar imagery (Ps. 45:6–9).

The second part of the poem is just as typically Isaianic (vv. 6–9). Verse 9 may be a late addition, but the references to Jerusalem ("my holy mountain") and "the knowledge of the Lord" forge a link with verses 1–5 and ensure that the stanzas are taken together as two aspects of the one vision. It is usually assumed that the prophecy is primarily concerned with the restoration of peace between man and nature. This view of paradise regained appears elsewhere in Biblical tradition: Job 5:23, for example, envisages an idyllic world where stones never break the farmer's ploughshare and wild beasts leave his animals to graze in peace. In the Wisdom literature, however, which has obvious affinities with the style and imagery of this passage, the world of nature is more often cited to illustrate social, moral or political truths, than as a subject in its own right. Proverbs contains many examples: e.g. birds, ants, gazelles in 6:1–8, and ravens, vultures, eagles, serpents, ants, badgers, locusts, lizards, lions, cocks and he-goats in 30:17–31. References to wolves are usually about fierceness and oppression (e.g. Gen. 49:27; Zeph. 3:3), while "a lamb led to the slaughter" stands for helplessness (e.g. Jer. 11:19). It seems therefore more likely that this prophecy is not literally about the taming of wild animals and the removal of natural dangers from the countryside, but about a new age in which old enmities will be forgotten, the mighty will live peacefully with the weak (v. 6), ruthless exploiters of the poor and needy will change their habits (v. 7), and the vulnerable will be immune from danger (v. 8). Verse 9 sums it all up in the two words translated "hurt" and "destroy": there will be no more ill-treatment or corruption in Zion. Nature conservancy and animal rights may be part of such a vision, but in a world where minorities are still persecuted, and nations still kill each other in war, they are surely not at the centre of it. It is the vision of a new world characterized by justice, righteousness and peace, a world ruled by an ideal king, the Messiah, son of David, and a world in which the people (not the animals) "shall be full of the knowledge of the Lord as the waters cover the sea."

A MESSIANIC SIGN TO THE NATIONS

Isaiah 11:10–16

[10]In that day the root of Jesse shall stand as an ensign to the peoples; him shall the nations seek, and his dwellings shall be glorious.

[11]In that day the Lord will extend his hand yet a second time to recover the remnant which is left of his people, from Assyria, from Egypt, from Pathros, from Ethiopia, from Elam, from Shinar, from Hamath, and from the coastlands of the sea.

[12]He will raise an ensign for the nations,
   and will assemble the outcasts of Israel,
  and gather the dispersed of Judah
   from the four corners of the earth.

[13]The jealousy of Ephraim shall depart,
   and those who harass Judah shall be cut off;
  Ephraim shall not be jealous of Judah,
   and Judah shall not harass Ephraim.

[14]But they shall swoop down upon the shoulder of the Philistines in the
      west,
   and together they shall plunder the people of the east.

> They shall put forth their hand against Edom and Moab,
>   and the Ammonites shall obey them.
> ¹⁵And the Lord will utterly destroy
>   the tongue of the sea of Egypt;
> and will wave his hand over the River
>   with his scorching wind,
> and smite it into seven channels
>   that men may cross dryshod.
> ¹⁶And there will be a highway from Assyria
>   for the remnant which is left of his people,
> as there was for Israel
>   when they came up from the land of Egypt.

The last prophecy in Isaiah 1–12 (chapter 12 is a hymn of thanksgiving) finally leaves behind any hope that an actual king will bring peace and justice to Judah and translates the dynastic language into a transcendent, messianic dream, in which the exiles will return from the ends of the earth, Israel will be united and all the enemies of God's people will be destroyed. The world to which such a prophecy was addressed is thus very different from the world of ancient Israel that we have in mind so far. No longer is there a king on the throne of David, God's people are already scattered to the four corners of the earth, and beleaguered Judah is even able to consider joining forces with Ephraim—the Jews with the Samaritans—to fight off the assaults of their enemies. In other words this prophecy comes from the Second Temple period, which begins with the rebuilding of the Temple in Jerusalem in 515 B.C., and includes the New Testament period down to A.D. 70 when the Roman legions destroyed the Temple for the second time. It will be no surprise to find the beginnings of apocalyptic style and imagery here, and close parallels with the Books of Haggai, Zechariah, Joel and Daniel.

"The root of Jesse" does not refer to an actual "branch" or "shoot" from David's family tree, but to the roots of that line firmly planted in Jerusalem. He is not pictured any more as himself achieving anything, but stands as a "signal" or a "sign" to the nations. They will flock to it as they will to Zion in 2:2–3, and they will find rest and glory. The last words in the verse (literally, "and his rest will be glorious") add two keywords to the picture. "Rest" is associated with the promised land as God's dwelling place (Ps. 95:11; 132:14) and generally with peace and security (e.g. Ps. 23:2; 1 Kings 8:56). "Glory" often means no more than "beauty", like the splendour of the newly built Temple in Hag. 2:7–9, or the majesty of a king (e.g. 1 Chron. 29:12, 28). But applied to God it transcends human analogies (Exod. 24:16–17), and in later descriptions of the world to come "glory" refers to a quality that "no eye has seen, nor ear heard" (1 Cor. 2:9). So Isa. 11:10 looks like an early intimation of the glory of the Messianic Age (John 1:14).

"In that day" (v. 11) introduces a second feature of the Messianic Age, the ingathering of the exiles. The "remnant" theme, taken up from 10:20–23, and the Shearjashub account in 7:1–9, here has a totally positive meaning, "survivors". Probably Assyria and Egypt were the only two places mentioned in the original text (as in v. 16), and it is interesting to note the thinking behind the additional list. Pathros and Ethiopia (Cush in Hebrew) are the regions of Egypt farthest away from Jerusalem; and Syene (Isa. 49:12) was situated in Pathros. Similarly Elam and Shinar were regions in the south of Mesopotamia, beyond Assyria, and Babylon was situated in Shinar (Gen. 11:1–9). Hamath in Syria is the nearest point to Israel, and the coastlands (Isa. 41:1; 49:1), which included Cyprus, Greece, Italy, even Spain, the most distant. One can also recognize in the list references to the "four corners of the earth" (v. 12): Hamath—North, Egypt—South, Elam and Shinar—East, "the coastlands of the sea"—West.

The bitter enmity between Jews and Samaritans that lies behind the longing for reconciliation expressed in verse 13 goes back to the early years of the restoration after the Babylonian Exile at the latest. We have come across it already in Isaianic tradition (e.g. 8:14; 9:8–21; 10:27(?)), and it was obviously exacerbated by the rebuilding of a Temple at Jerusalem in spite of opposition from Sanballat, governor of Samaria (Neh. 2–6).

The five peoples mentioned in verse 14 represent the traditional enemies on Israel's frontiers. Their subjugation, expressed in suitably vivid terms, amounts to the restoration of David's Golden Age, since only he succeeded in subduing them all at the same time and extending his frontiers to incorporate their lands. Furthermore Edom, Moab and Ammon had annexed tracts of Judah's land at the time of the Babylonian conquest (2 Kings 24:2; Lam. 4:21), and this is by no means the most bitter or vengeful of the Biblical attacks upon such peoples. The fierce language of Jeremiah 47–49 comes from the same period, as do the extraordinarily vicious attacks in the exilic chapters of Isaiah (e.g. 49:22–26; 51:21–23). One must offset such passages against the wistful longing for a day when "nation shall not lift up sword against nation, neither shall they learn war any more" (2:4).

At first sight verse 15 seems confused: what is the River? Why seven channels? Is the verse exclusively about the Exodus from Egypt? But we must realize that there are two sources for the imagery, not only Israelite legend, but also ancient near-eastern mythology. A similar amalgam appears in 51:9–11, and pure mythology in 27:1. The first part of the verse describes the victory of Yahweh over the powers of chaos, symbolized by the mythical monsters Sea (Yam) and River (Nahar). Psalm 74:13–14 is a good parallel:

> Thou didst divide the sea by thy might,
>   thou didst break the heads of the dragons in the waters.

An ancient Canaanite example from the Ras Shamra tablets, in which Baal is the speaker, is even more illuminating:

> Have I not slain Sea, beloved of El?
> Have I not annihilated River, the great god?
> I have slain the crooked serpent, the foul-fanged with seven heads.

Israelite tradition then applies this cosmic victory to the victory of their God, Yahweh, over the Egyptians, and the dry land that appears when Sea is destroyed becomes the route whereby they escape from slavery and oppression and "come to Zion with singing" (51:11). The "scorching wind" comes from the myth (Gen. 1:2; Dan 7:2), "in sandals" (translated "dryshod" in the RSV) comes from the Exodus story (Exod. 12:11). The prophet is describing nothing less than a New Exodus and a New Creation (Isa. 65:17) in one. The New Exodus will be from Assyria because that is the oppressor in Isaiah 1–12; and the returning exiles, "the remnant which is left of his people", will process back to Jerusalem on a highway specially built for them:

> "Prepare the way for the people;
> build up, build up the highway,
> clear it of stones,
> lift up an ensign over the peoples." (62:10; cf. 40:3; 19:23)

Just as the Lord built them a way through the Red Sea, "the waters being a wall to them on their right hand and on their left" (Exod. 14:22, 29), so now a highway will be built to take them in safety out of Assyria.

There have been some rather confusing images and allusions in this last prophecy. But in the end a clear highway opens up from oppression to freedom, and those of God's people who have followed that road will readily understand what the next chapter is about.

THE WELLS OF SALVATION

Isaiah 12:1–6

> ¹You will say in that day:
> "I will give thanks to thee, O Lord,
> for though thou wast angry with me,
> thy anger turned away,
> and thou didst comfort me.
>
> ²"Behold, God is my salvation;
> I will trust, and will not be afraid;
> for the Lord God is my strength and my song,
> and he has become my salvation."
>
> ³With joy you will draw water from the wells of salvation. ⁴And you will say in that day:
> "Give thanks to the Lord,
> call upon his name;

make known his deeds among the nations,
    proclaim that his name is exalted.

[5]"Sing praises to the Lord, for he has done gloriously;
    let this be known in all the earth.
[6]Shout, and sing for joy, O inhabitant of Zion,
    for great in your midst is the Holy One of Israel."

Chapter 12 gives Israel's response to the mighty acts of God which culminate in the New Exodus (11:11–16). It rounds off the first part of the Book of Isaiah by drawing together, in two short songs of thanksgiving, the twin themes of God's wrath "kindled against his people" (5:25), and his triumphant victory which set them free. The language provides continuity both with what goes before ("in that day"; "thy anger turned away" (5:25; 9:12, 17, 21; 10:4); "exalted" (2:11, 17); "Zion"; "the Holy One of Israel") and even more with what comes later in the book ("comfort me" (40:1), salvation, singing, rejoicing, telling the nations, shouting for joy).

More significant than these verbal correspondences is the reference to the Exodus ("he has done gloriously", Exod. 15:1, 6, 11, 21) which picks up a motif from chapter 11 and points forward to a major development of that motif in chapters 40–55. The same applies to the central Isaianic theme of "faith" (v. 2) introduced in chapters 1 and 7, prominent in 36–37, and further developed throughout 40–66; and to the affectionate way in which Jerusalem is addressed (v. 6), pointing back to the "faithful city" poem in chapter 1 and the Zion poems in 2 and 4, and forward to later, equally beautiful and familiar examples such as "Awake, awake, put on your strength, O Zion" (52:1), and "Arise, shine; for your light is come" (60:1).

The two songs (vv. 1–2 and 4–6), like many Isaianic poems, have much in common with the Psalms, and probably have a liturgical origin. Allusions to the Exodus traditions, both in Exod. 15 and Psalms such as 105, 106 and the "Hallel Psalms" (113–118, and 136), perhaps suggest the Passover as the original occasion for which they were written although, unlike the Hallel Psalms, they are not now part of the Jewish Passover ritual as we know it. The introductory rubrics, "You [singular] will say on that day..." (v. 1), and "you [plural] will draw water... and will say..." (vv. 3–4) confirm the songs' liturgical connections. Verse 3 was in fact recited at the Feast of Tabernacles when water from the pool of Siloam was used in the temple ritual. John 7:37–38 may contain an allusion to this.

"I will give thanks..." occurs three times in the Hallel Psalm 118 (vv. 19, 21, 28), and the same Psalm has "Give thanks to the Lord" twice (vv. 1, 29), corresponding to verse 4. Of course the verb occurs many times in the Psalms, but in Isaiah only here and 25:1 ("praise"), 38:18, 19. It can mean both "praise" and "confess", the connection being that true thanksgiving involves acknowledging one's unworthiness. Indeed there are examples in Biblical tradition of a sinner glorifying and praising God for his justice at the very moment of his punishment or execution (e.g. Josh 7:19–21 (the story of Achan at Jericho); Ezra 9; Neh. 9; Dan. 9). In the present context this explains the reference to God's anger at the very beginning of the thanksgiving. Most of Isaiah 1–12 is about sin and judgment; in this closing chapter Israel penitently remembers the rod of God's anger (10:5), but is comforted by the visions of hope in chapters 2, 4, 9 and 11.

Most of verse 2 also comes from the Hallel Psalm 118 (especially verses 14 and 21). "My strength and my song" also occurs in the "Song of the Sea" (Exod. 15:2). "Salvation" (Heb. *yeshu'ah*) is the keyword, however, repeated twice both here and in Ps. 118, then taken up in the beautiful imagery of the next verse. It is at the heart of a whole family of Biblical names and words: Isaiah, Hosea, Joshua and Jesus are all names associated with "salvation", as is the cultic shout "Hosanna!", first occurring in Psalm 118:25 (and the Tabernacles liturgy), then in Christian Palm Sunday traditions (Matt. 21:9). Words for "save", "salvation", "victory" and the like, derived from the same root, are amongst the commonest theological terms in the Old Testament, especially in Psalms and the later sections of the Book of Isaiah, but this is the first appearance in Isaiah. "Salvation" or "victory" is first and foremost something that comes from God the Saviour alone (45:21); other gods cannot "save" (45:20); Assyria cannot "give victory" (Hos. 14:3); no human agent can claim saving power (Judg. 7:2). It is therefore closely connected in many passages, as here, with "trust" and "faith": e.g. "In returning and rest you shall be saved; in quietness and trust shall be your strength" (30:15). Most commonly it refers quite explicitly to an act or acts of divine intervention on behalf of justice, and so comes near to "righteousness" (see on 1:26). "He has become my salvation" therefore means "he has intervened on my behalf" when I was in danger or oppressed (v. 2; Ps. 118:14, 21).

"The wells of salvation" recall the "wells" that sprang out of the rock in the wilderness and perhaps also "the cup of salvation", both alluded to in the Hallel Psalms (114:8; 116:13). Later in Isaiah the image reappears in more elaborate forms: 41:17–20 is one colourful example, and 55:1 another of a different kind: "Ho, everyone who thirsts, come to the waters". In John 4, Jesus (*Yeshua*ʿ) speaks of "a spring of water welling up to eternal life" (v. 14): the joy of drawing from that kind of well is the subject of the song in Isaiah 12 too.

The second song (vv. 4–6) is again in the language of the Hallel Psalms: Ps. 118 begins and ends with "Give thanks to the Lord", and "call on the name of the Lord" appears three times in Ps. 116 (vv. 4, 13, 17). Verse 5 contains another clear echo of the "Song of the Sea": "I will sing to the Lord because he has triumphed gloriously" (Exod. 15: 1, 21). Again it is with the Psalms and later Isaianic tradition that these verses have the closest affinities (e.g. Isa. 25:1; 54:1). The most striking correspondence is the leap from the Exodus to Zion. Isa. 51:9–11 illustrates this beautifully, as we have seen, combining the age-old myths about God's victory over the Sea with the redemption of Israel and her jubilant return from exile. This "New Exodus" can be applied to the experience of all "exiles" when their oppressor is defeated; to the Exodus of Jews from Nazi Germany in the 1930s and 1940s; in Negro spirituals to the liberation of Black American slaves; and in Christian hymns to the liberation from sin and death achieved by Christ: e.g.

O come, O come, Immanuel,
And ransom captive Israel,
That mourns in lonely exile here
Until the Son of God appear.
　Rejoice! rejoice! Immanuel
　Shall come to thee, O Israel.

O come, thou Rod of Jesse, free
Thine own from Satan's tyranny;
From depths of hell thy people save,
And give them victory o'er the grave:
　Rejoice! . . .

The hymnic language of Isaiah 12 is just such a statement of faith in God's power to overcome evil, by sending a royal saviour to establish a world-wide kingdom of peace and justice, starting in Jerusalem. In the Gospels it is the aged Simeon who first recognizes the connection between the child Jesus (*Yeshua'*) and the Isaianic concept of salvation (*yeshu'ah*):

"Lord, now lettest thou thy servant depart in peace,
　according to thy word;
for mine eyes have seen thy salvation
　which thou hast prepared in the presence of all peoples,
a light for revelation to the Gentiles,
　and for glory to thy people Israel." (Luke 2:29–32)

One might say chapter 12 adds a "Hosanna" (Ps. 118:25) to the "Sanctus" of chapter 6.

AN ORACLE CONCERNING BABYLON

Isaiah 13:1–5

¹The oracle concerning Babylon which Isaiah the son of Amoz saw
²On a bare hill raise a signal,
　cry aloud to them;
wave the hand for them to enter
　the gates of the nobles.
³I myself have commanded my consecrated ones,
　have summoned my mighty men to execute my anger,
　my proudly exulting ones.

⁴Hark, a tumult on the mountains
  as of a great multitude!
Hark, an uproar of kingdoms,
  of nations gathering together!
The Lord of hosts is mustering
  a host for battle.
⁵They come from a distant land,
  from the end of the heavens,
the Lord and the weapons of his indignation,
  to destroy the whole earth.

A new title introduces eleven chapters of "Oracles" nearly all of which concern foreign nations. Jeremiah 46–51 and Ezekiel 25–32 are similar collections, but the Isaianic one is the longest and most elaborate. It deals directly with Babylon, Philistia, Moab, Damascus, Ethiopia, Egypt, Arabia and Tyre, in a long series of prophecies arranged roughly under the headings "The oracle concerning Babylon" (13:1), "An oracle concerning Moab" (15:1) and so on (14:28; 17:1; 19:1; 21:1, 11, 13; 22:1; 23:1). What are we to make of eleven chapters of taunts and insults directed at foreigners? Is this anything more than nationalist propaganda?

It may be that the origin of such outbursts is to be found in a situation where Israel was beleagured by a foreign power, threatened with oppression or even extinction. We know of parallels from other parts of the ancient near east, such as the Egyptian "Execration Texts" from the twentieth century B.C., in which Egypt's enemies are systematically cursed in time of war. If such were the case, it would be right to sympathize with the plight of the people concerned, but not to expect to find in them anything enlightening or relevant for our own day. Such an approach, however, smacks of the Marcionite heresy condemned by the early Church, according to which the Old Testament has been superseded by the New and should not be used in church at all! It is due to a lack of appreciation of the structure and purpose of the Old Testament texts. Our task is to read and understand the meaning of the texts as we have them now, not to reconstruct the earliest and crudest stage in their history. In fact these long and important sections in three Major Prophets add at least two significant dimensions to our understanding of the prophetic literature.

First, the Book of Isaiah is primarily about Judah and Jerusalem. It is doubtful if the foreign nations ever heard a word of it. We have just worked through twelve chapters of the most biting attacks on "the people of Judah". The oracles concerning the foreign nations are no worse and no better than these. The crimes of the foreign nations are the same as those of Judah— arrogance, greed, cruelty, injustice—and must be punished as Judah's must be. But here is the crux: if the foreign nations are punished for their crimes against God and man, how much more severely shall Judah be punished? At the end of these collections the prophet turns to his audience and says in effect, as Nathan said to David, "Thou art the man!" (2 Sam. 12:7). The climax of Amos' prophecies against the nations in 1:3–2:3 is his devastating attack on his own people: "For three transgressions of Judah/ Israel and for four, I will not revoke the punishment . . . " (2:4–5, 6ff.). After their oracles on the foreign nations, Jeremiah describes the fall of Jerusalem (52) and Ezekiel turns to rebuke his own people (33–34). After the great "Apocalypse" on the ultimate faith of all nations (in Isaiah 24–27), we have in chapters 28–31 a collection of Woe-sayings and other doom-laden prophecies addressed to Israel and Judah quite matching anything in chapters 1–12. Taunts and gloating may be in these oracles, but everywhere there is the implicit warning soon to be made explicit, "You are no better, O Israel, and deserve to die."

The other consequence of the inclusion of these oracles in our Bibles is that they claim total supremacy, not for Israel—"lest they vaunt themselves and say, 'My own hand has delivered me' " (Judg. 7:2)—but for Israel's God. Later we shall hear repeated many times "There is no God but me" (e.g. 45:5, 6, 14, 21, 22). For the moment we are presented with a picture of Israel's God, our God, judging all the nations, using them for his purposes, controlling them, destroying them. The point is made both cumulatively in the series of oracles we are considering at the moment (13–23), and collectively in 24–27 where all the nations together are the object of divine intervention. Jerusalem, "the holy mountain" (27:13), stands at the centre of the world scene; nations rise and fall around it; and "on this mountain the Lord of hosts will make for all peoples a feast of fat things..." (25:6). We—and the prophets—may be wrong, but we believe in one God, creator of heaven and earth, and Isaiah chapters 13–23 provide a spectacular way of expressing that belief.

"Oracle" (v. 1) strictly speaking means the actual words of a deity, communicated through the medium of a priest or priestess, as at ancient Delphi, or a prophet as here. The explicit mention of Isaiah's name again, as in the first verses of chapters 1 and 2, makes the point that the prophet's visions extend beyond Jerusalem and Judah to include the nations of the world as well (see on 1:1).

The series starts with Babylon, because when the book that began with Isaiah of Jerusalem was reaching its final form, Babylon, not Assyria, was the arch enemy, being responsible, under Nebuchadnezzar, for destroying the Temple in 586 B.C. Since then many others have taken over its role, the Romans for their destruction of the Second Temple in A.D. 70, the Christian Church for persecuting the Jews throughout the Middle Ages, and the Nazis who were responsible for the extermination of six million Jews in Europe between 1939 and 1945. But Babylon remains the supreme symbol of human wickedness (e.g. Rev. 17–18), being first in Isaiah's list and forming an extended climax in Jeremiah's (50–51). Egypt and Assyria can receive God's blessing (Isa. 19:24–25), but Babylon is never forgiven.

The first part of the oracle describes the massing of a great army. No names are given until verse 17 where the Medes are mentioned, conquerors of Babylon, but we may assume that the army's objective is Babylon. On the other hand the language and imagery suggest that her attackers are more than Medes and Persians: "My mighty men" and "my proudly exulting ones" (v. 3) are giants and angels according to one ancient tradition; and certainly verses 6–16 transcend the bounds of human history. At all events this is God's army, armed with "the weapons of his indignation" (v. 5), advancing on Babylon. "My consecrated ones" (v. 3) is a title that anticipates exilic references to Cyrus, king of the Medes and Persians, as the Lord's "anointed" (45:1). Jeremiah 51 contains similar language in describing the downfall of Babylon:

> Set up a standard on the earth,
>> blow the trumpet among the nations;
> prepare the nations for war against her,
>> summon against her the kingdoms. (v. 27)

"Prepare" in the Jeremiah passage is the same word as "consecrated" in this. Joel 3:9 takes up the same theme.

"The mountains" (v. 4) and "a distant land from the end of the heavens" (v. 5) allude to the appearance on the scene of a new power, from the mountainous country east of Assyria and Babylon, known today as Iran. Cyrus (550–530 B.C.), and his equally famous successors Darius the Great (522–486) and Xerxes (486–465), established an empire that stretched from the Indus valley in the east to the frontiers of Greece in the west. According to traditional commentaries "the whole earth" (v. 5) means the Babylonian Empire, destroyed by Cyrus in 538 B.C. The verse might also be applied to the transformation of the world brought about by Persian achievements, both political and cultural. But most likely verse 5 points forward to the cosmic imagery of the next section.

THE DAY OF THE LORD

Isaiah 13:6–22

> 6Wail, for the day of the Lord is near;
>> as destruction from the Almighty it will come!
> 7Therefore all hands will be feeble,
>> and every man's heart will melt,
> 8 and they will be dismayed.
> Pangs and agony will seize them;
>> they will be in anguish like a woman in travail.
> They will look aghast at one another;
>> their faces will be aflame.
>
> 9Behold, the day of the Lord comes,
>> cruel, with wrath and fierce anger,

to make the earth a desolation
and to destroy its sinners from it.
¹⁰For the stars of the heavens and their constellations
will not give their light;
the sun will be dark at its rising
and the moon will not shed its light.
¹¹I will punish the world for its evil,
and the wicked for their iniquity;
I will put an end to the pride of the arrogant,
and lay low the haughtiness of the ruthless.
¹²I will make men more rare than fine gold,
and mankind than the gold of Ophir.
¹³Therefore I will make the heavens tremble,
and the earth will be shaken out of its place,
at the wrath of the Lord of hosts
in the day of his fierce anger.
¹⁴And like a hunted gazelle,
or like sheep with none to gather them,
every man will turn to his own people,
and every man will flee to his own land
¹⁵Whoever is found will be thrust through,
and whoever is caught will fall by the sword.
¹⁶Their infants will be dashed in pieces
before their eyes;
their houses will be plundered
and their wives ravished.

¹⁷Behold, I am stirring up the Medes against them,
who have no regard for silver
and do not delight in gold.
¹⁸Their bows will slaughter the young men;
they will have no mercy on the fruit of the womb;
their eyes will not pity children.
¹⁹And Babylon, the glory of kingdoms,
the splendour and pride of the Chaldeans,
will be like Sodom and Gomorrah
when God overthrew them.
²⁰It will never be inhabited
or dwelt in for all generations;
no Arab will pitch his tent there,

no shepherds will make their flocks lie down there.
²¹But wild beasts will lie down there,
and its houses will be full of howling creatures;
there ostriches will dwell,
and there satyrs will dance.
²²Hyenas will cry in its towers,
and jackals in the pleasant palaces;
its time is close at hand
and its days will not be prolonged.

"Wail!" (Heb. *helilu*) introduces our second major "Day of the Lord" poem; the first was 2:12–19. Here it is addressed to the Babylonians; elsewhere it is addressed to the Philistines (14:31) and "the ships of Tarshish" (23:1, 6, 14). Actually half of the Biblical occurrences of the word are in oracles against the foreign nations (Isa. 13–23, Jer. 46–51 and Ezek. 25–32). Most of the rest are in "Day of the Lord" poems (e.g. Ezek. 30:2; Joel 1:5, 11, 13; Zeph. 1:10, 11). It sets the scene in descriptions of human helplessness and terror. It is not a cry for help because no help is possible. The context shows that it is a yell of fear or pain: "arms fall limp" (Jerusalem Bible) (better than "hands will be feeble", RSV), hearts melt, there is dismay, anguish, "faces are like flames" (i.e. pale yellow, not "aflame", RSV) . . . This poem, and others like it, may originally have been independent compositions, drawing on traditional ways of thinking about the confrontation between good and evil. In the present context it is best to take it as focusing on the dramatic downfall of Babylon in 538 B.C., but of course, as we saw, Babylon has a symbolic, almost mythical significance, and her fall, accompanied by earthquakes (v. 13) and miraculous signs in the sky (v. 10), means the triumph of Israel's God over the powers of evil at all times.

"Destruction from the Almighty" (v. 6) contains a word play that recognizes in this ancient name for God, in Hebrew "Shaddai" (Gen. 17:1; 28:3), a clue to his nature, since "destruction, violence" in Hebrew is *shod*. In fact the name, which occurs only here in Isaiah, probably meant "God of the mountain" (cf. Ps. 48:1–3; Isa. 8:18). Ancient commentators understood it as "the One who is all-sufficient", hence "Almighty". But the frightening, destructive power of "Shaddai" appears not only here but in Job where it is a frequent name for God: e.g. "God has made my heart faint; the Almighty has terrified me" (23:16). So the word play in Isa. 13:6 certainly has a point.

Verses 9–16 may like verses 6–8 have been an originally independent "Day of the Lord" poem, very like Joel 1 and 2 and Isa. 24:1–13—but again it has been deliberately placed in the context of this "oracle concerning Babylon", and the gruesome last verse particularly encourages us to compare it with Psalm 137 ("By the waters of Babylon"), which ends in a similar vein. Its world-wide significance is also evident; the day of the Lord is coming "to make the earth a desolation and to destroy its sinners from it" (v. 9)—not just the sinners of sixth-century B.C. Babylon.

The participation of sun, moon and stars is common to many of these descriptions (e.g. Isa. 24:23; Joel 2:30–32; Luke 23:45), and instantly raises them out of the realm of ordinary human history into a history of the mighty acts of God. The darkened sky recalls the appearance of God to Moses at Sinai (e.g. Exod. 20:21) and, in the Psalms, to other theophanies as well (e.g. Ps. 18:7–11). But probably the ultimate source of this imagery is to be found in Job and the Psalms, where it describes suffering (e.g. Job 23:17) and in particular the suffering of the wicked: e.g.

> They meet with darkness in the daytime,
> and grope at noonday as in the night. (Job 5:14; cf. Ps. 35:6)

This of course is the significance of darkness in Amos 5:18–20 too, the earliest "Day of the Lord" passage:

> Is not the day of the Lord darkness, and not light,
> and gloom with no brightness in it?

It then follows that in the New Age, when evil has been finally destroyed, there will be no darkness; thus

> Your sun shall no more go down,
> nor your moon withdraw itself;
> for the Lord will be your everlasting light
> and your days of mourning shall be ended.
>
> (Isa. 60:20; cf. Rev. 22:5)

The finality of the act of divine intervention described in these passages, that is to say, their ultimate significance for all people, is expressed in various ways. It is God himself who is speaking: "I will punish the world" (v. 11). It is God who is now the only actor on the stage: there is no mention of a huge army, or of angels, or even of a messianic saviour. Lastly, it is the whole world that is to be punished: the fall of Babylon is only the start.

Verse 12 is about refining. Daniel's visions contain similar imagery (11:35; 12:10), with the difference that here Daniel's "those who are wise" (that is, the pure metal, refined in the fire of God's judgment) will be "more rare than fine gold". Wisdom tells us:

> My fruit is better than gold, even fine gold,
>   and my yield than choice silver. (Prov. 8:19)

The Book of Job contains a beautiful poem on the same theme (28:12–19). "Gold of Ophir" was specially valuable, having been imported via the Gulf of Aqaba (1 Kings 9:26–28) from some distant country. In ancient times this was thought to be India; more recently Southern Arabia and East Africa have been proposed, but like "ships of Tarshish" and "cedars of Lebanon" it is the legendary aura of the phrase that gives it its meaning rather than its precise location.

Verses 17–22 focus on Babylon and the foreign power that is to destroy her. Jeremiah's oracle against Babylon contains the same prediction (51:11), and we shall meet it again in 41:2–4 and 44:28–45:13. On the rise of Cyrus the Great and the Medes and Persians during the middle of the sixth century B.C., see on 13:1–5. They are mentioned in connection with the destruction of Nineveh, the Assyrian capital, in 612 B.C. as well (2 Kings 17:6). Their present objective, Babylon, with its "Hanging Gardens", one of the Seven Wonders of the ancient world, is richly described as "the glory of the kingdoms, the splendour and pride of the Chaldeans". "Chaldeans" is the name given to Nebuchadnezzar's subjects, that is to say, the Babylonians of the sixth century B.C. Now it is their turn to "become like Sodom and Gomorrah", and this time there will be no survivors (Gen. 18:22–

33; Isa. 1:9). No one will live there; no passing bedouin will even want to stop overnight there; the shepherds will keep their sheep away from the deserted site.

The details of verses 21 and 22 are uncertain: e.g. NEB identifies the "wild beasts" as "marmots" and the "howling creatures" as "porcupines"! But the point of the description is clear enough. In verse 21 there is a picture of desert life, with birds and animals, rarely seen anywhere near human habitation, making themselves at home, and satyrs, some kind of Pan-like spirits (Lev. 17:7), dancing about among the ruins. The animals mentioned in verse 22 are scavengers, normally familiar enough on the outskirts of a city, but now moving about freely in the centre. As in 34:11–15 the poet wishes us to imagine the mighty ruins of Babylon coming to life again under new management, her human occupants having been weighed in the balance and found wanting.

HOW YOU ARE FALLEN FROM HEAVEN!

Isaiah 14:1–21

[1]The Lord will have compassion on Jacob and will again choose Israel, and will set them in their own land, and aliens will join them and will cleave to the house of Jacob. [2]And the peoples will take them and bring them to their place, and the house of Israel will possess them in the Lord's land as male and female slaves; they will take captive those who were their captors, and rule over those who oppressed them.

[3]When the Lord has given you rest from your pain and turmoil and the hard service with which you were made to serve, [4]you will take up this taunt against the king of Babylon:

"How the oppressor has ceased,
    the insolent fury ceased!
[5]The Lord has broken the staff of the wicked,
    the sceptre of rulers,
[6]that smote the peoples in wrath
    with unceasing blows,
that ruled the nations in anger
    with unrelenting persecution.
[7]The whole earth is at rest and quiet;

they break forth into singing.
8The cypresses rejoice at you,
    the cedars of Lebanon, saying,
 'Since you were laid low,
    no hewer comes up against us.'
9Sheol beneath is stirred up
    to meet you when you come,
 it rouses the shades to greet you,
    all who were leaders of the earth;
 it raises from their thrones
    all who were kings of the nations.
10All of them will speak
    and say to you:
 'You too have become as weak as we!
    You have become like us!'
11Your pomp is brought down to Sheol,
    the sound of your harps;
 maggots are the bed beneath you,
    and worms are your covering.

12"How you are fallen from heaven,
    O Day Star, son of Dawn!
 How you are cut down to the ground,
    you who laid the nations low!
13You said in your heart,
    'I will ascend to heaven;
 above the stars of God
    I will set my throne on high;
 I will sit on the mount of assembly
    in the far north;
14I will ascend above the heights of the clouds,
    I will make myself like the Most High.'
15But you are brought down to Sheol,
    to the depths of the Pit.
16Those who see you will stare at you,
    and ponder over you:
 'Is this the man who made the earth tremble,
    who shook kingdoms,
17who made the world like a desert
    and overthrew its cities,
 who did not let his prisoners go home?'

¹⁸All the kings of the nations lie in glory,
    each in his own tomb;
¹⁹but you are cast out, away from your sepulchre,
    like a loathed untimely birth,
  clothed with the slain, those pierced by the sword,
    who go down to the stones of the Pit,
    like a dead body trodden under foot.
²⁰You will not be joined with them in burial,
    because you have destroyed your land,
    you have slain your people.

  "May the descendants of evildoers
    nevermore be named!
²¹Prepare slaughter for his sons
    because of the guilt of their fathers,
  lest they rise and possess the earth,
    and fill the face of the world with cities."

The famous taunt-song against the fallen king of Babylon (vv.
4*b*–21) is preceded by three and a half verses of prose introduction. Their purpose is to provide continuity with what goes before
and to give the song a context. In the midst of the preceding scene
of world-wide destruction and desolation (13:9–16) the Lord will
have compassion on Israel: he will set them in their own land and
give them rest. The picture of returning exiles, joined by aliens,
served by those who were once their oppressors, and free at last
from pain and turmoil, has many close parallels in chapters
40–55, and is one of the features that give unity to the Book of
Isaiah.

"Aliens" (v. 1) (Heb. *gerim*), an important term in Israelite
law, were originally non-Israelites living in Israel and possessing
certain rights and privileges. Like everyone else, for example,
they had to observe the Sabbath law (Exod. 20:10), although not
the food laws (Deut. 14:21). Later the term came to mean "proselyte" and probably has that meaning here: "the house of Jacob/
Israel" (vv. 1–2) will be enriched and strengthened by foreign
converts. One might add that these are the same people who, in
2:2–5, say:

  Come, let us go up to the mountain of the Lord,
    to the house of the God of Jacob;

that he may teach us his ways
   and that we may walk in his paths.

The last detail in this description of the "New Israel" is that,
when they are finally settled in their own land again, they will sing
"this taunt [song] against the king of Babylon" (v. 4). Again there
is a parallel in Isaiah 47, although there the taunts are aimed at
the city rather than her king. That song begins: "Come down and
sit in the dust, O virgin daughter of Bablyon". In both cases the
taunt-song is in the form of a funeral lament (like Lam. 1–2; 2
Sam. 1:19–27) and provides an opportunity for the author to tell a
tale of haughty ambition and failure. But its purpose is to celebrate rather than mourn, because the deceased was the king of
Babylon.

There has been much discussion as to whether the subject of
this long and colourful poem can be identified in history. It need
not originally have been about an actual king of Babylon at all,
since there are no historical details and the only mention of his
name is in the title (v. 4), which could well have been added later.
Thus although Nebuchadnezzar (605–562 B.C.) and Nabonidus
(555–539) have been proposed, it might be more appropriate to
cite the quite unhistorical legend of Belshazzar's Feast (Dan. 5)
as the most illuminating parallel in terms of dramatic force and
prophetic significance: "that very night Belshazzar the Chaldean
king was slain" (5:30).

A feature of this type of lament is the use of direct speech.
Babylon herself speaks several times in the lament in chapter 47,
for example, and in Lamentations 1 and 2 there are speeches by
Jerusalem, her starving children (2:12), mocking passers-by
(2:15) and gloating enemies (2:16). In this respect, as in others,
Isaiah 14 is a rich example. The first stanza (vv. 4–8) ends with the
words of jubilant cypresses and cedars of Lebanon: "Since you
were laid low, no hewer comes against us." The prophecy in 9:4
has been fulfilled: the oppressor's staff and sceptre are finally
broken, and "the whole earth is at rest and quiet" (v. 7). Who
better than the earth's majestic trees to celebrate the fact?

The second stanza (vv. 9–11) moves to the underworld, where

it is the turn of the "shades" to greet the fallen king: "You too have become as weak as we! You have become like us! (v. 10). "Sheol" can be conceived as a monster with an insatiable appetite (5:14), or a hunter (Ps. 116:3). Here it is probably a monarch (as in 28:15,18), surprised to learn of the king of Babylon's death. He immediately wakes up his subjects, the "shades" (Heb. *re-pha'im*), feeble ghosts that are all that remain of those who were once "leaders of the earth" and "kings of the nations" (v. 9). We shall meet the rephaim again in chapter 26:

> They are dead, they will not live;
>> they are shades [*repha'im*], they will not arise . . . (26:14)

Here they greet the new arrival with derision, observing that in death the strong and the weak are one. In Job's words:

> The small and the great are there,
>> and the slave is free from his master. (3:19)

And the king of Babylon is distinguished from the other royal rephaim who address him: they sit on thrones (v. 9), while he is to lie on a bed of maggots and worms.

In the third stanza (vv. 12–15) the words of the king himself are quoted to give us an insight into the enormity of his blasphemous ambitions. The language he uses, like that used of the king of Tyre in Ezek. 28:11–19, comes from ancient Canaanite mythology. "The mount of assembly in the far north" (Heb. *zaphon*: cf. Ps. 48:2), for instance, was the Mount Olympus of Canaanite mythology, home of the gods. "The heights of the clouds" is another example, as Amos 4:13, Mic. 1:3 and Job 9:8 show. A regular description of the Canaanite god Baal was "Rider on the clouds", a phrase that is applied to the God of Israel in Psalm 68:4 and 33 (RSV). "The Most High" was also a Canaanite title of God as the Melchizedek legend suggests (Gen. 14:19–20). But the sin of the king of Babylon was universal: Adam and Eve too, at the serpent's bidding, sought to become "like God" (Gen. 3:5). The builders of the Tower of Babel had similar ambitions (Gen. 11:1–9). "How are you fallen from heaven, O Daystar, son of Dawn!" So the fate of the king who thought he was a god is described. *Helel ben-Shahar*, "Daystar, son of Dawn", a satirical name given to the king, is made up of two more Canaanite deities. *Helel* has traditionally been understood as Venus, "the morning star" or "Lucifer", which would fit the idea of the falling of a deity (e.g. Hephaestus) or an angel (e.g. Satan; Luke 10:18) from heaven to hell or "the Pit" (v.15).

The last speakers in the poem are unnamed onlookers or passers-by (vv. 16–17). The scene is not necessarily Sheol again (vv. 9–11); it appears to be a battlefield littered with corpses, among them that of the king of Babylon: "Is this the man who made the earth tremble, who shook kingdoms, who made the world like a desert...?" To be deprived of a decent burial was considered a hideous fate, especially for a king: Jeremiah's prophecy concerning Jehoiakim makes this very clear (Jer. 22:19). In verse 19 the Hebrew text has "like a loathed branch", which would suggest the last and most useless member of the Babylonian royal family, good for nothing but to be thrown away or burnt. Some scholars, worried by the use of the word for "loathed" or "abominable" in this context, read "loathed untimely birth" (RSV) or "loathed carrion" (NEB; Jerusalem Bible). "The stones of the Pit" merely add a grim detail to the description of stony Sheol.

The whole poem ends with a curse, but not simply of the king of Babylon, rather of all like him: so perish all evil-doers and their descendants! (vv. 20b–21). A number of Biblical psalms and hymns end on a universalizing note like this, e.g. Ps. 104:35. Psalm 2 is a less hostile example: "Blessed are all who take refuge in him" (v. 11). The Song of Deborah does exactly what our Isaianic poem does, ending:

> "So perish all thine enemies, O Lord!
> But thy friends be like the sun as he rises in his might." (Judg. 5:31)

ORACLES AGAINST BABYLON, ASSYRIA AND PHILISTIA

Isaiah 14:22–32

²²"I will rise up against them," says the Lord of hosts, "and will cut off from Babylon name and remnant, offspring and posterity, says the

Lord. 23And I will make it a possession of the hedgehog, and pools of water, and I will sweep it with the broom of destruction, says the Lord of hosts."

24The Lord of hosts has sworn:
  "As I have planned,
    so shall it be,
  and as I have purposed,
    so shall it stand,
25that I will break the Assyrian in my land,
    and upon my mountains trample him under foot;
  and his yoke shall depart from them,
    and his burden from their shoulder."
26This is the purpose that is purposed
    concerning the whole earth;
  and this is the hand that is stretched out
    over all the nations.
27For the Lord of hosts has purposed,
    and who will annul it?
  His hand is stretched out,
    and who will turn it back?

28In the year that King Ahaz died came this oracle:
29"Rejoice not, O Philistia, all of you,
    that the rod which smote you is broken,
  for from the serpent's root will come forth an adder,
    and its fruit will be a flying serpent.
30And the first-born of the poor will feed,
    and the needy lie down in safety;
  but I will kill your root with famine,
    and your remnant I will slay.
31Wail, O gate; cry, O city;
    melt in fear, O Philistia, all of you!
  For smoke comes out of the north,
    and there is no straggler in his ranks."

32What will one answer the messengers of the nation?
  "The Lord has founded Zion,
    and in her the afflicted of his people find refuge."

The first of these three oracles (vv. 22–23) serves to remind us that the long taunt-song was about Babylon, which has not been mentioned by name since verse 4. The very different style, however, including the formula "says the Lord (of hosts)" (which we last met in 3:15), suggests that it is independent of it. It tells of four acts of divine intervention by which Babylon will be destroyed. First, the Lord of hosts will "rise up against them" like an enemy in the night (Judg. 20:5; Ps. 27:3). This provides a nice link with the preceding song, which had ended with the threat that evil-doers may "rise and possess the earth". Then he will obliterate every trace of Babylon: both idioms are strikingly alliterative: *shem ushear* ("name and remnant") and *nin weneked* ("offspring and posterity"). Next he will transform the site of Babylon into the haunt of hedgehogs. Finally, in an unusual image drawn from daily life, he will sweep them away like dirt, thus preparing the site for new occupants. The closest Old Testament parallels are the striking picture of God wiping "Jerusalem as one wipes a dish, wiping it and turning it upside down" (2 Kings 21:13), and the more frequent image of the wicked being swept away by the wind like chaff (e.g Ps. 1:4).

The oracle against Assyria is short and simple, a clear indication that when the oracles against foreign nations were collected together the mighty Assyrian Empire, which plays so central a role in eighth-century prophecy, was no more. It is introduced as an oath; cf. 5:9; Amos 4:2; 6:8; 8:7. There are obvious allusions to other Isaianic prophecies: verse 25 clearly picks up the imagery of 9:4; the outstretched hand of God (vv. 26–27) recalls the refrain running through the prophecies of chapters 9 and 10. The striking statement in this piece of anti-Assyrian polemic is in verse 25: "I will break the Assyrian *in my land* ..." The defeat of Assyria is to take place in Israel. Like 10:15–19, this is not a prophecy about the fall of Nineveh: the little Book of Nahum is about that. It must be about the miraculous defeat of the Assyrian army under Sennacherib in 701 B.C. From the standpoint of Jerusalem and Judah, that was the point at which Assyria was broken, his yoke removed from the people's neck and his burden from their shoulder; that was the point at which God's purpose was fulfilled (vv. 24, 26, 27), not at the fall of Nineveh in 612 B.C.

"My land ... my mountains" are wistful ways of referring to

the land of Israel, perhaps reflecting the nostalgia of exiles in Babylon. This certainly applies to 49:11 and 65:9, and to the poignant prophecies addressed to "the mountains of Israel" in Ezekiel 36. When one mentions some of them by name, the phrase becomes still more emotive—Hermon, Carmel, Tabor, Gilboa, Nebo, Sinai, Moriah, Zion and the Mount of Olives—every one rich in associations:

> But you, O mountains of Israel, shall shoot forth your branches, and yield your fruit to my people Israel; for they will soon come home.
>
> (Ezek. 36:8)

Psalms like 121 and 125 give further indications of the overtones present in the reference to "my mountains".

Verse 26, like parts of the preceding taunt-song, adds that what happened to Assyria, when they tried to capture Jerusalem, will happen to the whole earth. The history of Israel is a paradigm of the history of the human race; that is how it came about that Exodus, Jerusalem, Zion, Babylon and the like can express deep spiritual, religious and political ideals and realities, and how indeed in modern times Auschwitz has become a universal symbol of what racism, not only anti-semitism, can ultimately lead to.

The oracle against Philistia (vv. 28–32) is regarded by many nowadays as an authentic utterance of the prophet Isaiah. A date that would fit the oracle quite well is 722 B.C., the year of the death of the Assyrian king Shalmaneser V. In that year, rejoicing that this "rod" which smote them was broken (v. 29), the Philistines rebelled, only to be crushed, as the prophet predicted, by Shalmaneser's successor, Sargon II "out of the north" (v. 31). The "messengers" in verse 32 would then be Philistine envoys sent to persuade Hezekiah to bring Judah in on the side of the rebels. Isaiah's advice to Hezekiah, like his advice to Ahaz twelve years earlier (ch. 7), and to Hezekiah twenty-one years later (chs. 36–37), was "trust in God; he founded Zion; he is her refuge and her strength" (cf. Ps. 46). If we took verse 28 as being roughly equivalent to "In the early years of Hezekiah's reign", that historical reconstruction would fit.

The enduring significance of this prophecy, however, removed from its original context and placed, like its parallels in Jer. 47, Ezek. 25:15–17 and Amos 1:6–8, in a series of oracles against foreign nations, lies in the symbolic imagery used. It is not just concerned with what happened in 722 B.C. Thus traditional Jewish and Christian commentators, taking account of other relevant Biblical texts, have recognized in the sequence of three enemies in verse 29, each more frightening than the last—"the rod . . . the adder . . . a flying serpent"—three branches from the noble stem of Jesse: Ahaz, collaborator with Assyria (2 Kings 16), Hezekiah who "smote the Philistines as far as Gaza and its territory, from watchtower to fortified city" (2 Kings 18:8), and the Messiah, son of the David who slew more Philistines than anyone else (1 Sam. 17–19; 2 Sam. 5:17–25; 8:1). Others see in these verses a progression from "the rod" wielded under Hezekiah (2 Kings 18:8) to the more terrifying "adder", "flying serpent" and "smoke from the north" (v. 31), which they see as appropriate descriptions of Assyrian invaders (cf. 11:14). The Philistines are not mentioned again in the Book of Isaiah.

The three species of snake in verse 29 are arranged in order of deadliness. The first, "serpent", is a generic term for all snakes noted for their cunning (Gen. 3:1; Matt. 10:16); the second, "adder" or "cockatrice" (AV), a species of poisonous viper, figures prominently in Biblical sayings: e.g. "At the last it bites like a serpent and stings like an adder" (Prov. 23:32; cf. Isa. 11:8; 59:5; Jer. 8:17). The third is described as a "fiery serpent [Heb. *saraph*] that flies", and refers to a mythical creature in which are combined the deadly cunning of the first, the venom of the second and the terrifying fire of the winged seraphim (see on 6:2). Winged snakes appear in Assyrian iconography, which was no doubt familiar to eighth-century B.C. Judeans, and would give added point to the image as applied to Assyrian invaders "from the north".

The poem is in two parts, each beginning with taunting imperatives: "Rejoice not, O Philistia, all of you . . ." (v. 29) and "Wail, . . . cry . . . melt in fear, O Philistia, all of you" (v. 32). "All of you" stresses that all five chief Philistine cities are included

(Amos 1:7–8; 6:2). Each part then portrays the fate of the Philistines in graphic imagery—snakes in the first, smoke in the second—then, by way of contrast, confidently describes the peace and security of Jerusalem (v. 32), refuge for the poor and needy (v. 30). Philistia will be destroyed (v. 30), her ambassadors will fail (v. 32), but "the Lord has founded Zion. . . ."

A LAMENT FOR MOAB—I

Isaiah 15:1–16:14

¹An oracle concerning Moab.
   Because Ar is laid waste in a night
      Moab is undone;
   because Kir is laid waste in a night
      Moab is undone.
²The daughter of Dibon has gone up
      to the high places to weep;
   over Nebo and over Medeba
      Moab wails.
   On every head is baldness,
      every beard is shorn;
³in the streets they gird on sackcloth;
      on the housetops and in the squares
      every one wails and melts in tears.
⁴Heshbon and Elealeh cry out,
      their voice is heard as far as Jahaz;
   therefore the armed men of Moab cry aloud;
      his soul trembles.
⁵My heart cries out for Moab;
      his fugitives flee to Zoar,
      to Eglath-shelishiyah.
   For at the ascent of Luhith
      they go up weeping;
   on the road to Horonaim
      they raise a cry of destruction;
⁶the waters of Nimrim
      are a desolation;
   the grass is withered, the new growth fails,

the verdure is no more.
⁷Therefore the abundance they have gained
    and what they have laid up
 they carry away
    over the Brook of the Willows.
⁸For a cry has gone
    round the land of Moab;
 the wailing reaches to Eglaim,
    the wailing reaches to Beer-elim.
⁹For the waters of Dibon are full of blood;
    yet I will bring upon Dibon even more,
 a lion for those of Moab who escape,
    for the remnant of the land.

¹They have sent lambs
    to the ruler of the land,
 from Sela, by way of the desert,
    to the mount of the daughter of Zion.
²Like fluttering birds,
    like scattered nestlings,
 so are the daughters of Moab
    at the fords of the Arnon.
³"Give counsel,
    grant justice;
 make your shade like night
    at the height of noon;
 hide the outcasts,
    betray not the fugitive;
⁴let the outcasts of Moab
    sojourn among you;
 be a refuge to them
    from the destroyer.
 When the oppressor is no more,
    and destruction has ceased,
 and he who tramples under foot
    has vanished from the land,
⁵then a throne will be established in steadfast love
    and on it will sit in faithfulness
    in the tent of David
 one who judges and seeks justice
    and is swift to do righteousness."

⁶We have heard of the pride of Moab,
    how proud he was;
of his arrogance, his pride, and his insolence—
    his boasts are false.
⁷Therefore let Moab wail,
    let every one wail for Moab.
Mourn, utterly stricken,
for the raisin-cakes of Kir-hareseth.

⁸For the fields of Heshbon languish,
    and the vine of Sibmah;
the lords of the nations
    have struck down its branches,
which reached to Jazer
    and strayed to the desert;
its shoots spread abroad
    and passed over the sea.
⁹Therefore I weep with the weeping of Jazer
    for the vine of Sibmah;
I drench you with my tears,
    O Heshbon and Elealeh;
for upon your fruit and your harvest
    the battle shout has fallen.
¹⁰And joy and gladness are taken away
    from the fruitful field;
and in the vineyards no songs are sung,
    no shouts are raised;
no treader treads out wine in the presses;
    the vintage shout is hushed.
¹¹Therefore my soul moans like a lyre for Moab,
    and my heart for Kir-heres.
  ¹²And when Moab presents himself, when he wearies himself upon the high place, when he comes to his sanctuary to pray, he will not prevail.

    ¹³This is the word which the Lord spoke concerning Moab in the past. ¹⁴But now the Lord says, "In three years, like the years of a hireling, the glory of Moab will be brought into contempt, in spite of all his great multitude, and those who survive will be very few and feeble."

The author of these prophecies shows remarkable sympathy for the plight of the Moabites. There is no gloating here: chapter 15 is a genuine lament, not a parody like the one over Babylon in chapter 14; and cries of anguish like "My soul mourns like a lyre for Moab" (16:11; cf. 15:5; 16:9) make this "oracle concerning Moab" different from the others. The same applies to Jeremiah 48 where some of the same words are repeated and the conclusion is actually a prophecy of hope. Commentators have cited this as evidence for the superiority of Israelite prophets over prophets in neighbouring countries. For example, the Moabites hired the prophet Balaam to curse Israel (even although he found it impossible to do so: Num. 22–24), while here an Israelite prophet weeps over the sufferings of Moab. Elsewhere some fiercely anti-Moabite feeling is expressed, as in the tale of how they got their name (Gen. 19:30–37) and the account of David's treatment of Moabite prisoners of war (2 Sam. 8:2). In Deut. 23:3 they are specifically excluded from the congregation; and other references to Moab in Isaiah (11:14; 25:10) are hostile. So we must assume that this oracle reflects a situation where Moab's sufferings were so intense that even Israel wept for them. Respect for their territorial sovereignty (Deut. 2:8–9) and the tender treatment of Ruth the Moabitess (Ruth 1–4; Matt. 1:5) point in the same direction. But whatever the reason for including this lament over Moab in a series of oracles on the foreign nations, it has the effect of transforming them from primarily polemical attacks into a more thoughtful commentary on the fate of other parts of God's world.

No historical situation can be certainly identified to fit the disasters described. It is unlikely that it was Judah's fault. 2 Kings 3:21–24 and 2 Chron. 20:22–23 describe a Judean success there, but it would be odd to find Judah weeping over a military engagement which they had won. By paying tribute to the Assyrians, the Moabites, like Jerusalem, escaped destruction by Sennacherib in 701 B.C. Contemporary Assyrian records, however, tell of a defeat at the hands of some other invaders, probably from the south or east (as prophesied in Isa. 11:14 and Ezek. 25:8–11). The place-names in 15:1–4 depict a route from the south. This kind of sudden invasion is referred to several times in the Bible: e.g. that of "the Midianites, the Amalekites and all the peoples of the East" in the Gideon legend (Judg. 6–8); and the Sabaeans' attack on Job's property (Job 1:13–15). Whatever God chooses to use as the rod of his anger, it is terrifyingly effective.

The geography of the lament is also impossible to reconstruct precisely. Verses 1–4 have a clear enough structure: Kir (or Kir-hareseth: 16:7) was a major city in the south of Moab, Dibon has been identified as an important city in the central region, and Medeba, Nebo (the hill from which Moses viewed the promised land: Deut. 34), Heshbon and Elealeh are all in the north of the country. The invasion thus appears to have begun with a night attack on the southern frontier, but it soon overtook the length and breadth of the country. The "Brook of the Willows" marked the border with Edom in the south: verse 7 thus graphically portrays the end of the raid, marked by the invader's departure laden with Moabite booty. Most of the places to which the frightened Moabites vainly fled, situated in the desolate region south of the Dead Sea, have enticingly appropriate names: Zoar, "small" (Gen. 19:22); Eglath, "calf [to be slaughtered]" (1 Sam. 16:2; Jer. 34:18–19); Luhith, another "small" place; Horonaim, "caves"; Nimrim, "leopards". Perhaps their meaning is more important than their location, which in most cases is unknown.

The language and imagery are exceptionally powerful. The intensity of the mourners' feelings, both Moabite and Israelite, is heightened by the accumulation of words for "weep, wail, cry, melt in tears" and the like. The peculiarly expressive word *helil*, "wail" (see above on 13:6) occurs three times (15:2,8). Other outward manifestations of grief include shaving the beard and putting on sackcloth (15:2–3). Scenes of grief are everywhere— "in the streets . . . on the housetops and in the squares . . . as far as Jahaz [unknown]". "The grass is withered, the new growth fails, the verdure is no more" (15:6)—surely not to be taken literally, but as a further sign of the finality of Moab's defeat (cf. 40:6–8; Pss. 37:2; 103:15). "The waters of Dibon are full of blood" (v. 9) similarly recalls the first Plague of Egypt (Exod. 7:10–24), and the state of Jerusalem in the days of Manasseh (2 Kings 21:16), rather than the actual effect of mass slaughter on the country's water supply. Finally, the lion in verse 9 (like the one in 21:8; see RSV footnote) has aroused much discussion: NEB removes it entirely from the text, substituting "I have a vision of..." Some identify the "lion" with Nebuchadnezzar (Jer. 4:7), others with Judah (Gen. 49:9). It certainly ends the lament with a terrible warning: there is worse to come. Maybe the thought of a "remnant" has affected the transmission of the text (as in 6:13). But as it stands the closest and most grisly parallel would be Amos 3:12:

> As the shepherd rescues from the mouth of the lion two legs, or a piece of an ear, so shall the people of Israel who dwell in Samaria be rescued...

A LAMENT FOR MOAB—II

Isaiah 15:1–16:14 *(cont'd)*

Moab was once part of David's kingdom and the next section of the "oracle" (16:1–5) appears to allude to that Golden Age as a possible source of hope for the defeated Moabites. The prophet first speaks of the Moabite refugees sending tribute to the king of Israel, as in the old days when Mesha king of Moab sent "a hundred thousand lambs and the wool of a hundred thousand rams" (2 Kings 3:4). From Zoar, Eglath, etc. where the refugees were hiding, the quickest route to Jerusalem was round the south end of the Dead Sea "from Sela (= Edom) by way of the desert" (v. 1). The security of "the daughter of Zion", that is, Jerusalem, is contrasted to the panic and vulnerability of "the daughters of Moab at the fords of Arnon", that is, the main cities in the centre of the country. He then addresses his own people, calling upon them to show justice and mercy to "the outcasts of Moab", and predicting an end to oppression and the establishment of a kingdom of steadfast love, faithfulness, justice and righteousness, in which they can share. Most of the language of this speech is already familiar from the earlier chapters of Isaiah (see on 1:26). The rights and privileges of the "sojourner" or "proselyte" (v. 4) were discussed in connection with 14:1. The difference is that here all these ideals and attitudes are applied to the Moabites, which is unusual, especially in the oracles against the nations, but nonetheless significant for that.

An important theological term that occurs here for the first time in Isaiah is "steadfast love" (RSV), "mercy" (AV), "mutual trust" (NEB) (Heb. *hesed*). There are a number of words for "love" in Hebrew, and this one is distinguished from the rest by its consistent association with "faithfulness, loyalty, devotion"; *hesed* is the cement that holds communities, families and other relationships together. It is particularly frequent in the Psalms where it refers both to the devotion of the Psalmist (a "devotee") to God, and to the love of God that he can rely on, come what may (Pss. 5:7; 18:50). In the present context, as in many passages, it is concentrated in the throne of David at Jerusalem:

> Great triumphs [*yeshu'ot*] he gives to his king,
>> and shows steadfast love to his anointed,
>>> to David and his descendants for ever. (Ps. 18:50)

It is not a common term in Isaianic tradition, but there are some beautiful examples: e.g.

> For the mountains may depart
>> and the hills be removed,
> but my steadfast love shall not depart from you,
>> and my covenant of peace shall not be removed,
>>> says the Lord, who has compassion on you. (54:10; cf. 54:7–8)

The submission of Moab to Davidic sovereignty in their hour of need is a mixed blessing: it gives them hope of justice and protection, but at the same time it marks the end of their proud independence. Verse 6 recalls, not unsympathetically, that it was Moab's arrogant boasting that brought about their downfall. "Boasts" is a rare Hebrew word, but well enough known to make other suggestions (e.g. "strength", NEB) needless. It occurs in Job 11:3 where it refers to the almost blasphemous "nonsense" (NEB) talked by Job. The speakers ("we have heard") are perhaps giving Jerusalem's response to the request for help in the preceding verses.

Verses 7–11 return to lament with another verse about wailing. In the RSV the wailers are not Moabites as in 15:2 and 8, but sympathetic witnesses of Moab's plight: "let every one wail for

Moab". This would follow on from the prophet's cries in 15:5 and his intercession for them in 16:3–5. The actual Hebrew text is less sympathetic: "therefore shall Moab howl for Moab, every one shall howl" (AV). But that could well be due to later scribal interference. It is easier to envisage a scribe changing a friendly text about Moab to a more hostile one than the other way round. The close parallel in Jer. 48:29–33 is further evidence that the verse originally referred to other people, presumably the prophet's Judean audience, lamenting for Moab, not the Moabites themselves. The lament comes immediately after a description of their sins, and therefore amounts to: "If only Moab had not been so proud and insolent!"

The last part of the lament mourns the destruction of the vineyard of Moab. The appropriateness of this telling image for the land of Moab stems partly from the legend about the drunkenness of Lot, the father of Moab and Ammon (Gen. 19:30–38), and partly no doubt from the rich vines that once grew in Moab (although little trace of high quality viticulture remains today). As in chapter 5, the language is allusive and metaphorical. First, "raisin-cakes of Kir-hareseth": this surely means "Kir-hareseth, famous for its raisin cakes", a delicacy referred to several times in the Old Testament (e.g. Hos. 3:1; Song of S. 2:5), and wistfully recalling the comfort and luxury of happier times.

The "vine of Sibmah" (vv. 8, 9), filling the country and spreading its shoots abroad as well, symbolizes its economic strength and prosperity, now tragically destroyed. The places mentioned, Heshbon, Sibmah and Elealeh, were situated in the land of Reuben and Gad (Josh. 13:15–28), that is, in the northern part of Moab. The phrase "lords of the nations" who "struck down its branches" gives no clue to the identity of the invaders, but their battle-cry, heard just at the time of the grape harvest (v. 9), vividly marks the beginning of Moab's downfall. Harvest thanksgiving celebrations are a frequent motif in prophecies of hope (e.g. 9:3) and other joyful hymns: e.g. "Thou hast put more joy in my heart than they have when their grain and their wine abound" (Ps. 4:7; cf. Ps. 126:6). But instead, this year the "vintage shout" (v. 10) will be drowned by a "battle shout" (v. 9; the same Hebrew word *hedad* does duty for both), and the fields, vineyards and wine-presses will fall silent.

The final refrain of the lament (v. 11) introduces a beautiful but, in the RSV translation, enigmatic image, that of a lyre, which can hardly be said to "moan" and which is not usually associated with grief. Some change the Hebrew text and read "wails like a pipe". The verb, however, sometimes means "to be moved, in tumult"; it is used of a busy city (Isa. 22:2), the nations of the world (Ps. 46:6), enemies (Ps. 83:2), and the waves of the sea (Isa. 17:12; 51:15). Applied to "soul, heart", as here and in other passages (Jer. 31:20; Song of S. 5:4), it surely must mean "quiver" (Jerusalem Bible) or "throb (NEB) like [the strings of] a lyre".

The name Kir-heres clearly refers to the town Kir-hareseth (v. 7), and the variation in the name may be a kind of word play. *Heres* means a "piece of broken pottery", and so Kir-heres means in effect "a city reduced to rubble" (Isa. 30:14).

Verse 12 looks like a prose comment on 15:2: no amount of prayer and repentance on the part of the Moabites will change their ultimate fate. Another prophet deprives himself, in God's name, of the power of prayer: "Do not pray for this people, or lift up cry or prayer for them, and do not intercede with me, for I do not hear you" (Jer. 7:16). The weariness of ineffective prayer and ritual, both for the worshipper and for God, is noted elsewhere in Isaiah (e.g. 1:14–15; 47:12–13).

The last saying in "the oracle concerning Moab" (v. 13) is also negative. It contains an unusual opposition between what has been said before, and a new prophecy for the future. The effect is to change the whole oracle into an oracle of doom, since the implication is that the preceding prophecies, in which there were threads of sympathy and hope, are now out of date. This addition could thus have been made by the same hand as the one that altered verse 7 (see above). The crux of the addition is in the time-scale: "like the years of a hireling" the time has been calculated very accurately, and the day of reckoning is near at hand. The same idiom occurs at the end of the oracle concerning Arabia (21:16–17). In both the "remnant" idea holds out but the feeblest hope: no Moabite or Arab scribe has had the opportunity to do to these texts what a Jewish scribe has done to 6:13 or 7:21–22.

PROPHECIES AGAINST SYRIA AND ISRAEL

Isaiah 17:1–11

¹An oracle concerning Damascus.
  Behold, Damascus will cease to be a city,
    and will become a heap of ruins.
²Her cities will be deserted for ever;
    they will be for flocks,
    which will lie down, and none will make them afraid.
³The fortress will disappear from Ephraim,
    and the kingdom from Damascus;
  and the remnant of Syria will be
    like the glory of the children of Israel,

                    says the Lord of hosts

⁴And in that day
    the glory of Jacob will be brought low,
    and the fat of his flesh will grow lean.
⁵And it shall be as when the reaper gathers standing grain
    and his arm harvests the ears,
  and as when one gleans the ears of grain
    in the Valley of Rephaim.
⁶Gleanings will be left in it,
    as when an olive tree is beaten—
  two or three berries
    in the top of the highest bough,
  four or five
    on the branches of a fruit tree,

                 says the Lord God of Israel.

⁷In that day men will regard their Maker, and their eyes will look to the Holy One of Israel; ⁸they will not have regard for the altars, the work of their hands, and they will not look to what their own fingers have made, either the Asherim or the altars of incense.

⁹In that day their strong cities will be like the deserted places of the Hivites and the Amorites, which they deserted because of the children of Israel, and there will be desolation.

¹⁰For you have forgotten the God of your salvation,
   and have not remembered the Rock of your refuge;
therefore, though you plant pleasant plants
   and set out slips of an alien god,
¹¹though you make them grow on the day that you plant them,
   and make them blossom in the morning that you sow;
yet the harvest will flee away
   in a day of grief and incurable pain.

The first six verses of the "oracle concerning Damascus" appear to belong to the Syro-Ephraimite crisis of 735–732 B.C., when Syria (capital: Damascus) and Israel or Ephraim (capital: Samaria) formed an alliance against Judah (see on chapters 7–8 above). They consist of two short prophecies about Damascus (vv. 1–3) and Israel ("the glory of Jacob") (vv. 4–6), and may have been uttered by Isaiah some time before the subjugation of Damascus by the Assyrian army in 732 B.C. The picture of deserted ruins where animals can lie down without being disturbed by human intruders (vv. 1–2) is already familiar from chapter 13. This example is shorter and very abrupt. The first words of verse 2 are rather odd: in Hebrew they mean "the cities of Aroer are deserted" (RSV, footnote). Since Aroer is one of the Moabite cities conspicuous by its absence from the preceding chapters, it could be that the whole verse is misplaced. Others suggest emending the words "cities of Aroer" to "her cities . . . for ever" (RSV, NEB, Jerusalem Bible). The letters are similar in Hebrew. Perhaps the meaning as it stands is simply that the cities of Damascus will be as deserted as those of Moab.

"The fortress" (v. 3) probably refers to the Syrian capital, Damascus, which was the instigator of the ill-fated Syro-Ephraimite plan (7:5); but Samaria is also a possibility. One fate will befall Syria—or what is left of it ("the remnant")—and Israel ("the glory . . ."). This must be the meaning, and it is interesting to note that the word "remnant" (Heb. *shear* as in Shearjashub), parallel to "glory", clearly in this context has a positive meaning. But both will be "brought low" (v. 4).

The second half of this prophecy fills out and explains the full import of the first. Indeed, although entitled "An oracle concerning Damascus", the prophecy as a whole is more interested in Israel. After an introductory formula, "and in that day", linking the two parts, "the glory of Jacob" takes up a phrase from the preceding verse and the rest of the prophecy is concerned with the "remnant" idea with which the previous section ended. In verse 4 we are probably meant to imagine Jacob, the prosperous old father of Joseph and his brothers, reduced to skin and bone, stripped of his fine raiment ("glory") and clad in the garments of a pauper—a vivid metaphor for the downfall of Israel.

The similes in verses 5 and 6 are no less effective. A shorter version of the same appears in 24:13. A cornfield after the reapers have finished with it, an olive grove after all but a few olives on the topmost branches have been harvested—that is what Israel will look like when the Assyrians have finished with it. Some pointed details make it all the more biting: the word for "gather" in several contexts means "to destroy" as in Zeph. 1:2–3 (RSV "sweep away") and Ezek. 34:29 (RSV "consumed"). The "beating" of the olive trees has obvious violent overtones: the same word is used of felling trees in 10:34. The Valley of Rephaim was the scene of one of David's victories (2 Sam. 5:17–25) a few miles south of Jerusalem; but it could be taken to mean "Valley of the dead" (see on 14:9 above). The last word of the prophecy points remorselessly at Ephraim (Gen. 41:52) and the "house of Joseph", another name for the Northern Kingdom: "Joseph is a fruitful bough..." (Gen. 49:22). Such is the word of judgment from the "Lord God of Israel" (v. 6); Damascus was addressed by the "Lord of hosts" (v. 3).

"In that day" introduces an additional prophecy in prose, unlike the preceding ones, and reflecting a rather different situation (vv. 7–8). Such an attack on idolatry is commoner in the later chapters of the book (e.g. 44:9–20; 51:13; 54:5), where the leap of faith from polytheism to monotheism involves denial of the very existence of gods other than Yahweh (45:5, 6, 14, 21, 22). Where "the Holy One of Israel" (see on 1:4) is identified with the

Maker of all things, then idols and "the work of men's hands" are nothing.

According to Jewish law, traceable back to Josiah (late seventh century B.C.), no altars were permitted apart from the one that stood outside the door of the Temple of Solomon at Jerusalem. This applied to the altars at Bethel, Samaria, Gilgal and all the other ancient sanctuaries in the Northern Kingdom, criticized in this verse. Asherim were trees or wooden objects set up at many sacred sites in ancient Israel, often alongside a standing stone or pillar (e.g. Judg. 6:25–32; Deut. 12:3). In the Canaanite religion the stone object, sometimes carved, stood for the male god Baal, and the wooden object, called by her name, for Asherah the mother goddess, consort of El, father of the gods. The last cultic object referred to in verse 8 (Heb. *hammanim*) is rarely mentioned in the Old Testament, but probably denotes another type of idol, perhaps also representing a male god (e.g. Baal) alongside Asherah (Isa. 27:9; 2 Chr. 34:7). Among Israel's northern neighbours Hamman is an epithet for Baal. Traditionally *hammanim* has been translated "sun-images" or "altars of incense", but there is little to support either suggestion. Whatever they were, and that is for the archaeologists to tell us, collectively such "idols" can delude:

> Woe to him who says to a wooden thing, Awake:
> to a dumb stone, Arise!
> Can this give revelation? (Hab. 2:19)

If the Holy One of Israel created all things, then it follows that worshipping anything other than him is blasphemous as well as absurd. As the Moabites in their time of need turn to Jerusalem for help (16:1), so "in that day" the people of Ephraim will turn to the Holy One of Israel and the people of God will again be one.

But verses 9–11 take away that hope: "their strong cities will be deserted", their land devastated because they forgot the God of Israel. Probably at one time verses 10–11 followed on from verses 1–6; as it stands the insertion of 7–9, raising hopes and then dashing them, makes the "day of grief and incurable pain" (v. 11) all the more bitter. Neither the "Hivites" nor the "Amorites" appear in the Hebrew text which means "like deserted forests and hill-tops" (see RSV, footnote), a vivid enough variation on a theme already familiar to us (e.g. 17:2; 13:21–22), although it does not fit well with the second half of the verse. The Hivites and the Amorites were in the land of Canaan before the Israelites arrived (Josh. 9:1–2), and their ruined cities, abandoned "because of the children of Israel" (v. 9), provided a cautionary parallel: if you continue to worship idols like these people, this is what will happen to you too! In this case most modern translations follow the Greek version where the two idolatrous peoples are mentioned.

There is a dramatic contrast in verse 10 between, on the one hand, Israel's God, described in uniquely Israelite terms as "God of salvation" (see on 12:2–3) and "Rock of refuge" (see on 8:14) and, on the other, Adonis, the Greek name for Baal or Tammuz. He is described here as *Na'aman* (RSV "pleasant") and as "an alien god". The reference is to the cult of a male deity, representing some form of life-force, and worshipped in Syria, Phoenicia, Palestine and Cyprus throughout Biblical times. His death, corresponding to the harvesting of the crops, was mourned especially by women (Ezek. 8:14), and the planting of special cuttings in sacred gardens (the "pleasant plants" of v. 10) was an important part of the ritual for ensuring his resurrection to new life. These and other references to such practices (e.g. 1:29; 65:3; 66:17) cannot be dated with any certainty, but they probably belong to the Second Temple period, when Baals and Asherim (v. 8) were less common. In an age where horoscopes, oriental pseudo-cults and irrational prejudices of all kinds often determine people's attitudes and actions more than the fear of God which is the beginning of wisdom, these prophecies are not so irrelevant as they might seem at first sight.

PROPHECIES AGAINST ASSYRIA AND ETHIOPIA

Isaiah 17:12–18:7

[12]Ah, the thunder of many peoples,
    they thunder like the thundering of the sea!

Ah, the roar of nations,
  they roar like the roaring of mighty waters!
¹³The nations roar like the roaring of many waters,
  but he will rebuke them, and they will flee far away,
chased like chaff on the mountains before the wind
  and whirling dust before the storm.
¹⁴At evening time, behold, terror!
  Before morning, they are no more!
This is the portion of those who despoil us,
  and the lot of those who plunder us.

¹Ah, land of whirring wings
  which is beyond the rivers of Ethiopia;
²which sends ambassadors by the Nile,
  in vessels of papyrus upon the waters!
Go, you swift messengers,
  to a nation, tall and smooth,
to a people feared near and far,
  a nation mighty and conquering,
  whose land the rivers divide.

³All you inhabitants of the world,
  you who dwell on the earth,
when a signal is raised on the mountains, look!
  When a trumpet is blown, hear!
⁴For thus the Lord said to me:
 "I will quietly look from my dwelling
  like clear heat in sunshine,
  like a cloud of dew in the heat of harvest."
⁵For before the harvest, when the blossom is over,
  and the flower becomes a ripening grape,
he will cut off the shoots with pruning hooks,
  and the spreading branches he will hew away.
⁶They shall all of them be left
  to the birds of prey of the mountains
  and to the beasts of the earth.
And the birds of prey will summer upon them,
  and all the beasts of the earth will winter upon them.

⁷At that time gifts will be brought to the Lord of hosts
from a people tall and smooth,
  from a people feared near and far,

a nation mighty and conquering,
   whose land the rivers divide,
to Mount Zion, the place of the name of the Lord of hosts.

The next title does not appear till 19:1, and it is therefore natural to take two passages together: 17:12–14 and 18:1–7. They both begin with the conventional prophetic introduction "Woe...!" (AV) (RSV "Ah!") and concern mighty and fabulous nations: Assyria, although it is not actually named, and Ethiopia, a "land of whirring wings... a nation mighty and conquering". Furthermore both passages exult in the unique supremacy of Zion: 17:14 triumphantly alludes to the miraculous deliverance of Jerusalem in 701 B.C. (see 37:36), while 18:7 looks forward to a time when Ethiopia will join Moab (16:1) in bringing tribute to "Mount Zion, the place of the name of the Lord of hosts" (cf. 45:14).

In the first of the two prophecies the original Assyrian connection is unmistakable, not only in verse 14 but also in the picture of mighty waters, sweeping into Judah and swirling round the city of Jerusalem "reaching even to the neck" (8:7–8). The stilling of the tempest at the "rebuke" of God, however, goes far beyond the immediate circumstances of 701 B.C.: at creation God imposed his authority on the sea (Ps. 104:5–9); he did the same at the Red Sea (Ps. 106:9–12). The defeat of the Assyrians was only one manifestation of the power of the Creator of heaven and earth. This is a frequent theme in Isaianic tradition: e.g. "Behold, the nations are like a drop from a bucket, and are accounted as the dust on the scales..." (40:15). "Chaff" is also a popular simile, applied to Assyria in a close parallel in 29:5–8, and to Israel's enemies in general in 41:15: "You shall thresh the mountains and crush them, and you shall make the hills like chaff". In Psalms and the Wisdom literature the image is widened to include mankind in general, whose lives are at the mercy of God and as frail and transitory as moths: "between morning and evening they are destroyed" (Job 4:19–20; cf. 21:18; Ps. 35:5). Israel's history has much to tell us about God's dealings with mankind in general, not just Israel and her ancient near-eastern neighbours.

Chapter 18 begins, like chapter 16, with the arrival of foreign ambassadors in Jerusalem. In 16, the Moabites were pleading for help in their time of need; here the mighty Ethiopians are in all probability trying to persuade Judah to join them in a revolt against the Assyrians. Chapters 20 and 31 contain other prophecies about Ethiopia and Egypt and the same theme runs through them all: "Woe to those who go down to Egypt for help and rely on horses, who trust in chariots..." (31:1). The date of such a revolt is not known. It was certainly during the reign of Hezekiah (725–697 B.C.), but whether the passage comes from the earlier revolt which ended in Sargon's destruction of Ashdod in 711 B.C. (20:1), or the later one, which culminated in Sennacherib's invasion of Judah in 701 B.C., cannot now be ascertained. Egypt was ruled by an Ethiopian dynasty during Isaiah's lifetime, and this is reflected in the fact that Egypt and Ethiopia are mentioned in one phrase in chapter 20, and also grouped together here (chapters 18–19).

The description of the Ethiopians in this prophecy is full of vivid details which suggest that somewhere in its transmission there has been an eye-witness. Isaiah himself probably saw the ambassadors when they reached Jerusalem, but he may also have watched their ships sailing into port either on the Mediterranean or in Elath on the Gulf of Aqaba (2 Chron. 26:2,6). Here they come from the Nile (v. 2) to a Mediterranean port. It has been suggested that "wings" in verse 1 refers to the sails of Ethiopia's elegant ships. In that case "whirring" might be better translated "clattering". The word usually denotes the sound of a bell or cymbal, but can mean "to quiver" (Hab. 3:16) and has provided the name of a type of locust (Deut. 28:42). "The land of whirring wings" has thus also been understood to refer to the presence of locusts, mosquitoes and other noisy-winged insects in Ethiopia. A third possibility is to be found in the AV rendering: "Woe to the land shadowing with wings..." The suggestive phrase certainly starts off the description of the distant Ethiopians on a suitably mysterious and exotic note.

"The rivers of Ethiopia" included the Blue Nile and the White in modern Sudan, as well as the Barka, Awash, Rebi Shebeli and other rivers that flow through modern Ethiopia and Somalia, since *Cush*, the Biblical name translated "Ethiopia", covered a much wider area than modern Ethiopia. Small skiffs made of woven papyrus were familiar in ancient Egypt, though it is most unlikely that it was in such boats that the ambassadors came to Judah. The appearance of the tall, gleaming, black Ethiopians elicited comments from many ancient writers: Herodotus, for instance, writing in fifth-century B.C. Greece, described them as "the tallest and most beautiful of men". Jeremiah 13:23 is another comment on the physical appearance of Ethiopians, which like parts of the Queen of Sheba legend, is less flattering. The word translated "mighty" occurs only here and is very difficult: other suggestions are "speaking a foreign language" (like "barbarian") and "that measures its enemies with a line" (as David did to the Moabites: 2 Sam. 8:2). Once again the exotic foreign nation elicits rare and mysterious words from the author.

The prophet's reaction to the arrival of these exciting visitors is threefold. First he orders messengers to take Judah's answer swiftly to Ethiopia; then he calls upon the inhabitants of the whole world to witness what is about to happen; and finally he delivers the word of God (v. 4). The parallels in chapters 6 and 40 make it likely that the "swift messengers" in verse 2 are angels: in each case the prophet overhears God's instructions to members of his heavenly court. Verse 3 is typically Isaianic, putting into a universal context the theological realities revealed in Judah.

A "signal" and "trumpet(-call)" introduce the divine oracle in verse 4, like the sound of the trumpet that miraculously grew louder and louder on Mount Sinai (Exod. 19:19). A comparison between a trumpet-call and the revealed word of God appears in Amos too:

> Is a trumpet blown in a city,
>   and the people are not afraid? . . .
> Surely the Lord God does nothing,
>   without revealing his secret
>   to his servants the prophets. (3:6–7)

The oracle itself is one of the most beautiful and effective in the whole Book of Isaiah. Above all the turmoil of human affairs,

God quietly keeps watch—it is an expression of faith in God like 7:4–9, 28:16 and 30:15. God's "dwelling", whether in the Temple at Jerusalem or in heaven (see on 6:1), is a place that is firmly established, built on solid foundations which nothing can move, like his throne in Psalm 93:2. The images of "clear [dazzling] heat" and "cloud of dew" are striking. The first is visual and compares the clarity and stillness of a hot summer's day, undisturbed by even the slightest breath of wind, to the vision of the Almighty, in all his glory, source of light and peace for a perplexed and troubled world. The dew in the second image is perhaps more tactile: as after a long day's work in the heat, the cool of the evening refreshes and revives, so the wisdom of God, made available through his servants the prophets, gives strength and courage to those in need. It may have been addressed originally to Hezekiah, unsure what to answer the Ethiopian ambassadors, but it certainly speaks volumes to those who hear the prophet's words today.

Verses 5 and 6 speak of judgment upon "those who go down to Egypt for help" (30:1). The trees themselves are not cut down as in other prophecies (10:33–34); but their shoots and branches, perhaps the ill-advised allies of Ethiopia, are at the mercy of vandals wilfully damaging ripening fruit-trees, and of birds of prey and wild beasts making their home in the ruined fields and vineyards.

Like verse 3, the last verse brings the whole prophecy into line with Isaianic tradition by placing Mount Zion in the centre of the picture. The proud Ethiopians who came to pressurize Judah in verse 1 now come to Jerusalem with tribute. This is developed in 45:14 where they also acknowledge Yahweh as the One True God. The verse also identifies God's "dwelling" (verse 4) with the Temple at Jerusalem, and rounds off the passage in typically Isaianic style (cf. 4:2–6).

THE DISINTEGRATION OF EGYPT

Isaiah 19:1–15

[1]An oracle concerning Egypt.
  Behold, the Lord is riding on a swift cloud

and comes to Egypt;
and the idols of Egypt will tremble at his presence,
and the heart of the Egyptians will melt within them.
²And I will stir up Egyptians against Egyptians,
and they will fight, every man against his brother
and every man against his neighbour,
city against city, kingdom against kingdom;
³and the spirit of the Egyptians within them will be emptied out,
and I will confound their plans;
and they will consult the idols and the sorcerers,
and the mediums and the wizards;
⁴and I will give over the Egyptians
into the hand of a hard master;
and a fierce king will rule over them,
says the Lord, the Lord of hosts.

⁵And the waters of the Nile will be dried up,
and the river will be parched and dry;
⁶and its canals will become foul,
and the branches of Egypt's Nile will diminish and dry up,
reeds and rushes will rot away.
⁷There will be bare places by the Nile,
on the brink of the Nile,
and all that is sown by the Nile will dry up,
be driven away, and be no more.
⁸The fishermen will mourn and lament,
all who cast hook in the Nile;
and they will languish
who spread nets upon the water.
⁹The workers in combed flax will be in despair,
and the weavers of white cotton.
¹⁰Those who are the pillars of the land will be crushed,
and all who work for hire will be grieved.

¹¹The princes of Zoan are utterly foolish;
the wise counsellors of Pharaoh give stupid counsel.
How can you say to Pharaoh,
"I am a son of the wise,
a son of ancient kings"?
¹²Where then are your wise men?
Let them tell you and make known

what the Lord of hosts has purposed against Egypt.
13The princes of Zoan have become fools,
    and the princes of Memphis are deluded;
those who are the cornerstones of her tribes have led Egypt astray.
14The Lord has mingled within her
    a spirit of confusion;
and they have made Egypt stagger in all her doings
    as a drunken man staggers in his vomit.
15And there will be nothing for Egypt
    which head or tail, palm branch or reed, may do.

The centre-piece of the prophecies about Ethiopia and Egypt in chapters 18–20 is a long "oracle" concerning Egypt alone. It is in two distinct parts: verses 1–15 are in poetry and consist of three stanzas depicting the breakdown of Egyptian society in vivid but traditional style—trembling idols, the drying up of the Nile, a new Pharaoh and the stupidity of his wise men. The second part (vv. 16–25) is in prose and consists of five very unusual prophecies introduced by "In that day . . ." As in some earlier chapters (e.g 7,10,17), it seems most likely that the "In that day" prophecies are later additions, commenting on the first part and introducing quite new images and ways of thinking, in this case unique in Old Testament prophecies about Egypt.

The first stanza (vv. 1–4) begins with a traditional picture of God's cloud-chariot arriving in Egypt:

There is none like God, O Jeshurun,
    who rides through the heavens to your help
    and in his majesty through the skies. (Deut. 33:26; cf. Ps. 68:33)

His appearance confounds the Egyptians: their idols, notoriously elaborate symbols of childish folly (cf. Wisdom of Solomon 15:14–19), tremble like the foundations of the Temple in Isaiah's vision (6:4); then the people themselves lose heart, confronted by the Holy One of Israel. He has come to plunge the country into civil war and anarchy (v. 2). A number of Israel's legendary victories were won in this way: e.g. Gideon's victory over the massed armies of the Midianites, the Amalekites and the people of the East (Judg. 7:22), and Saul's over the Philistines (1 Sam. 14:20). It is one way of making the point that the victory is not Israel's or some other human agent's, but God's (Judg. 7:2; Ps. 83:9–12).

Without a strong central government the fiercely independent cities and regions of Upper and Lower Egypt were only too ready to turn against each other, demoralized and perplexed. There were then two alternative sources of help, the first comforting but totally useless—idols, sorcerers, mediums and wizards (v. 3) —the second cruelly efficient—"a hard master . . . a fierce king" (v. 4). There has inevitably been much speculation as to who this was and what the events described in verses 2–4 refer to. It could refer to the unsettled period of the 22nd and 23rd Dynasties which lasted from about 750 B.C. until powerful Ethiopian kings eventually imposed a firm central government on the whole country by about 710. Shabako (*c.* 716–695) would then be the successful but unpopular foreigner described as "a fierce king" in verse 4. At all events repressive foreign rule was to be Egypt's punishment, whether or not the "rod of God's anger" (10:5) in this case was an Ethiopian or someone else. A change of government meant oppression and slavery for the Hebrews in Egypt (Exod. 1:8); now it was the Egyptians' turn to suffer a similar fate. Such is the justice of God.

Just as the trembling idols in verse 1 symbolize frightened Egyptian society, so now the dried-up Nile is an obvious image for disruption and death. The tropical rain that every year floods the valleys of the Blue Nile, the White Nile and the Atbara in the Sudan and Ethiopia from June to September, brings life one thousand five hundred miles down the Nile valley to Egypt. Before the building of the great modern dams, variations in the annual rainfall could lead to disaster for the whole country. So the element of hyperbole in the present graphic description is limited to the fact that the main river itself never dried up completely, though the vast network of "branches" and canals certainly did with inevitable and devastating effects on plant and animal life. Crops of corn, flax and cotton (v. 9) would be wiped out, so that weavers and flax-workers would be unemployed and destitute, not only fishermen.

Verse 10 makes it clear that the poem is not simply concerned with dried-up rivers and unemployed fishermen, but with the total breakdown of Egyptian life. "The pillars of the land", that is Egypt's leaders, together with the workers, add up to the whole of Egyptian society. The word translated "pillars" is rare in the Hebrew Bible, where it happens to occur once as "foundations" (Ps. 11:3) and once as part of the anatomy (Isa. 20:4). The word may once have meant "spinners" (NEB) or "weavers" (Jerusalem Bible), but as it has been traditionally understood it makes excellent sense and gives the prophecy a sting in its tail.

The third object of the prophet's scorn, after the trembling idols in verses 1–4 and the dried-up Nile in verses 5–10, is the fabled "wise men" of Egypt. The ineptitude of these distinguished members of Pharaoh's establishment is ridiculed more than once (Gen. 41:8; Exod. 7:11–12); and the fact that Egypt produced some of the best writers and politicians of the ancient near east, some of whom had an influence on Israelite culture (e.g. Prov. 22:17–24:22 shows clear dependence on Egyptian models), is hardly relevant here. Her philosophers cannot cope with the present political crisis, and they have no idea "what the Lord of hosts has purposed against Egypt" (v. 12). The prophet's challenge to human wisdom recalls the divine rhetoric of the Book of Job (e.g. 38:4,18,21) or, still more apposite, the ridicule of idols later in the present book: e.g. "Tell us what is to come hereafter, that we may know that you are gods" (41:23). The image of the staggering drunkard is a standard example of indiscipline in the Wisdom literature and thus all the more biting here, applied to the kind of men who gave us that literature (cf. Prov. 23:29–35). The final verse of the stanza, like verse 10, emphasizes the totality of the disaster: the whole of society is involved. The idiom occurs also in 9:14.

The two place-names, Zoan and Memphis (vv. 11,13), denote cities that were important throughout Egyptian history. Zoan (Greek Tanis) was the site of the Hyksos capital (Avaris) from about 1750 to 1550 B.C., and under the name Raamses features in the Exodus narrative (Exod. 1:11). In the eighth century it was also capital of Egypt under the Ethiopian kings and gave its name to the Tanite Dynasty. Memphis was the most important city in Egypt during the Old and Middle Kingdoms, that is, down to about 1750 B.C. Both Zoan (Tanis) and Memphis continued to flourish in Greek and Roman times.

It is noteworthy that this whole prophecy about Egypt has little in common with the earlier Exodus traditions. There is no mention of Egypt's oppression of Israel as a reason for their present sufferings, and the place-names and other circumstantial details are different. It might almost be a different country: indeed the country where, from the sixth century B.C. on, Jews settled happily and built up the thriving community to which the next section is probably addressed.

A BLESSING ON EGYPT

Isaiah 19:16–25

16In that day the Egyptians will be like women, and tremble with fear before the hand which the Lord of hosts shakes over them. 17And the land of Judah will become a terror to the Egyptians; every one to whom it is mentioned will fear because of the purpose which the Lord of hosts has purposed against them.

18In that day there will be five cities in the land of Egypt which speak the language of Canaan and swear allegiance to the Lord of hosts. One of these will be called the City of the Sun.

19In that day there will be an altar to the Lord in the midst of the land of Egypt, and a pillar to the Lord at its border. 20It will be a sign and a witness to the Lord of hosts in the land of Egypt; when they cry to the Lord because of oppressors he will send them a saviour, and will defend and deliver them. 21And the Lord will make himself known to the Egyptians; and the Egyptians will know the Lord in that day and worship with sacrifice and burnt offering, and they will make vows to the Lord and perform them. 22And the Lord will smite Egypt, smiting and healing, and they will return to the Lord, and he will heed their supplications and heal them.

²³In that day there will be a highway from Egypt to Assyria, and the Assyrian will come into Egypt, and the Egyptian into Assyria, and the Egyptians will worship with the Assyrians.

²⁴In that day Israel will be the third with Egypt and Assyria, a blessing in the midst of the earth, ²⁵whom the Lord of hosts has blessed, saying, "Blessed be Egypt my people, and Assyria the work of my hands, and Israel my heritage."

The abrupt change of tone as well as style between the two parts of the "oracle concerning Egypt" must be explained by the fact that the Egyptians in Part 2 are not the same as those in Part 1. Gone are the idolaters, the fishermen, the weavers, the foolish "princes of Zoan" and their "hard master". In their place are Egyptians who speak Hebrew "and swear allegiance to the Lord of hosts" (v. 18), who humbly cry to the Lord for help and he sends them "a saviour" (v. 20). They are united with Assyria in their worship of the one true God, and along with Assyria and Israel receive a blessing from the Lord of hosts (vv. 24–25). Other prophecies end on such a triumphant note, describing the foreigners (e.g. Moabites in ch. 16; Ethiopians in 18:7) acknowledging the supremacy of the Holy One of Israel in Jerusalem. But this is very different: the worship of God takes place in Egypt, not on Mount Zion, and the foreigners are ranked above Israel in the blessing. There is only one explanation for this extraordinary shift of emphasis: the Egyptians referred to are Egyptian Jews, both converts to Judaism and Jewish expatriates.

There is ample evidence that, by the third century B.C., there was already established a significant Jewish presence in Egypt. This eventually rivalled the Palestinian community in some respects, as did the equally robust and creative Jewish community in Mesopotamia. Verse 18 indicates that the community was not yet Greek-speaking as it was by the middle of the third century when the first Greek translation of the Hebrew Bible (the Septuagint) was commissioned in Alexandria. It may be that these unusually interesting verses have been influenced by later events, such as the setting up of a Jewish Temple at Leontopolis about 145 B.C.; but it is likely that they were composed sometime before the end of the fourth century. There are other Isaianic texts from as late as this, as we shall see, but none later.

The keyword in the first of the five "In that day" prophecies is the word translated "terror" in verse 17. It occurs only here and is traditionally thought to be a noun from the verb "to reel . . . like drunken men" (Ps. 107:27), an image used three verses previously (19:14). The question still remains, however, why of all the words for "fear, terror, stagger, etc.", it is this unusual word that is selected here, and what is it exactly about "the land of Judah" (another expression that occurs only here in the Old Testament) that is going to become a terror to the Egyptians? It has been suggested that the verse depicts a time when Egyptian troops will be in the land of Judah and will suddenly be smitten by the hand of God, as the Assyrians were in 701 B.C. (chs. 36–37). This would certainly make sense of the verse in isolation, but it would then be the only prophecy in the chapter in which the land of Egypt is not the subject. In view of the last part of the verse in which "the purpose of the Lord of hosts" is mysteriously mentioned, we must rather think again of something extraordinary happening in Egypt, that is to say, the appearance of Jewish cities, Jewish religious communities, Jewish blessings, "in the midst of the land of Egypt" (v. 19). "The land of Judah" is going to spread across the Sinai desert into Egypt, and there it will unsettle the Egyptian host community with its strange forms of worship and festivals. The puzzling word "terror" in verse 17 is closely related to words for "festival" and "to celebrate": is it perhaps another celebration of the Passover that will strike terror into the Egyptians as it did in Exod. 12–15? Only this time the Exodus is from Judah to Egypt, not vice versa.

The problem in the second of these prophecies is the "City of the Sun". Of the five cities in Egypt which speak "the language of Canaan" three could well be the cities referred to in Jeremiah 43–44 as having a Jewish community in his day: Migdol and Tahpanhes (Greek *Daphne*) on the east of the delta, and Memphis further south (see on 19:13 above). A fourth could be Syene (or Elephantine), a Jewish colony six hundred miles upstream from Memphis, referred to by name in Ezek. 29:10 and Isa. 49:12, and perhaps included in the Jeremiah passage under the heading "the land of Pathros" (=Upper Egypt) (44:1). The fifth could be Heliopolis (Greek for "City of the Sun"), also mentioned in Jeremiah (43:13) and by its Egyptian name "On" in Gen. 41:50 and Ezek. 30:17. But why should one of the names be given such special emphasis here? In fact there is some evidence to suggest that the original text mentioned no names at all but described one of the cities as "the city of righteousness" (as in Isa. 1:26), that is to say, "a new Jerusalem", in line with the other extraordinary prophecies in this section. Understandably puzzled interpreters and translators of later generations changed the title to make it less incredible: the ancient Aramaic version of the Jews, for example, has "City of the Sun" (followed in RSV), while a more hostile "city of destruction" is preserved in the present Hebrew text (see AV).

The next prophecy (vv. 19–22) once again envisages the impossible happening: Egypt will have its own "salvation history". An altar will be set up like Abraham's at Shechem (Gen. 12:7), and a stone pillar like Jacob's at Bethel (Gen. 28:18). When they are in trouble, the Lord will send them a "saviour" as he did in the days of Moses, Joshua, Samson and the rest (Judg. 2:16–23). The Lord will make himself known as he did to David (2 Sam. 7) and Solomon (1 Kings 4). Sacrifices, burnt offerings and vows will be offered as in the Temple at Jerusalem. There will be disobedience and punishment as in the checkered history of Israel; but after suffering and destruction there will be repentance and healing (Deut. 30:1–10; 2 Kings 25:27–30; Isa. 53). To what extent this pattern was ever applied to the history of the Jews in Egypt cannot be determined, apart from the clues in "terror" (v. 17) and "City of the Sun" (v. 18) discussed above. In about 145 B.C. there was an attempt at setting up a "New Jerusalem" in Leontopolis, a city in the vicinity of Heliopolis. Jewish sources from the beginning of the Christian era tell of a Temple built there by the Zadokite priest in exile, Onias, son of Simon the High Priest described in Ecclesiasticus 50. Later commentators see Isa. 19 as referring to it, but even without this modest "fulfilment", the prophecy is a witness to the profound originality of certain strands within the Isaianic tradition.

The fourth prophecy (v. 23) takes the originality still farther. It imagines a day when the highway bringing the exiles back home (40:3; 62:10) will not stop in the land of Judah but will unite in one vast community the peoples of Egypt and Assyria, devoted to the worship of the Holy One of Israel. It is possible to connect this with the victories of Alexander the Great (333–323 B.C.) and his successors, the Ptolemies in Egypt and the Seleucids in Assyria, but the prophecy far transcends any actual historical event.

Finally, three peoples are united in a unique blessing (vv. 24–25): Egypt, Assyria and Israel. Influenced maybe by events in Egypt and Assyria, such as the success of Jewish communities there, but also inspired by a vision of a new world, like that in 2:2–4 and 66:22–23, the prophet breaks down age-old barriers and speaks of Egypt as "the people of God" and Assyria as "the work of his hands", intimate expressions normally reserved for Israel alone. The generosity of this world view, so often submerged under defensive attitudes and polarizations, rings true today as at any other time, and challenges us to apply it to relations, say, between Judaism, Christianity and Islam. How many Christians would be prepared to say, "In that day the Church will be the third with Egypt and Assyria, a blessing in the midst of the earth"?

PUT NOT YOUR TRUST IN EGYPT AND ETHIOPIA

Isaiah 20:1–6

¹In the year that the commander in chief, who was sent by Sargon the king of Assyria, came to Ashdod and fought against it and took it,—²at that time the Lord had spoken by Isaiah the son of Amoz, saying, "Go, and loose the sackcloth from your loins and take off your shoes from your feet," and he had done so, walking naked and barefoot—³the Lord said, "As my servant Isaiah has walked naked and barefoot for three years as a sign and a portent against Egypt and Ethiopia, ⁴so shall the king of Assyria lead away the Egyptians captives and the Ethiopians exiles, both the young and the old, naked and barefoot, with buttocks uncovered, to the shame of Egypt. ⁵Then they shall be dismayed and confounded because of Ethiopia their hope and of Egypt their boast. ⁶And the inhabitants of this coastland will say in that day, 'Behold, this is what has happened to those in whom we hoped and to

whom we fled for help to be delivered from the king of Assyria! And we, how shall we escape?' "

The last of the prophecies concerning Egypt and Ethiopia is different from the rest in various ways. It begins with a historical reference: "In the year that the commander in chief . . . came to Ashdod" (instead of "In that day . . ." or the like). Although it purports to be about Egypt and Ethiopia, it begins with references to Assyria and the Philistines, two foreign nations dealt with together elsewhere (14:24–32). It centres on a piece of extra-ordinary behaviour by the prophet, who "walked naked and barefoot for three years as a sign and a portent . . ." The prophet's objective in this prophecy is not primarily to comment on the fate of Egypt and Ethiopia, or indeed on that of Assyria and the Philistines, but to persuade his audience not to put their trust in foreign powers, a recurring theme throughout Isaiah's ministry (see also chs. 7 and 31).

The reason for its present position is of course partly its mention of four of the foreign nations just dealt with, namely, Assyria (14:24–27), Philistia (14:28–32), Ethiopia (18) and Egypt (19). But it has another function as well. There is a chronological sequence which runs through the book from "the year that King Uzziah died" (ch. 6) to "the year that King Ahaz died" (14:28), and from the year the Assyrians captured Ashdod (ch. 20) to "the fourteenth year of King Hezekiah" (ch. 36). Not much biographical material on the prophet has been preserved, but what there is has been arranged chronologically to root the prophecies in the life and times of Isaiah. The appearance of chapter 20 at this point, in the middle of a collection of, for the most part, undatable utterances, has the effect of reminding us of the important fiction that Isaiah the son of Amoz saw all these visions "concerning Judah and Jerusalem in the days of Uzziah, Jotham, Ahaz and Hezekiah, kings of Judah" (see commentary on 1:1).

Three distinct events are referred to in this short chapter, and the connection between them is not entirely obvious: (1) Sargon's capture of the Philistine city of Ashdod (v. 1); (2) the prophet's extraordinary behaviour which lasted three years (vv. 2–3); and

(3) the defeat of Egypt and Ethiopia by the king of Assyria. We know that Ashdod fell after three years' siege in 711 B.C., and that the third event took place in 701 B.C. Since this is still in the future (vv. 4–6) we are to assume that the background of the prophecy is sometime in the last decade of the eighth century, a time of increasing unrest in the Assyrian provinces, culminating in Hezekiah's revolt and the capitulation of Jerusalem in 701 B.C. (2 Kings 18:13–16). In that year Egypt too was defeated by Sennacherib at the battle of Eltekeh. The author or editor, looking back on all three events, wants us to see the hand of God in them and to listen to the words of the Lord as spoken by his servant the prophet (vv. 3–6). It may be that originally Isaiah's three-year sign had something to do with the three-year siege of Ashdod, and that "the inhabitants of this coastland" (v. 6) were the Philistines. But as the text has come down to us, verse 1 simply gives the date of the prophecy as ten years before its fulfilment, thereby emphasizing the exceptional powers of the prophet. Isaiah predicted the humiliating defeat of Egypt a good ten years before it happened. Verse 6 is then a cautionary comment on his audience's reaction: they did not believe him until it was too late, despite his extraordinary efforts to get the point across to them. "This coastland" in verse 6 is now Judah—will you never learn not to put your trust in human powers?

The siege of Ashdod is well documented in the Assyrian annals. According to his own account, Sargon himself (721–705 B.C.) commanded the Assyrian army, not his *tartan*, "commander-in-chief", as verse 1 states. But it may be that the Bible preserves the facts and Sargon is giving himself credit properly due to one of his officers. Ashdod was apparently the centre of anti-Assyrian opposition at this time, supported by, among others, the new and energetic Ethiopian dynasty in Egypt. In the event, however, for whatever reason, Egypt did not send help to Ashdod as they had hoped. Hence their cry of disillusionment and despair, "So this is what we put our trust in . . . Now how can we escape?" (v. 6—the Hebrew text does not actually say, "This is what has happened to . . .", RSV).

The "sign and portent" in verses 2–3 seems to contain two

"prophecies" in sequence. First, sackcloth denotes mourning (e.g. 2 Sam. 21:10) and must surely be a comment on the fate of Ashdod (cf. 14:29–31). Then, second, the mourner is stripped naked, mourning is superseded by humiliation: those who mourn the death of the Philistines—and that includes the Egyptians and Ethiopians—will themselves be defeated and led into degrading captivity. So the prophet represents by his actions the fate of the Philistines in the past, and that of the Egyptians and Ethiopians in the future. Such dramatic gestures are not uncommon in the Biblical accounts of prophetic behaviour: e.g. "Zedekiah the son of Chenaanah made for himself horns of iron and said, 'Thus says the Lord, With these you shall gore the Syrians until they are destroyed'." (1 Kings 22:11). Ezekiel stages an even more elaborate "acted parable" (Ezek. 12:1–16), and there are others (e.g. Jer. 13:1–7; 19).

It seems likely that at some stage in the history of this prophetic phenomenon people believed that, by sympathetic magic, the actions of a prophet had a direct effect on the subsequent course of events. Certainly the Biblical authors identify false prophets by their failure to predict the future correctly (Deut. 18:21–22; 1 Kings 22: 5–36). But there is no point in discussing whether Isaiah really went about Jerusalem for three years with nothing on. This is one of those stories, based on the fact of prophecy as a phenomenon in ancient Israel, that summons us to respect the authority of a man with some kind of extra powers, and to listen to what he says, rather than speculate about what he did. It is a warning about what happens to people who do not listen to what a prophet says (6:9–10). Do not trust the principalities and powers of this world, is what he is saying, however strong they may appear to be. In the end they will let you down as Egypt and Ethiopia let the wretched Philistines down, and you will be left by the roadside, like the man who fell among thieves (Luke 10:30–37), naked and ashamed. Who can you count on to help you then?

A VISION OF DESTRUCTION

Isaiah 21:1–10

> [1]The oracle concerning the wilderness of the sea.
> As whirlwinds in the Negeb sweep on,

    it comes from the desert,
      from a terrible land.
²A stern vision is told to me;
    the plunderer plunders,
      and the destroyer destroys.
Go up, O Elam,
    lay siege, O Media;
all the sighing she has caused
    I bring to an end.
³Therefore my loins are filied with anguish;
    pangs have seized me,
    like the pangs of a woman in travail;
I am bowed down so that I cannot hear,
    I am dismayed so that I cannot see.
⁴My mind reels, horror has appalled me;
    the twilight I longed for
    has been turned for me into trembling.
⁵They prepare the table,
    they spread the rugs,
    they eat, they drink.
Arise, O princes,
    oil the shield!
⁶For thus the Lord said to me:
"Go, set a watchman,
    let him announce what he sees.
⁷When he sees riders, horsemen in pairs,
    riders on asses, riders on camels,
let him listen diligently,
    very diligently."
⁸Then he who saw cried:
"Upon a watchtower I stand, O Lord,
    continually by day,
and at my post I am stationed
    whole nights.
⁹And, behold, here come riders,
    horsemen in pairs!"
And he answered,
    "Fallen, fallen is Babylon;
and all the images of her gods
    he has shattered to the ground."

¹⁰O my threshed and winnowed one,
   what I have heard from the Lord of hosts,
   the God of Israel, I announce to you.

The subject of the next "oracle" appears at first sight to be the fall of Babylon (v. 9), but in the first place Babylon's fate has already been very elaborately dealt with in this series (13:1–14:23), and secondly the prophecy is not entitled "The oracle concerning Babylon", but "The oracle concerning the wilderness of the sea". It is therefore not simply one of the oracles concerning the foreign nations. As in chapter 22, the title is taken from the prophecy itself, and instead of directing our attention at a particular foreign nation, it introduces one of the most vivid and moving descriptions of prophetic experience in the Bible, comparable to 1 Kings 19:9–18, Jer. 20:7–12 or the like. There are as many psychological, spiritual and mystical details in the chapter as there are references to the siege and fall of Babylon. The visionary elements in the passage bring it more in line with the apocalyptic material of chapters 24–27 than with the foreign nations in 13–33. Surely this is the explanation of the mysterious title: the mention of Babylon in verse 9 led to the placing of this passage here among the foreign nations, but the title reminds us that it is primarily about something else. It is the "Wilderness oracle", the one beginning "As whirlwinds in the Negeb . . .", a memorable title for a memorable vision.

The Hebrew text has "wilderness of the sea", which may conceivably at one time have been the equivalent of the Assyrian name for Babylon, *mat tamti*, "maritime plain" (Jerusalem Bible), the "sea" being the Persian Gulf. But this geographical meaning would soon be forgotten in Hebrew and is not attested anywhere else. As it stands, the phrase could mean the "distant wilderness" as in the post-Biblical Hebrew phrase *medinot ha-yam*, "distant lands" (lit. "countries of the sea"); or perhaps "the sea" stands for that awesome, formless reality, inhabited by dragons and monsters (27:1; 51:9–10; Amos 9:3), and experienced from time to time by the prophets (e.g. Jonah 2) and psalmists: "Out of the depths I cry to thee, O Lord" (Ps. 130:1;

cf. 18:16; 93:3). The whirlwinds and the desert reflect the proph-et's "stern vision", his pain, his dismay, his horror; is "the sea" in the title another image for his mental turmoil?

The "Wilderness oracle" begins with a description of the com-ing of this frightening experience to the prophet, "from the desert, from a terrible land", like "whirlwinds in the Negeb" (the desert to the south of Israel). The subject of the verse is singular ("it comes") and cannot refer to the approaching enemies of Babylon. It is the "stern vision" that dominates the first verse, as it does more than half of the prophecy.

A very small change in the text of verse 2 would give "the plunderer plundered, the destroyer destroyed" (cf. NEB), which would fit the latter part of the verse better. Babylon the plun-derer, which has caused so much sighing, will be herself de-stroyed. Elam and Media must be references to the armies of Cyrus, king of the Medes and Persians, who in 538 B.C. conquered Babylon. The present vision may well have come to the prophet in the years immediately preceding that date, since by then news of Cyrus' spectacular military successes in other parts of the Near East had certainly reached Babylon and struck fear into its leaders' minds. Similar predictions from about the same time appear in Isaiah 41:2–4 and 45:1–7, passages also set in exilic Babylon.

Again it is the prophet's own personal anguish, as he gets caught up in this horrific vision of destruction, that takes up the next two verses (3–4), not the fate of Babylon. The experience was almost more than he could bear; twilight, that is to say, calm after the dazzling sunlight of the vision, was so long in coming. Then in a few brief phrases (v. 5), the whole scene of an inter-rupted banquet is conjured up: the preparations, the eating and drinking, the sudden call to arms—"Arise, O princes". Daniel 5 is another example. Oiling the shields may have been a semi-religious rite (like breaking a bottle of champagne over the bows of a ship), rather than a process for improving their effectiveness or appearance, but there is little evidence in ancient literature for either explanation.

Verses 6–9 return to the prophet's experience again: "For thus

the Lord said to me, Go, set a watchman . . ." The Lord's speech
(vv. 6–7) is followed by two other speeches, one depicting the
approaching conquerors of Babylon (vv. 8–9a), the other an-
nouncing her fall (v. 9b). This type of debate between God and
his prophet, or between God and his angelic court, appears
elsewhere in Isaiah (6:1–13; 40:1–11), and presupposes a particular type of visionary experience. Who exactly is speaking in each
case is not always clear (see on 40:1–11 in volume 2). But what is
clear is that God speaks first (6:8; 40:1) and then several re-
sponses follow. Here God instructs the prophet to appoint a
watchman and prepare for a vision of horsemen and riders (as in
Ezekiel and the Apocalypse). The watchman takes up his position; and after a time the riders and horsemen appear. This
heralds the final vision of Babylon destroyed, her shattered
images lying on the ground.

According to the Hebrew text the speaker in verse 8 is "a lion"
(Heb. *arieh*). The Isaiah Scroll from Qumran reads "the seer" or
"the one who saw" (Heb. *ha-ro'eh*) and this is the text followed
by most modern translations (RSV, NEB, Jerusalem Bible).
With characteristic ingenuity, the rabbis interpreted the lion as
follows: following the Lord's instructions (vv. 6–7), Isaiah appointed Habakkuk the prophet to be his watchman, and he took
his stand on a watchtower to witness the fall of Babylon (Hab.
2:1). Why is Habakkuk called "lion"? Amos 3:8 compares a
prophet to a lion, and the numerical values of the letters of the
word for "lion" in Hebrew exactly add up to the numerical values
of the letters of Habakkuk's name! One might add that elsewhere
a lion stands for Judah (Gen. 49:9) and Jerusalem is called Ariel,
"the lion of God" (Isa. 29:1–2). The visionary, even apocalyptic
style of this passage means that we cannot entirely rule out the
possibility that it was a lion that appeared at this point in the
vision, whether as representing a prophetic figure, or as one more
detail in the horrific scene.

In verse 10, back on *terra firma* once more, the prophet comforts his people with a reassurance that all this news comes from
God: Babylon is soon to fall and their days of sighing (v. 2) will be
over. The compassionate way he addresses captive Zion as a girl

cruelly treated—"threshed with threshing sledges of iron"
(Amos 1:3)—and as a child constantly flayed on the threshing
floor of history ("winnowed one" is a weak translation of a
Hebrew expression meaning "child of the threshing floor")
makes this "oracle" unusually poignant. The prophet is appalled
by his vision of the coming fate of Babylon; but it means the end
of oppression and suffering for his people. The horrors of
Dresden and Hiroshima are matched only by the horrors of
Dachau and Auschwitz which preceded them and in a real sense
led to them, but they are still horrors.

PROPHECIES CONCERNING ARABIA

Isaiah 21:11–17

11The oracle concerning Dumah.
One is calling to me from Seir,
"Watchman, what of the night?
Watchman, what of the night?"
12The watchman says:
"Morning comes, and also the night.
If you will inquire, inquire;
come back again."

13The oracle concerning Arabia.
In the thickets in Arabia you will lodge,
O caravans of Dedanites.
14To the thirsty bring water,
meet the fugitive with bread,
O inhabitants of the land of Tema.
15For they have fled from the swords,
from the drawn sword,
from the bent bow,
and from the press of battle.
16For thus the Lord said to me, "Within a year, according to the
years of a hireling, all the glory of Kedar will come to an end; 17and the
remainder of the archers of the mighty men of the sons of Kedar will be
few; for the Lord, the God of Israel, has spoken."

After his second attack on Babylon, the prophet turns to Arabia in three short prophecies. Jeremiah's foreign nations include Arabia (49:28–33), but Ezekiel's and Amos' do not. Most of the Biblical references to Arabs and the other "sons of Ishmael" (Gen. 25:13 ff.) speak of camels (e.g. Gen. 37:25), trade in exotic products (Ezek. 27:20) and an independent lifestyle:

> He shall be a wild ass of a man, his hand against every man and every man's hand against him; and he shall dwell over against all his kinsmen. (Gen. 16:12)

Arab contacts with Jerusalem were for the most part limited to trading, and to find a historical context for these prophecies we have to look for a period when their paths crossed. There are two main possibilities. We know that the last of the Neo-Babylonian kings, Nabonidus (555–539 B.C.), invaded Northern Arabia and subjected the freedom-loving Arabs to servitude. He even set up his royal court at Tema (v. 14), leaving behind his son Belshazzar to act as regent in Babylon. That was thus a period when both Northern Arabia and Judah were united against a common oppressor, and looking forward to the fall of Babylon.

Another important period of direct contact between Judah and the Arabs was the time of rebuilding after the exile, when Ammonites, Arabs and "the rest of our enemies" (Neh. 4:7; 6:1) resented Judah's plans to rebuild Jerusalem and made life as difficult as they could for the returning exiles. Nehemiah's memoirs (esp. chs. 4–6) make it clear that feeling ran very high at the time, and against such a background one would expect in Judah's literature to find some bitter polemic. Sympathy in time of common crisis and fierce antagonism in time of hostility are both reflected in these three difficult prophecies.

A further complication arises when we turn to the first prophecy (vv. 11–12). Far more frequent and far more hostile are Judah's attacks on her closer neighbour Edom, "the sons of Esau" (Gen. 36). Edom figures prominently in other "foreign nations" prophecies (Jer. 49:7–22; Ezek. 25:12–14; 35; Amos 1:11–12; Obadiah; Mal. 1:2–5), as well as elsewhere in Isaiah (34; 63:1–4), but not here in Isaiah 13–23. Commentators from ancient times have therefore interpreted 21:11–12 as an oracle concerning Edom. The names Dumah and Edom are similar in Hebrew, and in Greek even more so. "Seir" in the first line of the oracle is the name given to the mountains of Edom (Gen. 36:9). Moreover, by about 200 B.C. Edom had been overrun by Nabataean Arabs so that the distinction between Arabs and Edomites was hard to define. Finally, *Dumah*, besides being an Ishmaelite place-name, means something like "silence, death", and would provide a bitter parody of the name "Edom". So it seems that a prophecy "from Seir" was first applied to the people of Northern Arabia, probably during the sixth-century Neo-Babylonian period, and then later used as anti-Edomite polemic when "Edomite" became synonymous with Israel's enemies (e.g. Rom. 9:13; Heb. 12:16; Ecclesiasticus 50:26). Herod the Great (Matt. 2:16), by the way, was an Edomite.

Without its title, the oracle in verses 11–12 has something of the mystical atmosphere of the preceding prophecy, and must be understood in that light. The one "calling to me from Seir" is certainly God or one of his heavenly messengers as in 6:3 and 40:3. That it is God himself in this case is suggested by the very ancient tradition that "the Lord came from Sinai, and dawned from Seir upon us" (Deut. 33:2; cf. Judg. 5:4; Hab. 3:3). This vision, like that of Moses, came "from Seir", but is not necessarily about Seir (Edom) or addressed to the Edomites. The prophet again overhears a mysterious dialogue between God and his "watchman", and like the Delphic oracle in ancient Greek tradition what he hears is ambiguous: the night is almost over, morning is coming. This would be good news for the oppressed: God "will help her at the break of day" (Ps. 46:5, NEB). But he goes on to say that night will return and they will need his word again. Perhaps the "Dumah oracle", the "Oracle of silence", is to be understood as a prophecy of judgment: a prophecy about continuous night, relieved only by momentary glimmerings of daylight. The last words of the prophecy, which are in Aramaic, not Hebrew, to add to the outlandish effect, seem to call for a change of heart, and thus correspond closely to the endings of some of the earlier prophecies in the series (e.g. 14:32; 16:1–5; 17:7–8; 18:7).

The "oracle concerning Arabia" (v. 13) takes us farther south into the north-western region of modern Saudi Arabia. The proud and wealthy trading communities established at the great oasis settlements such as Tema and Dedan have been attacked and destroyed, probably by Nabonidus' troops (see above), and the survivors driven into the desert without shelter and without food and water. "Thickets" suggest a scene of desolation like the Temple Mount after the Babylonians have finished with it (Mic. 3:12; RSV "wooded height") or vineyards and orchards laid waste and given to wild animals (Hos. 2:12; RSV "forest"). The word "Arabia" may mean "desert, steppe", in which case the title would refer to the scene of desolation with which the chapter began. "The wasteland oracle" certainly makes a good title, and is exactly in line with two other titles in this section (21:1; 22:1). Whether or not the prophecy can be fitted into some actual situation in ancient near-eastern history, it is yet another dramatic picture of the fate of the nations "in that day" (20:6; 22:8, 12, 20, 25; 23:15; 24:21, etc.).

The third prophecy (v. 16), introduced by a more conventional "Thus said the Lord . . .", concerns the fate of more "sons of Ishmael" (Gen. 25:13), the mighty men of Kedar. Kedar was the region of northern Arabia nearest to Judah and therefore often mentioned in such prophecies (cf. 42:11; 60:7; Jer. 49:28–33). In a short time, predicts the prophet, as predetermined as "the years of a hireling" (cf. 16:14), "all the glory of Kedar will come to an end"—a sentence which in Hebrew has a particularly harsh ring about it (*kalah kol-kebod kedar*). "Glory" conjures up the familiar picture of the camels, rich saddle-cloths, flowing robes, gold and silver ornaments, and above all the proud, independent bearing of "the sons of Ishmael", familiar to us from the old stories of Ishmael (Gen. 16), Joseph (Gen. 37:25), Gideon (Judg. 8:24), as well as from more recent "travellers' tales" such as those in Charles Doughty's *Travels in Arabia Deserta*. Again no reason for their downfall is given, no crimes listed. But it might be noted that many small kingdoms in this region flourished magnificently for a century or two, as the remains at Palmyra, Petra and elsewhere testify, and then disappeared as suddenly as they had come. This was a recurring phenomenon in the history of northern Arabia, and to the prophet was a telling illustration of how fragile is all human glory: "All flesh is grass, and all its beauty is like the flower of the field . . ." (40:6–8).

A PROPHECY AGAINST UNREPENTANT JUDAH

Isaiah 22:1–14

> [1] The oracle concerning the valley of vision.
>   What do you mean that you have gone up,
>   all of you, to the housetops,
> [2] you who are full of shoutings,
>   tumultuous city, exultant town?
>   Your slain are not slain with the sword
>   or dead in battle.
> [3] All your rulers have fled together,
>   without the bow they were captured.
>   All of you who were found were captured,
>   though they had fled far away.
> [4] Therefore I said:
>   "Look away from me,
>   let me weep bitter tears;
>   do not labour to comfort me
>   for the destruction of the daughter of my people."
>
> [5] For the Lord God of hosts has a day
>   of tumult and trampling and confusion
>   in the valley of vision,
>   a battering down of walls
>   and a shouting to the mountains.
> [6] And Elam bore the quiver
>   with chariots and horsemen,
>   and Kir uncovered the shield.
> [7] Your choicest valleys were full of chariots,
>   and the horsemen took their stand at the gates.
> [8] He has taken away the covering of Judah.

In that day you looked to the weapons of the House of the Forest, [9] and you saw that the breaches of the city of David were many, and you collected the waters of the lower pool, [10] and you counted the houses of

Jerusalem, and you broke down the houses to fortify the wall. ¹¹You made a reservoir between the two walls for the water of the old pool. But you did not look to him who did it, or have regard for him who planned it long ago.

¹²In that day the Lord God of hosts
    called to weeping and mourning,
    to baldness and girding with sackcloth;
¹³and behold, joy and gladness,
    slaying oxen and killing sheep,
    eating flesh and drinking wine.
"Let us eat and drink,
    for tomorrow we die."
¹⁴The Lord of hosts has revealed himself in my ears:
"Surely this iniquity will not be forgiven you
    till you die,"
    says the Lord God of hosts.

In these four short prophecies the prophet turns, as he did at the end of the vineyard parable (5:1–7), to his own audience in Jerusalem. The most significant difference between this "oracle" and the rest—and the same goes for the attack on Judah among Amos' foreign nations (2:4–5)—is the emphasis on Judah's spiritual crimes: their cowardice and empty pride (vv. 1–4), their stubborn dependence on human resources (vv. 8–11), their disobedience (vv. 12–13), their faithless fatalism (v. 13), their unforgivable and lethal iniquity (v. 14).

The collection has a very varied history. Verses 1–4 probably go back to Isaiah's own lifetime, possibly to the hollow victory over Sennacherib in 701 B.C. The references to Elam and Kir in verses 5–7 suggest that this description of siege and defeat comes from 586 B.C. The prose passage (vv. 8–11) reads like a later writer's comment on Judah's behaviour, drawing on familiar Isaianic themes (chs. 7 and 8). The concluding prophecy (vv. 12–14) seems to be a continuation of the first and like it could well be from Isaiah's own hand. The consistently foolish and godless behaviour of Judah links the collection together in one continuous sequence, as does the title "valley of the vision". This comes from verse 5 and vividly raises over the whole chapter the spectre of destruction: "of tumult and trampling and confusion in the valley of vision, a battering down of walls and a shouting to the mountains". There is no need to identify the valley, as the Jerusalem Bible does (Vale of Hinnom) or the ancient Greek version (Sion), any more than in the case of Ezekiel's "valley of dry bones" (Ezek. 37).

The first three verses are addressed to the city of Jerusalem, "the daughter of my people" (v. 4), as are so many of the later prophecies in this book (e.g. 40:9; 52:1–2; 60: 1–3). Here she is rebuked for indulging in victory celebrations when in fact her leaders had run away, and there had been casualties. The prophet's own assessment of the situation is that Jerusalem is destroyed; he laments while the rest of Jerusalem celebrates (v. 4). The bare survival of Jerusalem, amid the desolation of Judah (36:1), was scarcely cause for rejoicing. It was the result of Hezekiah's surrender to the Assyrians (2 Kings 18:13ff.), to the prophet a mark of unforgivable faithlessness. Later tradition built up that sorry tale into a colourful story of a miraculous deliverance (chs. 36–37). But in these interesting verses we have a glimpse into how things were at the time, and relics of the prophet's stern commentary on a situation that disgusted and saddened him.

Verses 5–7 are still addressed to Jerusalem. The description of the "day of the Lord God of hosts" is set in deliberate contrast to the description of the jubilant city in verse 2: the shouts, the tumult and the exultation of triumphant victory celebrations have turned into tumult of another kind, the trampling and confusion of siege panic and the shouts of pain and despair. The presence in the invading army of Elamites from the Persian highlands points to a period not earlier than the mid-seventh century B.C., since it was not until then that the Assyrians succeeded in subjugating them. Both Jeremiah (49:34–39) and Ezekiel (32:24–25) include Elam in their oracles against the foreign nations. The precise location of Kir is not known but it too comes into the picture during the Assyrian period (2 Kings 16:9). The Hebrew phrase that comes between the mention of Elam and Kir in verse 6 is difficult. One suggestion is that it means "chariots of Syria": adam ("men") and aram ("Syria") look very alike in Hebrew.

Verses 8–11 are about defence and protection: without God's protection, human defences are of no avail. In the words of Psalm 127: "Unless the Lord watches over the city, the watchman stays awake in vain." "Covering" (v. 8) is a very rare word, and perhaps deliberately alludes to the cloud spread over the Israelites in the wilderness (Ps. 105:39). The divine protection that saved Jerusalem in 701 (37:33–35) has been removed. The list of frantic human efforts to defend Jerusalem draws on architectural lore. "The House of the Forest" , an important part of the palace complex (1 Kings 7:2–5), was being used as an armoury. There is an allusion to the efforts of Hezekiah to improve the city's water supply (2 Kings 20:20), and a reference to attempts at reinforcing the city wall with stones taken from demolished houses. But throughout these verses the emphasis is on Judah's attitude to the crisis and to their God: "you *looked* . . . you *saw* . . . you *counted* . . . you *did not look* to him who did it or *have regard* for him who planned it long ago." This is a reproachful variation on the theme familiar to us from chapter 7 and continued in chapters 30–31 and 36–37: "Woe to the rebellious children, says the Lord, who carry out a plan, but not mine" (30:1).

The theme of Jerusalem's godlessness is continued in verses 12–14, linked with verses 1–4. Instead of mourning the dead and lamenting the destruction all round them, short-sighted Jerusalem is indulging in extravagant celebrations to mark the survival of their city, alone amid the devastation of Judah (36:1). The proper response to Hezekiah's capitulation to the Assyrian king and the catastrophe that had befallen all their neighbours was weeping and mourning, shaving the head and putting on sackcloth (cf. 2 Sam. 3:31–34). But Jerusalem disregards the word of God spoken by his prophet (v. 12) and abandons itself to eating and drinking. We must remember incidentally that it is "slaying oxen and killing sheep", like the killing of the fatted calf in the parable of the Prodigal Son (Luke 15:11–32), that makes these celebrations something special, not drinking wine. Meat was a rare delicacy in the ancient world, as it is today in the Third World.

The proverbial saying, "Let us eat and drink, for tomorrow we die", quoted by Paul in a discussion of life after death (1 Cor. 15:32), is also cited, in a variety of forms, in Ecclesiastes (e.g. 2:24; 3:12–13; 5:18; 8:15) and in the Wisdom of Solomon 2:1–9. It can be traced back to a famous song inscribed in the tomb of a fourteenth-century B.C. Egyptian harpist:

> Drink and be drunken; do not cease from festivity.
> Follow your desires while you are on earth...
> When a man goes, his possessions go.

In English literature there are some familiar examples too: e.g.

> Gather ye rosebuds while ye may,
> Old Time is still a-flying:
> And this same flower that smiles today,
> Tomorrow will be dying. (Robert Herrick, 1591–1674)

In some contexts such thoughts are not condemned, for they express determination to get the most out of the present and to combat the frustration and despair of this unpredictable life of ours. But in Paul and in Israel's Wisdom writings they are the defeatist mumblings of people without faith, in particular those who do not know or cannot believe in the possibility of a fuller life after death. In the context of the reckless banqueting of Jerusalem's leaders in the present chapter, they represent a turning away from God, from "the wells of salvation" (12:3), and that, to the prophet, was an unforgivable sin which they would bear with them till they died.

KEEPER OF THE KEYS OF DAVID

Isaiah 22:15–25

15Thus says the Lord God of hosts, "Come, go to this steward, to Shebna, who is over the household, and say to him: 16What have you to do here and whom have you here, that you have hewn here a tomb for yourself, you who hew a tomb on the height, and carve a habitation for yourself in the rock? 17Behold, the Lord will hurl you away violently, O you strong man. He will seize firm hold on you, 18and whirl

you round and round, and throw you like a ball into a wide land; there you shall die, and there shall be your splendid chariots, you shame of your master's house. [19]I will thrust you from your office, and you will be cast down from your station. [20]In that day I will call my servant Eliakim the son of Hilkiah, [21]and I will clothe him with your robe, and will bind your girdle on him, and will commit your authority to his hand; and he shall be a father to the inhabitants of Jerusalem and to the house of Judah. [22]And I will place on his shoulder the key of the house of David; he shall open, and none shall shut; and he shall shut, and none shall open. [23]And I will fasten him like a peg in a sure place, and he will become a throne of honour to his father's house. [24]And they will hang on him the whole weight of his father's house, the offspring and issue, every small vessel, from the cups to all the flagons. [25]In that day, says the Lord of hosts, the peg that was fastened in a sure place will give way; and it will be cut down and fall, and the burden that was upon it will be cut off, for the Lord has spoken."

This unusually interesting prophecy is addressed to a royal official, Shebna by name. It foretells his untimely death in a foreign land, and the subsequent exaltation of one greater than he, Eliakim, son of Hilkiah, in whose charge will be placed the keys of the kingdom of David. Verse 25 is almost certainly the comment of a later writer, foretelling the fall of Eliakim and with him the fall of David's kingdom. We might describe the passage as a "messianic prophecy" since it is concerned with the future establishment of the House of David—"a sure place . . . a throne of honour" (v. 23), and the royal figure at the centre described as "servant" of the Lord (v. 20) and "father to the inhabitants of Jerusalem and to the house of Judah" (v. 21), just like a Davidic king (e.g. Psalm 132; Isa. 37:35; 9:6). In Christian sources the prophecy points to "the holy one, the true one, who has the key of David, who opens and no one shall shut, who shuts and no one opens" (Rev. 3:7). So, while the rejection of Shebna at the beginning (vv. 15–19) and the ominous addition at the end (v. 25) explain the appearance of this prophecy in a series of attacks on the leaders of Judah and the other nations, this must not blind us to the firm messianic hope at its heart (vv. 20–24).

Shebna and Eliakim are mentioned together in the Biblical accounts of the traumatic events of the year 701 B.C. (36:3, 11, 22; 37:2). Since in all these passages Eliakim is "over the household" and Shebna a mere "secretary", Isaiah's prophecy is addressed to Shebna sometime before 701, by which time Shebna had been "thrust from his office . . . and cast down from his station" as the prophet foretold (v. 19). The office of "steward" or "keeper of the royal household" was a position of considerable authority in Judah, modelled almost certainly on the Egyptian system familiar to us from the Joseph story. Pharaoh appointed him "over his house" (Gen. 41:40) and Joseph later describes his own position as "a father to Pharaoh, and lord of all his house and ruler over all the land of Egypt" (45:8). This "high steward" was the administrator of the royal estate in Egypt, a very high-ranking official, occasionally even acting as regent for the king, and meriting a tomb of the most splendid quality. As well as the dozen or so references to the Hebrew equivalent of the office (e.g. 1 Kings 4:6; 18:3; 2 Kings 15:5), a sixth-century B.C. seal impression mentions a certain "Gedaliah who was over the household".

Most remarkable of all, a rock-cut tomb in the Kedron valley, dated to the time of Hezekiah, bears this inscription, unfortunately incomplete: "This is the tomb of [   ]a who is over the household". Perhaps this tomb was Shebna's and, standing empty years after his death, inspired the writer of the prophecy. We are to imagine the prophet pointing scornfully at the tomb: "What is the point of building yourself a tomb *here*," he cries ("here" is repeated three times in v. 16), "when you are destined to die in a foreign land far from *here*?" There is no suggestion that the prophet is condemning the man for building a particularly ostentatious tomb, or that he disapproves of sumptuous rock-cut tombs in general, for theological or aesthetic reasons! He is merely ridiculing the wasted effort and expense of a tomb that will never be used.

The image in verses 17–18 seems to be that of a person picking an insect off himself, rolling it up in a ball and throwing it as far away from himself as he can. A similar image appears in Jeremiah 43:12, and in a beautiful description of dawn shaking off the

creatures of the night in Job 38:12–15. The royal chariots and the
rest of the king's possessions in his charge will share his fate (v.
18).

The removal of Shebna, punished like the other leaders of
Judah for his self-sufficiency and ill-timed rejoicing ("for tomorrow we die": vv. 8–14), will leave room for "my servant Eliakim
the son of Hilkiah." "In that day" he will be clothed in Shebna's
official vestments and assume responsibility for the whole weight
of his "father's house" (v. 23). This is hardly an actual prediction
about a member of Hezekiah's government, but rather a prophecy about the miraculous survival of Jerusalem and the House of
David during the period of office of Eliakim. In him are invested
the powers and hopes of the House of David—hence the messianic interpretation of the passage. The vestments are those of
the priests and signify the permanence of the appointment as well
as its religious authority as coming from God (Exod. 29:5–9).
The "key of the house of David" is presumably a symbol of the
peculiar authority of this official, although it is nowhere else
mentioned in the Old Testament. The key to the gates and doors
of the royal palace, including no doubt those of the armoury and
the treasury, gave the holder enormous power. Thus "the key of
David" (Rev. 3:7) or "the keys of the kingdom" (Matt. 16:19)
became, in the hands of Jesus Christ and his Church on earth, a
telling symbol of the power to give entry into the kingdom of
heaven:

> O come, thou Key of David, come,
> And open wide our heavenly home;
> Make safe the way that leads on high,
> And close the path to misery:
> *Rejoice! rejoice! Immanuel*
> *Shall come to thee, O Israel.*

The image in verse 23, that of "a stake [or tent-peg] in a sure
place", to which Jerusalem, "a quiet habitation, an immovable
tent" (33:20), is firmly secured, is thoroughly Isaianic. We have
already considered "the faithful city" (1:21, 26) and the proverb,
"If you will not believe, surely you shall not be established"

(7:9): now Eliakim, keeper of the royal household, represents that stability amid the chances and changes of a troubled world. His very name means "God will establish" (1 Kings 2:4; Jer. 28:6). Verse 24 spells out his role in the House of David with a different image: the country will hang on his words, everything will depend on him, all the affairs of state right down to the smallest item of household management. Perhaps his fall is already foreshadowed in the description of the burden of his duties as "the whole weight of his father's house".

The final verse reads very much like the barbed comment of a later writer aimed at some actual person, an opponent perhaps or an unpopular official. It is written in a different style from what precedes it and the "peg" is not now a tent-peg, as it was in verse 23, but a peg hammered into a wall. "In that day" it comes away from the wall, and with it all that had been hung on it. The verbs do not add up to a very convincing picture—"give way . . . cut down . . . fall . . . cut off". But it served its purpose if it succeeded in challenging the view that any state official—Shebna, Eliakim or anyone else—can dominate the political scene indefinitely, and it certainly transforms the prophecy into the kind of warning against pride that the rest of the prophecies in this section contain. But the astonishing "messianic" promise concerning Eliakim the son of Hilkiah (vv. 20–24) still stands and, with that in mind, one can trace the messianic route still further, to the point at which, weighed down by the sins of the world, the servant falls to the ground. Then at last the burden that was upon him will be cut off—and "the servant of the Lord" exalted and lifted up (52:13): "He himself bore our sins in his body on the tree, that we might die to sin and live to righteousness" (1 Pet. 2:24; cf. Isa. 53:4–5).

WAIL, O SHIPS OF TARSHISH!

Isaiah 23:1–18

> [1]The oracle concerning Tyre.
> Wail, O ships of Tarshish,
>   for Tyre is laid waste, without house or haven!

From the land of Cyprus
   it is revealed to them.
²Be still, O inhabitants of the coast,
   O merchants of Sidon;
your messengers passed over the sea
³ and were on many waters;
your revenue was the grain of Shihor,
   the harvest of the Nile;
   you were the merchant of the nations.
⁴Be ashamed, O Sidon, for the sea has spoken,
   the stronghold of the sea, saying:
"I have neither travailed nor given birth,
   I have neither reared young men
   nor brought up virgins."
⁵When the report comes to Egypt,
   they will be in anguish over the report about Tyre.
⁶Pass over to Tarshish,
   wail, O inhabitants of the coast!
⁷Is this your exultant city
   whose origin is from days of old,
  whose feet carried her
   to settle afar?
⁸Who has purposed this
   against Tyre, the bestower of crowns,
  whose merchants were princes,
   whose traders were the honoured of the earth?
⁹The Lord of hosts has purposed it,
   to defile the pride of all glory,
   to dishonour all the honoured of the earth.
¹⁰Overflow your land like the Nile,
   O daughter of Tarshish;
   there is no restraint any more.
¹¹He has stretched out his hand over the sea,
   he has shaken the kingdoms;
the Lord has given command concerning Canaan
   to destroy its strongholds.
¹²And he said:
"You will no more exult,
   O oppressed virgin daughter of Sidon;
arise, pass over to Cyprus,
   even there you will have no rest."

¹³Behold the land of the Chaldeans! This is the people; it was not Assyria. They destined Tyre for wild beasts. They erected their siege towers, they razed her palaces, they made her a ruin.

¹⁴Wail, O ships of Tarshish,
  for your stronghold is laid waste.

¹⁵In that day Tyre will be forgotten for seventy years, like the days of one king. At the end of seventy years, it will happen to Tyre as in the song of the harlot:

¹⁶"Take a harp,
  go about the city,
  O forgotten harlot!
Make sweet melody,
  sing many songs,
  that you may be remembered."

¹⁷At the end of seventy years, the Lord will visit Tyre, and she will return to her hire, and will play the harlot with all the kingdoms of the world upon the face of the earth. ¹⁸Her merchandise and her hire will be dedicated to the Lord; it will not be stored or hoarded, but her merchandise will supply abundant food and fine clothing for those who dwell before the Lord.

The oracle concerning Tyre consists of two parts: first a long, poetic lament over the fall of Tyre and other wealthy and adventurous Phoenician seaports (vv. 1–14), and then a short appendix mainly in prose which foretells the restoration of Tyre to her former prosperity (vv. 15–18). Tyre is included among the foreign nations attacked by Amos (1:9–10), Joel (3:4–8), Zechariah (9:3–4), Jeremiah (25:22; 47:4) and, in the most elaborate example of all, Ezekiel (chs. 26–28). It comes at the end of the Isaianic oracles concerning the foreign nations (chs. 13–23), probably partly because the general arrangement seems to be geographical, starting with Babylon in the east (13–14) and concluding with Phoenicia and points west (23), and partly because of Phoenicia's world-wide horizons which then provide an appropriate transition to the eschatological prophecies that follow and that concern the whole world. It is no accident that the geography of the lament in chapter 23 takes in the whole of the Mediterranean, from Egypt in the south to Cyprus in the north, and from Tyre and Sidon in the east to Tarshish (in southern Spain) in the west.

The fact is that what happened in the Phoenician seaports affected the rest of the world. By the end of the eighth century B.C. the Phoenicians had established colonies in Cyprus, Greece, North Africa, Malta, Sicily and Spain, and taken the alphabet to Greece. By the fifth century B.C. they had circumnavigated Africa and visited Britain in search of Cornish tin. Phoenician dyes, ivories, wood and ships were familiar everywhere. In a way, when the prophets addressed Tyre or "the ships of Tarshish", they were addressing "the coastlands" (41:1, 5), "the ends of the earth" (41:5), "peoples from afar" (49:1).

There has been much discussion about possible historical events that could underlie the lament. The Assyrians invaded Phoenicia under Sennacherib in the years 705–701 B.C., and again under his successor Esarhaddon (681–669). Nebuchadnezzar (605–562) besieged the island city of Tyre for thirteen years (Ezek. 26:7ff.), although he failed to take it (Ezek. 29:17–20). Later Sidon fell to the Persian king Artaxerxes III in 343, and in 332 Tyre was conquered by Alexander the Great, after a seven-month siege during which he built the famous causeway linking Tyre to the mainland. The text, which is very difficult in places, shows signs of having been worked over more than once in the light of these and other traumatic events in Phoenician history, and since there are no unmistakable marks of Isaiah's own style in the lament, we may safely approach it as a rich and powerful prophetic comment on the fate of human enterprises in general, rather than seeking to identify detailed historical allusions.

Like the gates of the Philistines (14:31) and the trees of Lebanon (Zech. 11:2), the ships of Tarshish are summoned to join in the lament over the destruction of their harbour (v. 1) and their "stronghold" (v. 14): "Wail, O ships of Tarshish!" Tyre is obviously intended, as well as Sidon (v. 2), although it is not actually in the Hebrew text. Tarshish (possibly meaning "refinery") is identified with an important Phoenician settlement on the site of modern Cadiz in southwest Spain, from which silver, iron, tin and lead were exported in antiquity (Ezek. 27:12). But "ships of Tarshish" came to be used of any merchant ships, not necessarily literally from Tarshish or bound for Tarshish (e.g. 1 Kings 22:48). There is a beautiful description in Ezekiel 27.

"Cyprus" (RSV) is a translation of Hebrew *Kittim*, since Kition was the main city in Cyprus. The Kittim were close brothers of the people of Tarshish (Gen. 10:4), and in Biblical tradition later associated with the danger of foreign invasion, especially from Rome (Num. 24:24; Dan. 11:30). "Be still!" is related to the sinister word *dumah*, "silence, death" in 21:11. Shihor is translated "Nile" in Jer. 2:18 and trade between Egypt and Phoenicia is attested as far back as 3000 B.C.

Direct speech is typical of the lament, as we saw above (14:4–21), and first to speak in the present example (v. 4) is the sea, disowning her "daughters" in Sidon, Tyre and other Phoenician cities. Others emend the text to make Sidon the speaker, like Jerusalem in 49:14–21: "Sidon . . . cries in her disappointment" (NEB). Verses 6–9 follow the convention of summoning us to marvel at how the mighty princes and traders of Tyre are fallen (cf. 2 Sam. 1:19–27), and why: it is God's will to "put down the mighty from their thrones" (Luke 1:52; Isa. 2:12–19). Verse 7 is a poetic summary of the remarkable achievements of the Phoenician adventurers from the earliest times.

The last part of the lament describes the final humiliation of the Phoenician kingdoms under the outstretched hand of God (v. 11). Once again they will spread abroad, overflowing their land like the Nile (v. 10) but this time they will be going into exile. The land of Kittim (Cyprus) will give them no rest (v.12); they cannot return to their homeland because it is destroyed (vv. 11, 13–14); "the land of the Chaldeans" will be their home. This last phrase is synonymous with exile throughout Biblical tradition, and can hardly have any other meaning here, even although historically, as we saw, Nebuchadnezzar and his Chaldean army did not in fact succeed in taking Tyre.

"In that day" (v. 15) marks the end of the lament and the beginning of a prophecy that after seventy years the fortunes of Tyre will be restored. For seventy years she will be like an ageing prostitute, her former charm and self-respect forgotten. It is hard to think of a more painful image for humiliated Tyre. No doubt the cruel Hebrew song cited in verse 16 was used to get rid of pathetic, unattractive harlots desperate for custom in the streets of ancient Jerusalem. Other Biblical comments on the oldest profession are to be found in Proverbs chapters 5–7. As a metaphor for Jerusalem, the city that prostituted all the love and wealth lavished on her by God, it appears in a lurid allegory in Ezekiel 16. But the closest parallel to the Tyre passage is Revelation 18, where the subject is Babylon the great: "in one hour has thy judgment come!" (18:10).

The prophecy of restoration after seventy years may have been influenced by the historical fact that, about sixty years after Alexander destroyed Tyre, it was restored and given full autonomy by Ptolemy Philadelphus, but more likely this is the symbolic "seventy years" of exile familiar to us from Jer. 25:11. Verse 18 steers the prophecy round to include Judah and Jerusalem in the restoration of Tyre's fortunes. As we have seen, what happens in Phoenicia affects the rest of world. But this final detail recalls the golden age of Solomon, when it was King Hiram of Tyre who provided the skills and the materials for the building of the Temple (1 Kings 5–7), and ships of Tarshish that brought to Jerusalem once every three years gold, silver, ivory, apes, and peacocks (1 Kings 10:22). This is by no means the only prophecy against a foreign nation that ends up by becoming a prophecy of salvation for Jerusalem. To the gifts brought by the Moabites (16:1) and the Ethiopians (18:7) will be added the merchandise of Tyre—and if Ezek. 27:12–25 is anything to go on, that will herald the dawning of the messianic era:

> And I will shake all nations, so that the treasures of all nations will come in, and I will fill this house with splendour, says the Lord of hosts. (Hag. 2:7)

THE END OF THE WORLD

Isaiah 24:1–13

> [1]Behold, the Lord will lay waste the earth and make it desolate, and he will twist its surface and scatter its inhabitants.

²And it shall be, as with the people, so with the priest;
    as with the slave, so with his master;
    as with the maid, so with her mistress;
 as with the buyer, so with the seller;
    as with the lender, so with the borrower;
    as with the creditor, so with the debtor.
³The earth shall be utterly laid waste and utterly despoiled;
    for the Lord has spoken this word.

⁴The earth mourns and withers,
    the world languishes and withers;
    the heavens languish together with the earth.
⁵The earth lies polluted
    under its inhabitants;
 for they have transgressed the laws,
    violated the statutes,
    broken the everlasting covenant.
⁶Therefore a curse devours the earth,
    and its inhabitants suffer for their guilt;
 therefore the inhabitants of the earth are scorched,
    and few men are left.
⁷The wine mourns,
    the vine languishes,
    all the merry-hearted sigh.
⁸The mirth of the timbrels is stilled,
    the noise of the jubilant has ceased,
    the mirth of the lyre is stilled.
⁹No more do they drink wine with singing;
    strong drink is bitter to those who drink it.
¹⁰The city of chaos is broken down,
    every house is shut up so that none can enter.
¹¹There is an outcry in the streets for lack of wine;
    all joy has reached its eventide;
    the gladness of the earth is banished.
¹²Desolation is left in the city,
    the gates are battered into ruins.
¹³For thus it shall be in the midst of the earth
    among the nations,
 as when an olive tree is beaten,
    as at the gleaning when the vintage is done.

Chapters 24–27, although building on traditional prophetic images and ideas from Isaianic tradition and elsewhere, stand out from the rest of the book as quite distinctive in both style and content. They are concerned with the end of the world, the last judgment and the resurrection of the dead, and come most appropriately at the end of the prophecies about the foreign nations (13–23). They also come, most probably, at the end of the Isaianic tradition itself, written last of all in its long and complex process of composition, possibly as late as the fourth century B.C.

Since in several respects this striking section of the Book of Isaiah shows affinity with Daniel, 2 Esdras (4 Ezra), Enoch and the Book of Revelation, it has often been referred to, rather loosely, as the "Isaiah apocalypse", like the "Marcan apocalypse" in Mark 13. It is certainly "apocalyptic" in the sense of being about the end of the world. The resurrection of the dead and the last judgment are also frequent motifs in the true apocalypses, and so is the cosmic and astronomical imagery. But some of the main characteristics of apocalyptic literature—elaborate angelology, symbolic numbers, patterns in history, allusions to actual visions and other mystical experiences, and the effect of these on the visionary—are conspicuous by their absence. Maybe we have the seeds of apocalyptic eschatology in these chapters, but we are still dealing with prophecy, not so different from what comes before and after them in Isaiah. The difference is one of degree, not kind. The desolate earth, the city, the darkened sky, the interrupted banquet, the mountain of the Lord, the land of the dead, the slaying of the monster that is in the sea, the pleasant vineyard and the return of the exiles from Egypt and Assyria to Jerusalem—these are all familiar from the mainstream of prophetic tradition, especially Isaianic tradition. Woven together into a single unit, and set in a universal, eschatological context, they break new ground in the history of Old Testament prophecy, but do not yet qualify for the title apocalyptic. Even the universalism of these chapters has its roots firmly in chapter 2 and chapter 11. Only the eschatology is new: in this passage the prophet sees beyond the rise and fall of individual nations, even beyond death itself, to a new world where death will be swallowed up for ever (25:8) and the people of God will be summoned by a great trumpet (as on the day when liberty is proclaimed throughout the land: Lev. 25:9–10) "to come and worship the Lord on the holy moutain at Jerusalem" (27:13).

Chapter 24 sets the scene for the whole section and in a way forms the base on which the rest of the "apocalypse" is built. The major themes are introduced—the groaning of all creation (to use Pauline language: Rom. 8:22), the guilt of mortals, the last judgment, the reign of the Lord of hosts on Mount Zion. As we saw, the Tyre prophecy in chapter 23 ended on a universalist note (v. 17); but 24:1–6 leaves human history and human geography behind and summons us to picture a day when the whole earth will be laid waste, its surface twisted, its inhabitants scorched. Maybe originally some of the language and imagery referred to the destruction of the land of Judah, as in 1:7–9 or 6:11–12 or 8:22. But now we are no longer to think of the men of Judah or the daughters of Zion being punished by human powers. The whole earth is involved, as in the days of Noah (Gen. 6–9); and God has thrown away the rod of his anger (10:5) and, by his word, turned creation into chaos. All humanity is corrupt: nothing short of a new creation can save us (25:9).

The universalism of verse 2, where all religious, social and political differences between people are removed, and all human conventions and institutions destroyed, similarly goes far beyond prophecies about a messianic age (e.g. 9:1–7; 11:1–9), and can only be compared to visions of how things are after death, in Sheol (e.g. Job 3:17–19; Ecc. 3:19; Isa. 14:3–20). All are equally guilty. The land where they live has been polluted by their sin. The reference to an everlasting covenant in verse 5, applicable to all humanity, must be to the covenant with Noah (Gen. 9:8–17), and vividly highlights murder (Gen. 9:6) as the prime example of man's inhumanity to man. Bloodshed pollutes the earth (Ps. 106:38; Num. 35:33); the voice of a murdered man's blood cries from the ground (Gen. 4:10). Adultery and idolatry also pollute the earth (Jer. 3:2, 9), but in primeval stories like those about Cain and Noah, as also in these eschatological chapters where we are moving in a mythical world of vivid symbolism, it is murder that best symbolizes the breaking of the everlasting covenant. Earlier prophecies envisage a time when the whole world will be under the same law as Jerusalem (e.g. 2:3), but in this context we need not take the reference to "laws and statutes" in verse 5 too literally.

The related themes of the silencing of the vintage songs and the interrupted banquet (vv. 7-9) are already familiar to us from 16:8-11 and 22:12-14 (also Amos 5:16-17; 8:3), and prepare us for the eschatological banquet for all peoples in 25:6.

"The city of chaos" (v. 10) is a striking phrase, recalling both the beautiful "faithful city" poem in chapter 1 (vv. 21-26) and the second verse of the creation story (Gen. 1:2). There is no suggestion that we are intended to identify some historical event behind these verses: the city is a recurring theme in this "apocalypse" and others (Rev. 17-18) as a symbol of human society, and chaos is a graphic way to describe the end of civilization: every house boarded up, people wailing in the streets, no pleasure, no laughter, a scene of desolation and neglect, the city gates lying in pieces. This means the return to a world without cities (Gen. 4:17), without wine (Gen. 9:20-21), without joy (Gen. 3:6), without people (Gen. 1:26-28): in a word, a return to primeval chaos. Such is the fate of sinful humanity; but from such chaos will emerge a new city with walls of salvation and gates open for a righteous nation to enter (26:1-2).

Verse 13 picks up another image from earlier prophecy (17:6) and uses it to conclude the first part of this eschatological prophecy. People will be shaken off the earth like olives at harvest time. Only a very few will be left alive, like the few grapes left on the vines after the grape harvest.

THE LAST JUDGMENT

Isaiah 24:14-23

14They lift up their voices, they sing for joy;
  over the majesty of the Lord they shout from the west.
15Therefore in the east give glory to the Lord;

in the coastlands of the sea, to the name of the Lord, the God of
   Israel.
16From the ends of the earth we hear songs of praise,
      of glory to the Righteous One.
   But I say, "I pine away,
      I pine away. Woe is me!
   For the treacherous deal treacherously,
      the treacherous deal very treacherously."

17Terror, and the pit, and the snare
      are upon you, O inhabitant of the earth!
18He who flees at the sound of the terror
      shall fall into the pit;
   and he who climbs out of the pit
      shall be caught in the snare.
   For the windows of heaven are opened,
      and the foundations of the earth tremble.
19The earth is utterly broken,
      the earth is rent asunder,
      the earth is violently shaken.
20The earth staggers like a drunken man,
      it sways like a hut;
   its transgression lies heavy upon it,
      and it falls, and will not rise again.

21On that day the Lord will punish
      the host of heaven, in heaven,
      and the kings of the earth, on the earth.
22They will be gathered together
      as prisoners in a pit;
   they will be shut up in a prison,
      and after many days they will be punished.
23Then the moon will be confounded,
      and the sun ashamed;
   for the Lord of hosts will reign
      on Mount Zion and in Jerusalem
   and before his elders he will manifest his glory.

The last judgment will bring terror to the wicked; but it is also the
moment of final victory for the Righteous One (v. 16) and therefore a time for thanksgiving, a time to give glory to the Lord, the

God of Israel, a time to celebrate the coming of the kingdom of God in all its glory. The three short poems that make up the next section of the Isaiah "apocalypse", originally independent compositions in all probability, spell this out in vivid, allusive language.

First comes the song of thanksgiving (vv. 14–16) to be sung by the faithful remnant all over the world. These are the few olives left clinging to the tree after the beating and the shaking have stopped (v. 13). The phrase translated "in the east" (v. 15) is intriguing: literally it means "in/with the lights or fires". The word occurs in the singular four times in Isaiah, always translated "fire" (31:9; 44:16; 47:14; 50:11). The usual view that it must be a geographical term corresponding to the previous verse's "from the west . . ."—thus "in the fires", i.e. the tropics (AV) or "in the east" (RSV, NEB, Jerusalem Bible)—has little to commend it. Others have suggested "every morning", thinking perhaps of passages like 33:2 (literally, "in the mornings"). Could it be a reference to some torchlight ceremony or procession, as in the later Hebrew name for the Jewish festival of Hanukkah (John 10:22), which was called, from at least the time of Josephus, "the Feast of Lights" (see 2 Maccabees 1:18–2:18)? Or to sacrificial fire? Or perhaps to beacons spreading the news of victory round "the coastlands of the sea", from one end of the earth to the other? We might then translate verse 15: "Therefore light fires to glorify the Lord . . . "

The phrase translated "of glory to the Righteous One" (RSV) is also difficult. The first word means "beauty, splendour", especially the splendour of kings (e.g. 28:5) and kingdoms (e.g. 13:19; Jer. 3:19). In other apocalyptic language "the glorious land" or even just "the glory" is applied to the land of Israel (e.g. Dan. 8:9; 11:16, 14, 45). Here surely it alludes to the glorious reign of God which is to follow the terrifying upheavals in heaven and earth just described (vv. 3ff.). That these upheavals are planned and controlled by God is emphasized by the choice of the term "the Righteous One" to describe him. "True glory belongs to God" is thus a statement of faith concluding the first hymn of thanksgiving (vv. 14–16). Jonah's hymn ends on a very similar note ("Deliverance belongs to the Lord", 2:9), and like Jonah's hymn this one is sung in the midst of the terrors of God's judgment.

Although "the God of Israel" is mentioned by name (v. 15), we need not think only of Jewish exiles joining in the songs of praise. There is no hint of such exclusiveness in these eschatological poems. On the contrary, all the inhabitants of the earth will be involved in the judgment, and "all peoples" will take part in the eschatological banquet (25:6). There is a curious vacillation in the persons referred to in verses 14–16: "*They* lift up their voices . . . [*you*] give glory to the Lord . . . *we* hear songs of praise . . . but *I* say . . ." Whether or not this is actually the original text, it is an excellent grammatical device for stressing that everyone is participating, "them" as well as "us", "me" as well as "you".

"But I say . . ." introduces yet another problem. The interruption by the prophet recalls passages like 6:5 and 40:6, as well as more elaborate examples such as Daniel 10:16, which describe the impact of a vision on the visionary. But what he says here is shrouded in mystery—perhaps deliberately, as a look at the various modern English versions will show: "Enough, enough!" (Jerusalem Bible); "I pine away, I pine away!" (RSV, cf. AV); "Villainy, villainy!" (NEB). Most appropriate perhaps, in the light of the apocalyptic affinities of the passage, is the traditional Jewish view, followed by some modern scholars, that the words mean "My mystery is with me! my mystery is with me!" In that case the words are taken in a normal, post-Biblical Hebrew sense, influenced by the Aramaic of Daniel: e.g. "Then the mystery was revealed to Daniel in a vision of the night" (2:19; cf. 4:9).

The second poem in this section is a vivid description of the last judgment, packed with alliteration, allusive language and daring images (vv. 17–20). It begins with a striking chain of words beginning with the letters *pah*: *pahad* ("terror") . . . *pahat* ("pit") . . . *pah* ("snare"). There will be no escape: in Amos' words, it will be

as if a man fled from a lion,
and a bear met him;
or went into the house and leaned with his hand against the wall
and a serpent bit him. (5:19)

Jeremiah uses very similar language for the fate of the Moabites (48:40–44); see also Lam. 3:47. In the Damascus Scroll from Qumran, the three nouns are interpreted as the "three nets of the devil": fornication, riches and the profanation of the Temple, by which he ensnares Israel. But here the traps are set to catch all the inhabitants of the earth, not just Moab or Israel.

The "windows of heaven" and the "foundations of the earth" remind us that we are dealing with cosmic events comparable to primeval history. When the windows of heaven were opened in Gen. 7:11, the waters of the great deep, symbol of the powers of chaos (Gen. 1:2; Isa. 51:10; Jonah 2:5), burst forth and destroyed the world. That is what the last judgment is going to be like. "Earth", almost personified in verses 19–20, will be broken and shaken, reeling to and fro (AV, NEB), and swaying like a hut whose foundations have been undermined. Weighed down by her sin, she falls to the ground and cannot get up again.

The last poem (vv. 21–23), separated from the others by the formula "On that day", describes the defeat and imprisonment of "the host of heaven, in heaven, and the kings of the earth, on the earth", and the inauguration of the kingdom of God on Mount Zion. To understand the meaning of the poem, we must go first to Deut. 32:8, where the number of angels ("sons of God") is equal to the number of nations in the world; and then to the heartland of Jewish apocalyptic, where this world's battles are fought out behind the scenes, in heaven, and witnessed by visionaries, as in the Books of Daniel and Enoch. The nations of the world are guided by angels like Michael and the prince of the kingdom of Persia (Dan. 10:13), for example, or by "the dragon, that ancient serpent, who is the Devil and Satan" (Rev. 20:2–3). "On that day", when all the nations of the world are punished, the host of heaven will be punished too, "judged and found guilty ... cast into an abyss, full of fire and flaming, and full of pillars of fire" (Enoch 90:24; cf. Rev. 20:3, 7–10). Isa. 24:21–23 comes somewhere between Deuteronomy 32 and Enoch 90.

The enthronement of God upon Mount Zion, the dazzling climax of the passage, draws on the liturgical language of the Psalms (especially 47, 93, 97, 99) and the Sinai traditions: "And they [Moses and the elders] saw the God of Israel; and there was under his feet as it were a pavement of sapphire stone, like the very heaven for clearness" (Exod. 24:10). But again there are close parallels in Enoch and in Revelation (21:23; 22:5; cf. Isa. 60:19; Zech. 14:7): "And the city has no more need of sun or moon to shine upon it, for the glory of God is its light ..." (Rev. 21:23).

THE ESCHATOLOGICAL BANQUET

Isaiah 25:1–12

1O Lord, thou art my God;
  I will exalt thee, I will praise thy name;
 for thou hast done wonderful things,
  plans formed of old, faithful and sure.
2For thou hast made the city a heap,
  the fortified city a ruin;
 the palace of aliens is a city no more,
  it will never be rebuilt.
3Therefore strong peoples will glorify thee;
  cities of ruthless nations will fear thee.
4For thou hast been a stronghold to the poor,
  a stronghold to the needy in his distress,
  a shelter from the storm and a shade from the heat;
 for the blast of the ruthless is like a storm against a wall,
 5 like heat in a dry place.
 Thou dost subdue the noise of the aliens;
  as heat by the shade of a cloud,
  so the song of the ruthless is stilled.

6On this mountain the Lord of hosts will make for all peoples a feast of fat things, a feast of wine on the lees, of fat things full of marrow, of wine on the lees well refined. 7And he will destroy on this mountain the covering that is cast over all peoples, the veil that is spread over all nations. 8He will swallow up death for ever, and the Lord God will wipe away tears from all faces, and the reproach of his people he will take away from all the earth; for the Lord has spoken.
9It will be said on that day, "Lo, this is our God; we have waited for

him, that he might save us. This is the Lord; we have waited for him; let us be glad and rejoice in his salvation."

[10]For the hand of the Lord will rest on this mountain, and Moab shall be trodden down in his place, as straw is trodden down in a dung-pit. [11]And he will spread out his hands in the midst of it as a swimmer spreads his hands out to swim; but the Lord will lay low his pride together with the skill of his hands. [12]And the high fortifications of his walls he will bring down, lay low, and cast to the ground, even to the dust.

The spectacular vision of a banquet on Mount Zion, to which all people will be invited and at which death will be swallowed up for ever (vv. 6–9) is framed between a prayer of thanksgiving for God's power over the "cities of ruthless nations" (vv. 1–5), and a prophecy about the fate of one such nation (vv. 10–12). Mount Zion stands at the centre, scene of unrestrained rejoicing, symbol of life and salvation, surrounded by silent, dusty ruins where once the proud cities of the nations had stood.

The prayer begins with a confident expression of faith in God, derived from the Psalms (e.g. 118:28; 77:5; 78:12), but also rooted in Isaianic tradition. The prophecy in 12:1 is so to speak fulfilled here; the wonders planned by God belong to the description of the messiah in 9:6 (cf. 28:29); and "faithful and sure" are words from the very heart of Isaiah's prophetic message (e.g. 1:21, 26; 7:9; 30:15). There is even a kind of word play at the end of the verse like that in 7:9: *emunah omen*, literally "steadfastness (and) faithfulness".

Like Babylon in Revelation 18 and the "city of chaos" in 24:10, the city in verse 2 is a symbol, not a real, identifiable city, and its fall illustrates the vulnerability of civilization as we know it. No reason for the scenes of destruction is given. "The palace of aliens" refers no doubt to the foreign nations, attacked in chapters 13–23, and all heading for the same fate. But the rest of the poem draws a sharp distinction between the strong and ruthless, on the one hand, and the poor and needy, on the other. When justice is finally established in the earth, ruthless nations will fear God: Moabites (16:1–5) and Ethiopians (18:1–7), Nebuchadnezzar (Dan. 4:34–37), Darius (Dan. 6:25–28) and Cyrus (Ezra 1:2–4) will glorify his name.

The pile-up of images in verses 4 and 5 is typical of the language of the Psalms (cf. 18:2 and 22:12–21): God is a stronghold, a shelter (or refuge), a shade to the poor and needy; their enemies and oppressors are a tempest, desert heat, a noise. A short, somewhat unnecessary comment at the end of verse 4 explains that the threats and attacks of the ruthless (or "the terrible ones", AV) are like the wind beating against the walls of a house (cf. Matt. 7:24–27). But against the people of God no storm can prevail; the noise of the nations clamouring to break down the defences of the city of God is eventually subdued, and the tempest stilled.

"On this mountain" (v. 6) picks up the reference to Mount Zion that preceded the prayer of thanksgiving (24:23), and introduces four of the richest and most emotive verses in the entire Book of Isaiah. While in other descriptions of the coming of the nations to Jerusalem the emphasis is on what they can bring with them to enrich the lives of those who live there (e.g. 45:14; 60:3, 6–7; Hag. 2:7), here in verse 6, as in 2:2–4, they are to be welcomed with open arms to a banquet comparable to the messianic banquet in Luke 14:15–24. The banquet is brilliantly described in two words, each repeated twice: *shemanim* ("fat things") includes meat, fruit and vegetables, all sorts of choice dishes, rich and full of goodness ("marrow"); and *shemarim*, literally "dregs, lees", suggests unrestrained drinking (as in "drain it down to the dregs", Ps. 75:8) as well as the high alcoholic content and rich flavour of wine made from the lees. The prophet Ezekiel visualizes a similar scene (39:17–20).

The next two verses begin with the same word: "he will swallow up . . . the veil" (v. 7), "he will swallow up death" (v. 8). The two are usually taken together and the coverings in verse 7 interpreted as veils with which mourners cover their faces (e.g. 2 Sam. 15:30), or as shrouds wrapped round the dead bodies of the nations (Jerusalem Bible, NEB). But the terms used do not occur in the contexts of mourning, and the two verses need not refer to the same phenomenon. Could verse 7 not rather be taken as describing the moment when, like the elders in 24:23 (and Exod. 24:10), the eyes of the nations will be opened and they will behold the glory of the Lord of hosts? Surely Paul's vision of the new age throws more light on the Isaiah apocalypse than the Old Testament passages about mourning customs usually quoted: "... but when a man turns to the Lord the veil is removed ... and we all, with unveiled face, beholding the glory of the Lord, are being changed into his likeness from one degree of glory to another" (2 Cor. 3:16, 18).

The third of these memorable verses envisages a time when there will be no more death, no more weeping and no more shame. As in the two previous verses, the finality and totality of this vision are stressed: "for ever ... from all faces ... all the earth". The idea was a rare one in ancient Israel, although the seeds of it are to be found in passages like Prov. 3:18 and 8:35: "he who finds me [Wisdom] finds life". By New Testament times such passages were, like Isaiah 25, Dan. 12:1-4, Wisdom of Solomon 2:21-3:9 and 1 Cor. 15 (where Isa. 25:8 is actually quoted), interpreted eschatologically. The Isaiah Apocalypse leads the way out of ancient Israel, where the Old Testament originated, into Judaism and Christianity where it now belongs. We shall return to this subject in the commentary to chapter 26.

The last of the eschatological events (v. 9) is the jubilant response of the nations. The banquet, the vision of God's glory, the swallowing up of death for ever—these add up to the final mighty act in the salvation-history (Ger. *Heilsgeschichte*) of the world. This is what the world has been waiting for: now at last "let us be glad and rejoice in his salvation". Just as chapters 1-12 ended with a song of thanksgiving on the theme of "salvation" (*yeshu'ah*), so now that same rich term reappears in the celebration at the end of the second long division of the book (chs. 13-27). It occurs twice in this verse, and then again in the chorus with which the next chapter opens:

> We have a strong city;
>   he sets up salvation [*yeshu'ah*]
>   as walls and bulwarks. (26:1)

Only God can be the subject of the verb "to save": he alone feeds us (v. 6), reveals his glory to us (v. 7), rescues us from death (v. 8), answers our prayers (v. 9). That is what "salvation" means.

Verses 10–12 draw a vivid contrast between the mountain of the Lord, where such glorious events take place, and the dung-pit or cesspool where the wicked end up. Moab is a mere symbol in this context. Probably because of the law that "no Moabite shall enter the assembly of the Lord" (Deut. 23:3; Neh. 13:1), Moab was excluded from the eschatological banquet on the mountain of the Lord.

The Hebrew for "cesspool" looks like a pun on the name of the Moabite town of Madmen (Jer. 48:2) and may be another reason why Moab was selected. But the passage is about more than Moab. The repulsive picture of someone sinking in a cesspool recalls the plight of the Psalmist:

Save me, O God!
For the waters have come up to my neck.
I sink in deep mire,
where there is no foothold . . . (Ps. 69:1–2; cf. 40:2)

Like him he stretches out his hands in prayer (Isa. 1:15; Ps. 143:6; 1 Kings 8:22). But to no avail: his outstretched hands are more like a swimmer's than a supplicant's, and their frantic efforts, both to save himself from drowning and to attract a rescuer's attention, come to nothing. It is a horrible scene, but then the ultimate fate of the wicked must be depicted with as much vivid detail as that of the righteous. Just think of the works of Dante or Hieronymous Bosch, not to mention the bottomless pit in Revelation 9!

THE RESURRECTION OF THE DEAD

Isaiah 26:1–21

[1]In that day this song will be sung in the land of Judah:
"We have a strong city;
he sets up salvation
as walls and bulwarks.

²Open the gates,
    that the righteous nation which keeps faith
    may enter in.
³Thou dost keep him in perfect peace,
    whose mind is stayed on thee,
    because he trusts in thee.
⁴Trust in the Lord for ever,
    for the Lord God
    is an everlasting rock.
⁵For he has brought low
    the inhabitants of the height,
    the lofty city.
 He lays it low, lays it low to the ground,
    casts it to the dust.
⁶The foot tramples it,
    the feet of the poor,
    the steps of the needy."

⁷The way of the righteous is level;
    thou dost make smooth the path of the righteous.
⁸In the path of thy judgments,
    O Lord, we wait for thee;
 thy memorial name
    is the desire of our soul.
⁹My soul yearns for thee in the night,
    my spirit within me earnestly seeks thee.
 For when thy judgments are in the earth,
    the inhabitants of the world learn righteousness.
¹⁰If favour is shown to the wicked,
    he does not learn righteousness;
 in the land of uprightness he deals perversely
    and does not see the majesty of the Lord.
¹¹O Lord, thy hand is lifted up,
    but they see it not.
 Let them see thy zeal for thy people, and be ashamed.
    Let the fire for thy adversaries consume them.
¹²O Lord, thou wilt ordain peace for us,
    thou hast wrought for us all our works.
¹³O Lord our God,
    other lords besides thee have ruled over us,
    but thy name alone we acknowledge.

¹⁴They are dead, they will not live;
    they are shades, they will not arise;
  to that end thou hast visited them with destruction
    and wiped out all remembrance of them.
¹⁵But thou hast increased the nation, O Lord,
    thou hast increased the nation; thou art glorified;
    thou hast enlarged all the borders of the land.

¹⁶O Lord, in distress they sought thee,
    they poured out a prayer
    when thy chastening was upon them.
¹⁷Like a woman with child,
    who writhes and cries out in her pangs,
    when she is near her time,
  so were we because of thee, O Lord;
¹⁸ we were with child, we writhed,
    we have as it were brought forth wind.
We have wrought no deliverance in the earth,
    and the inhabitants of the world have not fallen.
¹⁹Thy dead shall live, their bodies shall rise.
    O dwellers in the dust, awake and sing for joy!
For thy dew is a dew of light,
    and on the land of the shades thou wilt let it fall.

²⁰Come, my people, enter your chambers,
    and shut your doors behind you;
  hide yourselves for a little while until the wrath is past.
²¹For behold, the Lord is coming forth out of his place
    to punish the inhabitants of the earth for their iniquity,
  and the earth will disclose the blood shed upon her,
    and will no more cover her slain.

Chapter 26 contains another song or psalm that the nations will sing when they gather in the land of Judah (cf. 25:9). The first part of the song (vv. 1–10) is about strength (v. 1), salvation (v. 1), faith (v. 2), trust (vv. 3–4), peace (v. 3), hope (vv. 8–9) and above all righteousness (vv. 2, 7, 9, 10). The righteous are those who will enter the gates of the city (v. 2); the righteous are those who will see the majesty of God (v. 10). The "righteous nation" in verse 2 is probably Israel, but in verse 10 they are joined by the

inhabitants of the world, and the preceding chapter makes it clear
that it is not just loyal Jews who are celebrating on Mount Zion
(25:6–7). As in the case of most of the Psalms, there is no sure
way of dating the poem, or of identifying any historical allusions
in it, such as the defeat of the "lofty city" in verse 5. Like the rest
of this "apocalypse" and many Psalms, it is rich in timeless
symbolic language and imagery.

The "strong city" poem (vv. 1–6), like the "faithful city"
lament in chapter 1, has a striking symmetry about it. Two verses
describe the walls and gates of the New Jerusalem (vv. 1–2),
corresponding to two verses describing the fall of Babylon (or
another "city of chaos", 24:10) (vv. 5–6). A "righteous nation"
ceremoniously processes into the one; while the poor and the
needy trample over the dusty ruins of the other. The divine
protection of the one—it has walls and bulwarks of salvation (v.
1)—is contrasted with God's annihilation of the other. Elsewhere
in Isaianic tradition Zion and salvation (*yeshu'ah*) are closely
linked: e.g.

> How beautiful upon the mountains
> are the feet of him who brings good tidings,
> who publishes peace, who brings good tidings of good,
> who publishes salvation,
> who says to Zion, "Your God reigns." (52:7)

When it was surrounded by enemy invaders, the word of the Lord
came to Isaiah: "For I will defend this city *to save it*, for my own
sake and for the sake of my servant David" (37:35). But the New
Jerusalem will transcend all that has gone before, as in 65:17ff.
and Rev. 21:1–4, where she is part of a new heaven and a new
earth.

Between the verses describing two cities comes an exquisite
passage about the perfect peace of those who trust in God. The
theme is familiar to us already (1:21, 26; 7:9; 25:1; and cf. 30:15),
but the language is new. It is derived from the Psalms (e.g.
118:19–20; 112:7; 143:8), but has no exact parallels. The Hebrew
for "perfect peace" is simply *shalom shalom*, the great emotive
term for fulfilment, abundance, well-being, security, repeated

twice. "Whose mind is stayed on thee" consists of but two words in Hebrew: the first really means "will, imagination", as in Genesis (6:5), and the second "dependent, supported, firm". Psalm 131:2 elucidates this verse with an unusually effective image:

> I have calmed and quieted my soul,
>   like a child quieted at its mother's breast.

Finally, God is "an everlasting rock", providing water in the wilderness (Exod. 17:6), shade in a thirsty land (Isa. 32:2, NEB), safety in a dangerous situation (Ps. 40:2), a secure foundation to build on (Matt. 7:24–25; 16:18): in short, someone we can rely on for ever.

Verses 7–10 take up the phrase "righteous nation" from verse 2, and consider it in what is more like a lament than a song of thanksgiving. It is out of such wistful yearning, in a world where the righteous suffer, that the triumphant cry of the martyrs developed: "Thy dead shall live!" (v. 19). "Righteousness", we must remember, does not mean "innocence, justice, obedience to the law, self-righteousness", or the like. This short poem makes it very clear what it means. It means a level path, a path illuminated by God's "judgments", that is, evidence of his involvement in human affairs. It means waiting for God, yearning for him in the night, directing one's life by his judgments. It means recognizing the hand of God in one's life and in the life of the world: that is how "the inhabitants of the world learn righteousness" (v. 9). It means seeing the majesty of the Lord. In other words "righteousness" is almost another word for "salvation". In some contexts the Hebrew word for "righteousness" (*tsedek*) is actually translated "victory" (e.g. 41:2), "deliverance" (e.g. 51:1, 5, 6, 8) and, in the plural, "the triumphs of the Lord" (Judg. 5:11). Woe to the wicked who turn away from the righteousness of God! Blessed are the righteous who have a share in that righteousness!

Verses 11–15 describe the "judgments" of God, those acts of divine intervention in the affairs of men by which he reveals himself to us: the wonders wrought by his "mighty hand and outstretched arm" (Exod. 6:6; Deut. 4:34), the zeal with which he fights for his people (Isa. 9:7; 37:32), the fire that consumes his enemies (10:16–17; Lev. 10:2). We know that he is "author of peace and lover of concord" (cf. v. 12), we acknowledge that he alone rules over us (v. 13), and we gladly attribute our prosperity and security to him (v. 15). We recognize his handiwork everywhere—"in all our works, begun, continued and ended in thee" (cf. v. 12). The wicked are not so: they are blind (v. 11) and dead, destroyed and forgotten (v. 14). Verse 14 recalls the fate of the king of Babylon, sarcastically welcomed to the land of the dead by the "shades" (14:9–10). The finality of the death of the wicked here draws on the old Wisdom traditions: e.g. "He who finds me [Wisdom] finds life . . . [but] all who hate me love death" (Prov. 8:35–36). But as we saw above (on 25:8), the belief that the righteous will never die (Wisdom of Solomon 3:1–4), or after death will rise to everlasting life (e.g. Dan. 12:2), gave such passages new significance.

One of the major factors in the emergence of this belief in an after-life for the faithful was the persecution and martyrdom of the righteous, particularly in the troubled Maccabean era in the second century B.C. when Daniel 12 was almost certainly composed. It is unlikely that the next passage (vv. 16–21) was composed as late as that, but the text as it stands must undoubtedly be interpreted in the light of that theological watershed, its original text and meaning being no longer accessible. First there is the sheer suffering: distress (Ps. 120:1), chastisement (Isa. 53:5), physical pain like that of a woman in labour (13:8; Ps. 48:6), frustration (v. 18). Then after a leap of faith between verses 18 and 19 comes a vision of the resurrection of "thy" dead. The Hebrew text, no doubt influenced by the second-century belief in individual resurrection, and also by the recurring intrusion of an individual's voice into this "apocalypse" (24:16; 25:1; 26:9, 20), has "together with *my body*, they shall rise". Most modern translations (RSV, NEB, Jerusalem Bible) try to remove this late stratum of tradition, both here and in similar passages elsewhere (e.g. Job 19:25–27; Isa. 53:11), by simply emending the text. Then we are left with a more conventional contrast between the final destruction of the wicked (v. 14) and, under the metaphor of "rising", of the return of Israel from exile, or her revival after a period of decline. Ezekiel's vision of the valley of dry bones (Ezek. 37) would be comparable, and it may be that the original text was along these lines. But we do not know precisely when to date it, and certainly the text as it stands comes closer to Daniel 12 than to Ezekiel 37. At all events the appearance of life-giving dew and the clear light of dawn in the "land of the shades" brings hope of some kind of life after death—as well as justice after injustice, since the wicked "will not live, they will not arise" (v. 14) while the righteous will "awake and sing for joy"

Originally perhaps verses 20-21 compared the final judgment of the world to the Passover, when Israel sheltered in their homes while the destroying angel (Exod. 12:23) executed judgment on the Egyptians. In its present context, however, it deals nicely with the problem of what happens between death and the resurrection of the dead. There will be a time of waiting, it explains; then in the words of another apocalypse "the chambers will give up the souls which have been committed to them, and the Most High shall be revealed on the seat of judgment..." (2 Esdras 7:32-33). See also Matt. 27:51-53.

THE RETURN TO JERUSALEM

Isaiah 27:1-13

¹In that day the Lord with his hard and great and strong sword will punish Leviathan the fleeing serpent, Leviathan the twisting serpent, and he will slay the dragon that is in the sea.

²In that day:
"A pleasant vineyard, sing of it!
³   I, the Lord, am its keeper;
    every moment I water it.
Lest any one harm it,
    I guard it night and day;
⁴   I have no wrath.
Would that I had thorns and briers to battle!

I would set out against them,
I would burn them up together.
⁵Or let them lay hold of my protection,
let them make peace with me,
let them make peace with me."

⁶In days to come Jacob shall take root,
Israel shall blossom and put forth shoots,
and fill the whole world with fruit.

⁷Has he smitten them as he smote those who smote them?
Or have they been slain as their slayers were slain?
⁸Measure by measure, by exile thou didst contend with them;
he removed them with his fierce blast in the day of the east wind.
⁹Therefore by this the guilt of Jacob will be expiated,
and this will be the full fruit of the removal of his sin:
when he makes all the stone of the altars
like chalkstones crushed to pieces,
no Asherim or incense altars will remain standing.
¹⁰For the fortified city is solitary,
a habitation deserted and forsaken, like the wilderness;
there the calf grazes,
there he lies down, and strips its branches.
¹¹When its boughs are dry, they are broken;
women come and make a fire of them.
For this is a people without discernment;
therefore he who made them will not have compassion on them,
he that formed them will show them no favour.

¹²In that day from the river Euphrates to the Brook of Egypt the
Lord will thresh out the grain, and you will be gathered one by one, O
people of Israel. ¹³And in that day a great trumpet will be blown, and
those who were lost in the land of Assyria and those who were driven
out to the land of Egypt will come and worship the Lord on the holy
mountain at Jerusalem.

The "Isaiah apocalypse" ends with a trumpet call summoning
Israel to return from exile to Jerusalem (v. 13). The slaying of
Leviathan and the dragon that is in the sea (v. 1) makes it possible
for them to cross over on dry land in a New Exodus (cf. 51:9–11).
The Lord's vineyard is planted again, without thorns and briers
(cf. 5:1–7), and Israel fills the whole world with its fruit (vv. 2–6).

The "people without discernment" (probably the Samaritans) will be shown no mercy (vv. 7–11); but the Jews will be gathered one by one and will "come and worship the Lord on the holy mountain at Jerusalem" (vv. 12–13). The wide horizons of earlier chapters in the section 13–26 are narrowed: Jerusalem and Judah again take the centre of the stage, where they were in chapters 1–12, and where they remain from now until the end of the book. After all, this is the "vision of Isaiah the son of Amoz, which he saw concerning Judah and Jerusalem" (1:1). Often the vision is concerned with the whole world (e.g. 11:9), indeed the entire universe at times (e.g. 1:2; 66:22), but "beginning at Jerusalem" (Luke 24:47).

The ancient myth about a battle between Israel's God and a monster known variously as Leviathan, Rahab, Yam (Hebrew for "sea") and Nahar (Hebrew for "river, flood"), and "the dragon that is in the sea", is referred to explicitly in several Old Testament passages (e.g Ps. 74:13–14; 89:9–10), and underlies a good many others (e.g. Gen. 1:2; Ps. 93:3–4). The Babylonians had a similar way of expressing their faith in the power of their God, Marduk, to overcome all evil: every year they represented the victory of Marduk over Tiamat, the monster of the deep, in a great liturgical drama, which ended with the triumphant shout "Marduk is king". The Canaanites, as we know from the tablets discovered at Ras Shamra (Ugarit), celebrated the victory of Baal over the monsters Yam and Nahar in a similar way. In the Old Testament we have Israel's version of this myth: e.g. in Psalm 93 which begins "The Lord is king!" (RSV "reigns") and continues

> The floods [*nahar*] have lifted up, O Lord,
>   the floods have lifted up their voice,
>   the floods lift up their roaring.
> Mightier than the thunders of many waters,
>   mightier than the waves of the sea [*yam*],
>   the Lord on high is mighty! (vv. 3–4)

What more spectacular way than this to express one's faith in the power of God to overcome evil, to defeat one's enemies, to prevent drought and famine, to conquer injustice, to forgive sin? The myth is not only about the creation of order out of chaos at the beginning of time: the Creator God acts in our lives time and time again. "The Lord is king!" is one way of declaring that "neither death, nor life, nor angels, nor principalities, nor things present, nor things to come, nor powers, nor height nor depth, nor anything else in all creation" (Rom. 8:38–9) can defeat him.

In Israel the myth developed in a unique direction, as an Isaianic example (51:9–11) illustrates:

Awake, awake, put on strength,
O arm of the Lord;
awake as in days of old,
the generations of long ago.
Was it not thou that didst cut Rahab in pieces,
that didst pierce the dragon?
Was it not thou that didst dry up the sea [*yam*],
the waters of the great deep [cf. Gen. 1:2; 7:11];
that didst make the depths of the sea a way
for the redeemed to pass over?
And the ransomed of the Lord shall return,
and come to Zion with singing...

The sea monster Yam has become identified with the Red Sea, and its defeat with the Exodus from Egypt. Elsewhere Rahab is identified with Egypt (e.g. Isa. 30:7), and the victory of God at the Red Sea ends with his enthronement as King for ever and ever (Exod. 15:18) just as in the ancient myth. In the present context too the final victory of Yahweh over Leviathan and the dragon that is in the sea means the defeat of Israel's enemies, so that "those who were lost in the land of Assyria..." can return to Zion (v. 13). If Rahab is Egypt, then there is some point in the rabbis' identification of Leviathan with Assyria, and "the dragon that is in the sea" with the Kittim or Romans (Num. 24:24; Dan. 11:30). For a sixteenth-century political philosopher (Hobbes), "Leviathan" meant the centre of absolute power. Such identifications are surely much closer to the author's intention in the

"Isaiah apocalypse" than are the equations with constellations (Serpens, Draco and Hydra) or with solar eclipses (cf. Job 3:3–10) suggested by some commentators. Later apocalyptic passages like Revelation 20 and the apocryphal 2 Esdras 6:49–52 confirm this.

The new "song of the vineyard" is very different from the old (5:1–7), and obviously intends us to contrast the two. Like the first song, it begins with a description of the care with which the vineyard is tended, and ends with the identification of the vine- yard as Jacob/Israel (v. 6; cf. 5:7). Verse 4, on the other hand, is completely new. God is not angry; the vineyard is producing good wine (the Hebrew of verse 2 actually has "vineyard of wine", not "pleasant vineyard"); there are no "thorns and briers" this time for him to attack and burn. Instead of bitterness and bloodshed, the new vineyard will be characterized by protection, peace (*shalom* repeated twice), and abundant success (vv. 5–6). The Hebrew of verses 4 and 5 is odd and may not be original, but the meaning is clear enough and the radical reinterpretation of NEB is neither linguistically nor theologically justified. Verse 6 follows 11:1–9 in picturing a kind of new life and hope that burgeons in Israel but affects the whole world. Where other vineyards failed (5:1–7; Ps. 80:8–13; Ezek. 19:10–14; Mark 12:1–9), this one will succeed.

Verses 7–11 appear to deal with a tragic schism within the people of God. They describe the exile of a "people without discernment" (v. 11), the destruction of their idols, and the defeat of their fortified city. The question at the beginning, however, and the implied question at the end, as to why God, who made them, did not have compassion on them, suggests that these people are close kinsmen of Israel. It seems natural to take the passage therefore as an early treatment of the Samaritan question. We have come across this already in various passages originally addressed to Ephraim (the Northern Kingdom) and its capital Samaria, but given added spice when read in the light of the Samaritan schism after the exile (e.g 9:8–10:4). Verse 7 comments on the fall of the Assyrians who had been responsible for the destruction of Samaria in 722–721 B.C. Now Samaria too has been rejected again. No doubt later commentators saw in this verse a reference to the destruction of Samaria by Judah's king John Hyrcanus in 108 B.C., a hideous illustration of how bitter relations between Jews and Samaritans had become by then. The enigmatic word translated "measure by measure" in verse 8 perhaps implies that the Samaritans were not destroyed immediately, as they deserved (v. 9), but given every opportunity to repent. There is a very similar discussion of how God treats his erring creatures in the apocryphal Wisdom of Solomon (11:21–12:2):

> Therefore thou dost correct little by little those who trespass,
> and dost remind and warn them of the things wherein they sin,
> that they may be freed from wickedness and put their trust in Thee, O
> Lord. (12:2)

In this case "they" are punished by exile to Assyria (2 Kings 17), described here as "his fierce blast in the day of the east wind" (v. 8). Their idols are smashed (v. 9); their city is deserted (v. 10), cut down like a tree fit only to be burned on the fire (v. 11). But they have no sense; they are unrepentant. The calf grazing in the ruins (v. 10) may be an ironical allusion to the source of their wickedness; for when Israel split off from Judah, their king Jeroboam made two calves of gold, and said to the people, "Behold your gods, O Israel . . ." (1 Kings 12:28; cf. Exod. 32:1–6).

The climax of the "apocalypse" is in two parts, the sifting out of Israel from among the nations (v. 12) and their triumphant return to Jerusalem (v. 13). The word for "lost" is used of sheep (Ezek. 34) and of Israel's "wandering", homeless ancestors from Syria (Deut. 26:5). "Those who were driven out to the land of Egypt" is perhaps a reference to that other tragic schism in Israel, the establishment of a rival Jewish Temple at Leontopolis (see on 19:18). The land that stretches from the Euphrates in Syria to the Egyptian frontier ("Brook of Egypt" is the Biblical term for Wadi El Arish) means the land ruled once by David and Solomon (1 Kings 8:65), the promised land at its greatest (Gen. 15:18). In the end, at the sound of the ram's horn (Lev. 25:9–10), that Golden Age will dawn again, and Israel will be one.

PRIESTS AND PROPHETS DRUNK WITH WINE

Isaiah 28:1–13

¹Woe to the proud crown of the drunkards of Ephraim,
   and to the fading flower of its glorious beauty,
      which is on the head of the rich valley of those overcome with
         wine!
²Behold, the Lord has one who is mighty and strong;
   like a storm of hail, a destroying tempest,
 like a storm of mighty, overflowing waters,
   he will cast down to the earth with violence.
³The proud crown of the drunkards of Ephraim
   will be trodden under foot;
⁴and the fading flower of its glorious beauty,
   which is on the head of the rich valley,
 will be like a first-ripe fig before the summer:
   when a man sees it, he eats it up
   as soon as it is in his hand.

⁵In that day the Lord of hosts will be a crown of glory,
   and a diadem of beauty, to the remnant of his people;
⁶and a spirit of justice to him who sits in judgment,
   and strength to those who turn back the battle at the gate.

⁷These also reel with wine
   and stagger with strong drink;
 the priest and the prophet reel with strong drink,
   they are confused with wine,
   they stagger with strong drink;
 they err in vision,
   they stumble in giving judgment.
⁸For all tables are full of vomit,
   no place is without filthiness.

⁹"Whom will he teach knowledge,
   and to whom will he explain the message?
 Those who are weaned from the milk,
   those taken from the breast?
¹⁰For it is precept upon precept, precept upon precept,
   line upon line, line upon line,
   here a little, there a little."

11Nay, but by men of strange lips
   and with an alien tongue
the Lord will speak to this people,
12   to whom he has said,
"This is rest;
   give rest to the weary;
and this is repose";
   yet they would not hear.
13Therefore the word of the Lord will be to them
   precept upon precept, precept upon precept,
line upon line, line upon line,
   here a little, there a little;
that they may go, and fall backward,
   and be broken, and snared, and taken.

In chapters 28–33 we return from the foreign nations (13–23) and the "apocalypse" (24–27) to the mainstream of Isaianic prophecy. The form of the prophecies as well as their content immediately suggests that they go back, in the main, to the eighth century B.C., like the bulk of chapters 1–12. There are a number of "Woe" prophecies (cf. 5:8); several are introduced by the formula "Therefore thus says the Lord . . ." or "Hear the word of the Lord . . ." Many of them are directed at drunkenness, injustice, dishonesty, hypocrisy, and other social evils. Jerusalem remains at the centre of the prophet's attacks, threatened by Assyria, tempted by offers of military aid from Egypt. Where there is hope, it comes from quietness and trust in God, not from horses and chariots, and in the form of a son of David who will establish a kingdom of peace and justice. As in chapters 1–12, there are indications that later writers—poets, prophets, commentators, editors from the seventh and sixth centuries—have had a hand in the composition of the text as we now have it. But the vivid imagination, penetrating criticisms and unshakable faith of the eighth-century originator of Isaianic tradition are recognizable throughout.

Chapter 1 introduced the subject of Israel's sins with the disgusting image of a diseased body, covered with sores and bleeding wounds. The present series of prophecies begins with an equally repulsive scene: a banquet at which the guests have got horribly drunk, and are staggering about in a stupor, unable to see or speak properly, vomiting all over the tables (vv. 7–8), shouting at the prophet (vv. 9–10). Perhaps originally this prophecy referred to an actual incident in Jerusalem, possibly even at a festive occasion in the Temple as prophets and priests are explicitly mentioned (v. 7). But as it stands now, at the beginning of a series of attacks on the dissipated, godless leaders of Jerusalem (v. 14), and coupled with a "Woe" prophecy against their northern neighbours (vv. 1–4), it provides a magnificently appropriate general introduction. Drunkenness, as we have seen, both in the prophets and the Wisdom literature, is a standard symbol of indiscipline and ineffectiveness, especially in the affluent echelons of society (e.g. 5:11–12). Verses 1–4 are about much more than drunkenness.

The attack on "the drunkards of Ephraim" (vv. 1–4) belongs to a large group of "Woe" prophecies, addressed to the men and women of high society in Jerusalem, Samaria, Bethel and other cities (e.g. Amos 6; Isa. 5:8–24). Again, perhaps it was actually delivered by Isaiah in the years leading up to the fall of Samaria in 722–721 B.C. But in its present context, addressed now to Jerusalem, after the Northern Kingdom had been destroyed, it has a different force: "Look what happened to your drunken kinsmen in the north!"

The "proud crown . . . of Ephraim" is the beautiful city of Samaria which stood on a hill at the head of a rich valley surrounded by cornfields and vineyards. But it has another meaning: as, when a banquet is over, garlands worn by the drunken revellers are thrown down and trampled on, even so Samaria is shortly to be "cast down to the earth with violence" (v. 2) and "trodden under foot" (v. 3). "The flower of her glorious beauty"—her ivory palaces (Amos 3:15), her splendid furniture (Amos 6:4–7), her festivals (Amos 5:21–23)—will fade. Like the first fig to ripen on a tree, Samaria will be greedily devoured as soon as someone spots her (v. 4). The "one who is mighty and strong" (v. 2) is Assyria, the rod of God's anger (10:5): the Assyrian army will sweep through the valley like a flood "reaching even to the neck" (8:7–8), or like a hailstorm battering down the flowers, crops and trees of Samaria.

Verses 5–6 tell of another crown of glory, one that will not easily be thrown away and trampled under foot, one that will restore to God's people justice, strength and something of their former beauty . . . the Lord of hosts is its name. This little prophecy of salvation certainly comes from a later age than the other "crown of glory" prophecy with which it is coupled, and summons us to see beyond the fall of Samaria—and indeed beyond the fall of Jerusalem (v. 22)—to a new beginning. That is what "the remnant of his people" refers to (see on 6:13).

With the words "These also . . ." the prophet turns angrily to the "men of Judah", as he did in 5:7, in particular priests and prophets. NEB finds in verse 7 more colourful information about the drunkards ("hiccuping in drunken stupor"). Most versions, however, take it as referring to the prophets' inability to carry out their duties properly ("they totter when they are having visions", Jerusalem Bible), and the priests' inability to make the correct pronouncements ("judgment"), that is, on matters of cultic purity and the like (e.g. Lev. 13: 27–28; Matt. 8:1–4). No doubt Hezekiah's misguided decision to join the Egyptians in rebelling against Assyria was backed up by his court prophets (cf. 1 Kings 22).

With striking imagination, the prophet then quotes the words of the drunkards (vv. 9–10): "Who's going to listen to him? Does he think we're babes in arms?" The fact that in their present state they were probably incapable of understanding much more than monosyllables gives their words a nice ironic touch. The older commentators used to try to make sense of the extraordinary gibberish in verse 10: (see AV, RSV). But since the verse comes between a reference to infants and a reference to a strange foreign language, it is surely to be taken as a string of meaningless syllables, mimicking Isaiah's ludicrous blabbering (as his opponents see it), and at the same time ridiculing the blurred and disjointed speech of the speakers; Jerusalem Bible merely transliterates: *kav lakav, kav lakav, sav lasav, sav lasav, zeer sham, zeer sham.* NEB, rather less imaginatively, paraphrases: "harsh cries and raucous shouts".

The scene ends with an ominous prophecy of judgment (vv. 11–13). God is going to address his people in a strange foreign language, and it will not be the innocuous gobbledygook of their own drunken priests and prophets. It will be the Assyrian language, the language of their conquerors. The scathing epithet "this people" is used by the prophet in his sternest comments on his fellow-countrymen (e.g. 6:9–10; 8:6, 11, 12). The words that the Lord might have spoken, "This is rest . . ." (v.12) are very beautiful both in their sound and in their associations: cf. "Blessed be the Lord who has given rest to his people Israel" (1 Kings 8:56). Isaiah 32:18, the familiar words of Psalm 23 (v.2) and Matthew 11:29 are other examples (see on 11:10). But instead, loud and hostile Assyrian voices will be heard in the land (36:4–10, 13–20; 37:10–13). The prophecy ends with no less than five verbs describing the fall of Jerusalem. They may have escaped, by the skin of their teeth, in 701 B.C. (chs. 36–38), but destruction came in 586 B.C. (2 Kings 25). The accumulation of images in 24:17–18 gives a similar effect in stressing the finality and inevitability of judgment.

A COVENANT WITH DEATH

Isaiah 28:14–29

[14]Therefore hear the word of the Lord, you scoffers,
    who rule this people in Jerusalem!
[15]Because you have said, "We have made a covenant with death,
    and with Sheol we have an agreement;
when the overwhelming scourge passes through
    it will not come to us;
for we have made lies our refuge,
    and in falsehood we have taken shelter";
[16]therefore thus says the Lord God,
    "Behold, I am laying in Zion for a foundation
    a stone, a tested stone,
a precious cornerstone, of a sure foundation:
    'He who believes will not be in haste.'
[17]And I will make justice the line,

and righteousness the plummet;
   and hail will sweep away the refuge of lies,
    and waters will overwhelm the shelter."
18Then your covenant with death will be annulled,
   and your agreement with Sheol will not stand;
  when the overwhelming scourge passes through
    you will be beaten down by it.
19As often as it passes through it will take you;
   for morning by morning it will pass through,
    by day and by night;
  and it will be sheer terror to understand the message.
20For the bed is too short to stretch oneself on it,
   and the covering too narrow to wrap oneself in it
21For the Lord will rise up as on Mount Perazim,
   he will be wroth as in the valley of Gibeon·
  to do his deed—strange is his deed!
    and to work his work—alien is his work!
22Now therefore do not scoff,
   lest your bonds be made strong;
  for I have heard a decree of destruction
    from the Lord God of hosts upon the whole land.

23Give ear, and hear my voice;
   hearken, and hear my speech.
24Does he who ploughs for sowing plough continually?
   does he continually open and harrow his ground?
25When he has levelled its surface,
   does he not scatter dill, sow cummin.
  and put in wheat in rows
   and barley in its proper place,
   and spelt as the border?
26For he is instructed aright;
   his God teaches him.

27Dill is not threshed with a threshing sledge,
   nor is a cart wheel rolled over cummin;
  but dill is beaten out with a stick,
   and cummin with a rod.
28Does one crush bread grain?
   No, he does not thresh it for ever;
  when he drives his cart wheel over it

with his horses, he does not crush it.
29This also comes from the Lord of hosts;
    he is wonderful in counsel,
    and excellent in wisdom.

The prophet now turns to Jerusalem's leaders; "scoffers", he calls them, a term very frequent in Proverbs: e.g. "Scoffers set a city aflame, but wise men turn away wrath" (29:8). The word means undisciplined (Prov. 13:1; 15:12), arrogant (Prov. 21:24) people who cause havoc in society, especially if they hold positions of authority. "Scoffing" and drunken brawls are not dissimilar (Prov. 20:1). Here it refers to the stubborn, short-sighted behaviour of those in Jerusalem who reject the way of faith and justice, and rush (v. 16) into some foolish course of action which is sure to lead the country into disaster.

The "covenant with death" and the "agreement with Sheol" can perhaps be identified with a treaty made between Hezekiah and the Ethiopian Pharaoh Tirhakah (cf. 37:9; 20:5; 31:1), which led to Sennacherib's devastating invasion of Judah in 701 B.C. (36:1). In the context of the Wisdom literature (where there are few such allusions to the history of Israel) a "covenant with death" would be a general description of any project doomed to end in failure, either because it is evil or because it is foolish, like the wretched young men lured into the house of Lady Stupidity (NEB) at the end of Proverbs 9, or tempted to throw in their lot with criminals (Prov. 1:10–19). This would be a more likely interpretation of the present passage than any involving reference to necromancy or the quest for immortality.

"The overwhelming scourge", or perhaps (originally) "the flood's lash" (vv. 17–18), may similarly be interpreted both as a historical reference to the Assyrian invasion (cf. 8:7–8) and as a general comment on the problems and disasters that these fools are confident they can withstand. The prophet's irony is again evident (as in v. 9) in the blatant mention of their own lies and deceit, and (in view of v. 17) it may be noted that the penalty for deceitfulness is death (Ps. 5:6).

The short and memorable passage introduced by "Thus says the Lord God . . . " (vv. 16–17) starts as a prophecy of salvation on the thoroughly Isaianic theme of Zion "the city of righteousness, the faithful city" (cf. 1:21–26), but ends with a sweeping prophecy of doom aimed at the "scoffers". The effect is to neutralize the scoffers' deceitfulness with faith and justice, before condemning it. The Hebrew phrase translated "tested stone" (RSV) has been much discussed. NEB in a typical break with tradition renders it "block of granite". The phrase is traditionally understood as "touchstone, criterion", which goes well with the references to a "plumbline" in the next verse: the lines of the city of righteousness are true and her proportions perfect because every stone is cut according to a touchstone. Others think rather of a firm foundation or a cornerstone, on which the whole building depends. Whatever the precise image, the stone bears the legend (three words in Hebrew): "He who believes will not be in haste" (or "waver" (NEB)). As in 7:9, there is a play on words here, since, in an architectural context, the Hebrew for "believe" could well have the more concrete meaning "stand firm" (as in Job 39:24).

What is meant, then, by "the stone that stands firm", the touchstone? Like the seven pillars of wisdom in Proverbs 9:1, interpreters apply it to whatever they believe to be the source of truth and justice. Thus some say it means the Torah (2:3), others Wisdom, others the Temple, others the Messiah—"that living stone, rejected by men (Ps. 118:22) but in God's sight chosen and precious" (1 Pet. 2:4). Surely in its Isaianic context it must refer to faith in God: "in quietness and in trust shall be your strength" (30:15; 7:9). Those who put their trust in lies (v. 15) or human powers (31:1) will be swept away and drowned (v. 17); those who trust in God and in his righteousness will stand secure Is this not a variation on the first verse of Psalm 127?

The remaining five verses of the prophecy (vv. 18–22) are rich in the imagery of doom and disaster. First, the treaty with Egypt will prove disastrous: Assyria will sweep through the area like a flood (see on v. 15) and no one will be able to rescue the cities of Judah (36:1). Verse 19 applies the prophecy to recurring disasters in the experience of his listeners, not only the events of 701 B.C.: "morning by morning . . . by day and by night" recalls in particular the "sheer terror" experienced by a prophet gripped by visions of death and destruction (e.g. 21:1–10), and bearing a "message" (cf. v. 9) of unremitting doom (e.g. 6:1–12; 50:4). Verse 20 follows that horror with a proverb: there is going to be no room to relax, like a bed that is too short, and nothing to protect yourself with, like blankets that are too narrow.

Next come two allusions to the legends of Israel's past (v. 21). First is David's victory over the Philistines when the Lord "broke through" his enemies "like a bursting flood" (2 Sam. 5:20)— Perazim actually means "breaking through". Second is Joshua's victory over the king of Jerusalem at Gibeon when "the Lord threw down great stones from heaven upon them . . . and they died" (Josh. 10:11), and "the sun stood still, and the moon stayed, until the nation took vengeance on their enemies" (10:13). But now the men of Judah are the enemies of the Lord, and it is they who are going to be the victims of flood and hailstones (v. 17). How strange that God should treat his own people in this way (v. 21)!

The final image in this rich prophecy is of prisoners' chains (v. 22). Again the prophet refers to his own experience of revelation (cf. v. 19): he knows that God has decided to destroy the whole land—Judah and Samaria and the "scoffers" are all tied up, like animals for the slaughter, in the midst of it.

The chapter ends with a parable (vv. 23ff.) that looks beyond the horrors of judgment (vv. 17*b*–22) to the happier times that must, in the nature of things, inevitably follow. First there is the ploughing season, and of course ploughing is a horribly vivid metaphor for oppression (cf. Ps. 129:3). But, like harrowing, it does not go on for ever (v. 24). Then the sowing season begins. It is important to appreciate the accuracy of these verses, because the wisdom of the peasant and the wisdom of God are being compared. Notice, for example, the distinction between the careless "scattering" of the relatively abundant herbs like dill and cummin, and the much more orderly sowing of wheat, barley and spelt (an inferior variety of barley) in verse 25. Similarly the different techniques for preparing them after they have been harvested are meticulously observed: cummin is easily separated from its delicate case by quite a thin cane; dill requires a stouter stick to dislodge the seed; bread grain has to be threshed by a horse-drawn threshing cart or sledge on a threshing floor. Again "threshing" is used metaphorically of torture and oppression (e.g. Amos 1:3; Isa. 41:15), and the point of the parable is clear. God in all his wisdom, like the skilful peasants, does not make us suffer more than we can bear. He knows our individual strengths and weaknesses; and he does not punish us for ever. Like ploughing and threshing, the sufferings have an end. In Shelley's words:

> The trumpet of the prophecy! O, Wind,
> If Winter comes, can Spring be far behind?

WOE TO ARIEL, THE CITY OF DAVID!

Isaiah 29:1–8

> [1]Ho Ariel, Ariel,
>   the city where David encamped!
> Add year to year;
>   let the feasts run their round.
> [2]Yet I will distress Ariel,
>   and there shall be moaning and lamentation,
>   and she shall be to me like an Ariel.
> [3]And I will encamp against you round about,
>   and will besiege you with towers
>   and I will raise siegeworks against you.
> [4]Then deep from the earth you shall speak,
>   from low in the dust your words shall come;
> your voice shall come from the ground like the voice of a ghost,
>   and your speech shall whisper out of the dust.
>
> [5]But the multitude of your foes shall be like small dust,
>   and the multitude of the ruthless like passing chaff.
> And in an instant, suddenly,
> [6] you will be visited by the Lord of hosts
> with thunder and with earthquake and great noise,
>   with whirlwind and tempest, and the flame of a devouring fire

⁷And the multitude of all the nations that fight against Ariel,
  all that fight against her and her stronghold and distress her,
  shall be like a dream, a vision of the night.
⁸As when a hungry man dreams he is eating
  and awakes with his hunger not satisfied,
 or when a thirsty man dreams he is drinking
  and awakes faint, with his thirst not quenched,
 so shall the multitude of all the nations be
  that fight against Mount Zion.

The "Ariel" prophecy is in two distinct parts: the first foretells a disastrous siege of Jerusalem (vv. 1–4), the second pictures a sudden change in Jerusalem's fortunes and the defeat of the besieging army (vv. 5–8). Such a sequence of events is described in chapters 36–37, which should be read alongside the present passage, although neither passage has much basis in historical fact. What actually happened in 701 was that when Sennacherib approached Jerusalem Hezekiah bought him off with "all the silver that was found in the house of the Lord, and in the treasuries of the king's house ... " (2 Kings 18:15), and Jerusalem survived "like a booth in a vineyard" (Isa. 1:8), alone out of all the cities of Judah (36:1). But the fact that she survived at all was something of a miracle, and a century later, in the light of the fall of Nineveh (Assyria's capital) in 612 and the upsurge of national feeling in Jerusalem associated with the reign of Josiah (640–609 B.C.) (2 Kings 22–23), the legend of the miraculous defeat of the Assyrians was born, and, needless to say, closely linked to the prophet laureate of Jerusalem, Isaiah.

A comparison between the two main Isaianic versions of the legend (29:1–8 and 36–37) highlights various differences. Of course one is a prophecy, in verse, and the other is written as a piece of historical narrative. But that is only a superficial difference, since in fact the prose account contains prayers (37:16–20), prophecies (37:21–35) and various Isaianic idioms (e.g. 37:31–32) not so different from what we get in 29:1–8. More significant is the fact that the poetic version preserves more of what actually happened than the prose version. The first four verses of chapter 29 spell out the horror of defeat with a vividness and pathos that suggest they are based on eye-witness accounts, while the prose version (36–37) written many years later, omits the passage about Hezekiah's surrender (2 Kings 18:14–16) altogether. The other important difference between the two is that, while in the prose account the human characters—Hezekiah, Sennacherib, the Rabshakeh, Eliakim, Shebna, "Tirhakah the king of Ethiopia", Isaiah—hold the centre of the stage until the very end (37:36), the Lord of hosts is the subject of 29:1–8. Thus, even though in this case we can identify actual historical events underlying the prophecy, the theme is not historical, but theological.

The word "Ariel" probably originally meant "altar-hearth", as in 2 Sam 23:20, Ezek. 43:15 and verse 2 of the present passage, and thus came to be a name applied to Jerusalem, the place where year by year the feasts were celebrated (v. 1*b*). In Hebrew, however, *ari'el* looks like a name meaning "lion of God" ("of God" as in Michael, Gabriel, Raphael, Ezekiel, Daniel, etc.), and that is how it has been understood since early times. Thus Jerusalem is called "lion of God" (="hero") because of her brilliant victory over Sennacherib. In the time of Christ, the Temple was called "Ariel" because it looked like a lion: the façade was large and imposing, the back of the building small and narrow. Still later, by the time of Shakespeare's *The Tempest*, Ariel was a spirit, or a ghost (cf. v. 4).

There is another play on words in verse 2: Ariel (=Jerusalem) is going to be like an *ariel* (=altar-hearth): that is to say, covered with smouldering ashes and reeking of blood; or perhaps a ghost, wailing and whispering ("squeaking", NEB). In both verses 2 and 3 God is the speaker, although the technical terminology might have fitted more naturally into prose narrative than prophecy. As Isaiah has argued so often before (e.g. 7:17–20; 8:7–8; 10:5), the Assyrian invasions are acts of God. Verse 4 depicts Jerusalem as defeated, lying in the dust, hardly able to speak (cf. 1:7–9). The macabre allusion to a "ghost", however, must not blind us to the fact that the scene is also one of penitence, preparing for the sudden upturn in Jerusalem's fortunes described in vv. 5–8. This is how, by faith, disaster and humiliation are transformed by God into the road to victory "for my own sake and for the sake of my servant David" (37:35).

The sudden appearance of the Lord of hosts amid thunder, earthquake, whirlwind and consuming fire, recalls his appearances to the Israelites at Mount Sinai (Exod. 19), to Elijah the prophet (1 Kings 19:9–12) and to the Psalmist in the Temple (e.g. Ps. 18:7–15), rather than to human enemies like Sennacherib and the Assyrians. According to 37:36 "the angel of the Lord went forth, and slew a hundred and eighty-five thousand in the camp of the Assyrians . . . " While such a statement could be applied to the onslaught of a plague or a sudden storm or the like, 29:6 completely transcends the realm of historical reality, and takes us rather into the world of Psalm 48:

> For lo, the kings assembled,
>   they came on together.
> As soon as they saw it, they were astounded,
>   they were in panic, they took to flight . . .
> As we have heard, so we have seen,
>   in the city of the Lord of hosts,
> in the city of our God,
>   which God establishes for ever. (vv. 4–8)

These are imaginative expressions of faith in God, of which Jerusalem, the city of God, is a symbol:

> Those who trust in the Lord are like Mount Zion,
>   which cannot be moved, but abides for ever. (Ps. 125:1)

Verse 7 develops the scene of the faithful city withstanding all attacks from the forces of evil ranged against her. The image of "a dream, a vision of the night" needs little comment: when the siege is over and peace restored, the people of Jerusalem will find it hard to believe that they had ever been surrounded by so immense a multitude of foreign nations (cf. Ps. 126:1). Verse 8 elaborates the image in another direction from the point of view of the frustrated ambitions of the enemy: victory had seemed so easy before the battle that they had come to imagine that the wealth of Jerusalem was already theirs. Defeat means the end of their glorious plans. It is like waking up to harsh reality after a beautiful dream. So shall it be with all who fight against God's people:

> These things shall vanish all;
>> The city of God remaineth!
>>> (Martin Luther)

HAVING EYES THEY SEE NOT

Isaiah 29:9–24

⁹Stupefy yourselves and be in a stupor,
  blind yourselves and be blind!
 Be drunk, but not with wine;
  stagger, but not with strong drink!
¹⁰For the Lord has poured out upon you
  a spirit of deep sleep,
 and has closed your eyes, the prophets,
  and covered your heads, the seers.

¹¹And the vision of all this has become to you like the words of a book that is sealed. When men give it to one who can read, saying, "Read this," he says, "I cannot, for it is sealed." ¹²And when they give the book to one who cannot read, saying, "Read this," he says, "I cannot read."

¹³And the Lord said:
 "Because this people draw near with their mouth
  and honour me with their lips,
  while their hearts are far from me,
 and their fear of me is a commandment of men learned by rote;
¹⁴therefore, behold, I will again
  do marvellous things with this people,
  wonderful and marvellous;
 and the wisdom of their wise men shall perish,
  and the discernment of their discerning men shall be hid."

¹⁵Woe to those who hide deep from the Lord their counsel,
  whose deeds are in the dark,
  and who say, "Who sees us? Who knows us?"
¹⁶You turn things upside down!
  Shall the potter be regarded as the clay;

¹⁰that the thing made should say of its maker,
　　"He did not make me";
　or the thing formed say of him who formed it,
　　"He has no understanding"?

¹⁷Is it not yet a very little while
　　until Lebanon shall be turned into a fruitful field,
　　and the fruitful field shall be regarded as a forest?
¹⁸In that day the deaf shall hear
　　the words of a book,
　and out of their gloom and darkness
　　the eyes of the blind shall see.
¹⁹The meek shall obtain fresh joy in the Lord,
　　and the poor among men shall exult in the Holy One of Israel.
²⁰For the ruthless shall come to naught and the scoffer cease,
　　and all who watch to do evil shall be cut off,
²¹who by a word make a man out to be an offender,
　　and lay a snare for him who reproves in the gate,
　　and with an empty plea turn aside him who is in the right.

²²Therefore thus says the Lord, who redeemed Abraham, concerning the house of Jacob:
　"Jacob shall no more be ashamed,
　　no more shall his face grow pale.
²³For when he sees his children,
　　the work of my hands, in his midst,
　　they will sanctify my name;
　they will sanctify the Holy One of Jacob,
　　and will stand in awe of the God of Israel.
²⁴And those who err in spirit will come to understanding,
　　and those who murmur will accept instruction."

Like the first eight verses of the chapter, verses 9–24 comprise a prophecy in two parts, the first made up of three short prophecies of judgment, very probably from the years leading up to 701 B.C. (vv. 9–12; 13–14; 15–16), and the second a fine prophecy of salvation reminiscent of parts of the "Isaiah apocalypse" (chs. 24–27) and "Deutero-Isaiah" (40–55). The pattern sin–judgment–hope recurs throughout the book, as it does in Deuteronomy, Jeremiah and elsewhere, strengthened, it seems, by each catastrophe that befell the Biblical writers. Whether this way of thinking goes back to Isaiah himself we do not know, because his mission was to say to his people, "Hear and hear, but do not understand; see and see, but do not perceive" (6:9), not to offer them hope of forgiveness.

The present example of the way Isaiah carried out that mission is very closely related to his vision in the Temple (6:1–13). The three prophecies all have the same subject: the blindness and lack of understanding of Judah's leaders. First, their blind folly (perhaps referring to the ill-fated negotiations with Egypt that led to Sennacherib's invasion in 701 B.C.) is so inexplicable and so catastrophic that it must be due to divine intervention (vv. 9–10). They are behaving as if they are in a drunken stupor, as though God had put them to sleep, so that they cannot see or understand the vision. It has been plausibly suggested that the words "the prophets" and "the seers" in verse 10 were added by a later commentator who interpreted the verse allegorically. Jerusalem Bible brackets them. However, the traditional view that the text as it stands is actually attacking the blindness of false prophets has much to be said for it, especially when verses 11–12 (also possibly a late addition) are taken into account. Their prophetic omniscience ("All prophetic vision", NEB), says he with heavy irony, is wasted on them—they are too drunk or stupid to know what to do when they receive a vision. Their plight is comparable to that of their drunken counterparts in chapter 28 (vv. 7–10).

The second prophecy (vv. 13–14) is also about blindness: because of the hypocrisy of "this people" their leaders will be deprived of the political acumen and resourcefulness needed to guide the country through a difficult crisis. Again the original context of these words may well have been the last years of the eighth century when irresponsibility and short-sightedness led to the devastation of Judah. But as it stands, it can be taken as a general attack on the lip-service of people who slavishly attend acts of worship and mouth the words of prayers and hymns, without taking seriously what they say and do. This is another reason for the prophetic attacks on ritualism. In chapter 1 it was injustice and oppression outside the temple worship that was criticized; here it is insincerity and lack of spirituality during worship.

Verse 13 ends with what looks very like a grotesque parody of the saying "Fear God, and keep his commandments" (Ecc. 12:13; Deut. 6:2). "The fear of God", which is the beginning of wisdom (Prov. 1:7; 9:10; Job. 28:28; Ps. 111:10), involves worshipping him in spirit and in truth, not merely conforming to prevailing social convention. The parody of the Exodus traditions in verse 14 recalls the strange acts of God in 28:21: the same God who in days gone by saved Israel by great signs and wonders (e.g. Exod. 15:11; Ps. 77:14) "will again do marvellous things with this people"—but this time it will bring them ignominious defeat.

The third prophecy is a Woe-saying (see on 5:8–25), addressed to a government that thinks it can get away with policies that are against the interests of the country and against the will of God, if they keep them secret (vv. 15–16). This sounds like another prophecy from the time of Sennacherib's invasion, although as it stands it draws from those dark days a lesson for people in general concerning their relationship to God. God is not mocked: that is the gist of this prophecy. First, like Amos (9:3) and the Psalmist (e.g. 64:5–6; 94:7), he ridicules the notion that we can act without regard for our ultimate answerability before God, and second, like Jeremiah (18:6; cf. Isa. 45:9), he mocks the idea that the creature can criticize its creator. The implication in both ideas comes near to atheism, the high-handed rejection of any authority or power beyond ourselves. No one can stop us; we have wisdom, skill, freedom, they said. The prophet's "Woe!" was soon to be fulfilled, however, and their arrogant deceit and impotence exposed.

The second part of this section is a prophecy of salvation (vv. 17–24). A new age will soon dawn when the inadequacies and injustices of the present will be miraculously replaced by joy and godliness. It will be as though the cedars of Lebanon started bearing fruit like vines and fruit-trees, and the vines and fruit-trees of Carmel began to produce timber like the forests of Lebanon (1 Kings 5:8–10). The Hebrew for "fruitful field" is *carmel*, and in this context, in parallel with Mount Lebanon, it surely refers to Israel's most fertile and beautiful mountain range (e.g. 35:2; Jer. 50:19; Song of S. 7:5). Although the scope of this prophecy is wider than the three judgment prophecies that precede it, the continuity is unmistakable. The sealed book (vv. 11–12) will be opened (v. 18); the eyes of the blind (vv. 9–10) shall see (v. 18); those who challenged the sovereign power of the Creator (v. 16) will look on the work of his hands and stand in awe of him (v. 23); those who err in spirit (v. 10) will come to understanding (v. 24); and those who murmur against the Lord (vv. 15–16) will accept instruction (v. 24).

Verses 19–21 introduce a new but very familiar subject: namely, the exaltation of the poor and needy, and the defeat of the ruthless, the scoffers (see on 28:14) and all who "watch to do evil" (RSV). The last expression really means "on the look out for evil" and may be interpreted either as "quick to see mischief", that is, in other people (NEB) or "disposed to evil" in general (Jerusalem Bible). Either way, it refers to the perversion of justice "in the gate" (="in court"), as in 1:23; 5:23; Amos 5:12–13. In the new age, all this will change. The God who "redeemed Abraham" will act again. As Abraham was rescued from the confusion of Babel (Gen. 11:31; 12:4; Wisdom of Solomon 10:5), from the idolatry of Mesopotamia (Josh. 24:2), and from the ordeal of having to slay his own son (Gen. 22; Wisdom of Solomon 10:5; Ecclesiasticus 44:20), so now his descendants, the sons of Jacob, will be rescued from frustration (the Hebrew means much more than "ashamed") and error. Then will Israel worship the Lord in the beauty of holiness, and, to quote Proverbs once more, accept Wisdom's invitation:

> Come, eat of my bread
>   and drink of the wine I have mixed.
> Leave foolishness, and live,
>   and walk in the way of insight. (9:5–6)

WOE TO THE REBELLIOUS CHILDREN

Isaiah 30:1–17

[1]"Woe to the rebellious children," says the Lord,
  "who carry out a plan, but not mine;
  and who make a league, but not of my spirit,

that they may add sin to sin;
²who set out to go down to Egypt,
without asking for my counsel,
to take refuge in the protection of Pharaoh,
and to seek shelter in the shadow of Egypt!
³Therefore shall the protection of Pharaoh turn to your shame,
and the shelter in the shadow of Egypt to your humiliation.
⁴For though his officials are at Zoan
and his envoys reach Hanes,
⁵every one comes to shame
through a people that cannot profit them,
that brings neither help nor profit,
but shame and disgrace."

⁶An oracle on the beasts of the Negeb.
Through a land of trouble and anguish,
from where come the lioness and the lion,
the viper and the flying serpent,
they carry their riches on the backs of asses,
and their treasures on the humps of camels,
to a people that cannot profit them.
⁷For Egypt's help is worthless and empty,
therefore I have called her
"Rahab who sits still."

⁸And now, go, write it before them on a tablet,
and inscribe it in a book,
that it may be for the time to come
as a witness for ever.
⁹For they are a rebellious people,
lying sons,
sons who will not hear
the instruction of the Lord;
¹⁰who say to the seers, "See not";
and to the prophets, "Prophesy not to us what is right;
speak to us smooth things,
prophesy illusions,
¹¹leave the way, turn aside from the path,
let us hear no more of the Holy One of Israel."
¹²Therefore thus says the Holy One of Israel,
"Because you despise this word,
and trust in oppression and perverseness.

and rely on them;
¹³therefore this iniquity shall be to you
    like a break in a high wall, bulging out, and about to collapse,
    whose crash comes suddenly, in an instant;
¹⁴and its breaking is like that of a potter's vessel
    which is smashed so ruthlessly
that among its fragments not a sherd is found
    with which to take fire from the hearth,
    or to dip up water out of the cistern."

¹⁵For thus said the Lord God, the Holy One of Israel,
    "In returning and rest you shall be saved;
    in quietness and in trust shall be your strength."
And you would not, ¹⁶but you said,
    "No! We will speed upon horses,"
    therefore you shall speed away;
and, "We will ride upon swift steeds,"
    therefore your pursuers shall be swift.
¹⁷A thousand shall flee at the threat of one,
    at the threat of five you shall flee,
till you are left
    like a flagstaff on the top of a mountain,
    like a signal on a hill.

We now come to a series of four more short prophecies of doom (vv. 1–5; 6–7; 8–14; 15–17), all of them probably containing the original words of Isaiah, followed, like all the other prophecies of doom in this section of the book, by an elaborate prophecy of salvation from a later age (vv. 18–33). Specific references to Egypt in the first two, and the general tenor of the other two, indicate that these four short pieces also come from the frantic period leading up to Sennacherib's invasion in 701 B.C. (cf.18:1–7; 28:14–22; 29:1–16).

The first in the series, like the first in the previous two series (28:1; 29:1; cf. 31:1; 33:1), is a Woe-saying. "Rebellious children" has a double meaning: in political terms Judah's leaders have joined Egypt in a rebellion against the Assyrians, while in theological or moral terms they have rebelled against God (cf. 1:2). Their policies are against God's will, in particular the treaty with Egypt, and if they persist with it they will be "piling sin upon sin" (NEB). Verses 2 and 4 refer to envoys sent by Hezekiah to Egypt, presumably in order to carry on negotiations begun by the Egyptian ambassadors who caused such a stir in Judah some years earlier (see on ch. 18). Their aim was now to seek military aid from Egypt, a policy ridiculed both by Sennacherib in his own record of events and throughout Isaianic tradition (e.g. 36:4–10). In the event, Sennacherib defeated the Egyptian army at Eltekeh shortly before he invaded Judah (cf. 37:9), and Isaiah's condemnation of his leaders was justified.

Emotive words like "refuge", "protection", "shelter", "shadow", "help", familiar from the Psalms where they refer exclusively to God (e.g. Ps. 121; 18:2), are here cynically applied to Egypt and neutralized by a string of ugly words for "shame", "disgrace" and "humiliation", drawn from the vocabulary of sexual and religious insults (e.g. 47:3; Prov. 6:32–33; Jer. 3:24–25). Zoan (called Tanis by the Greeks) was an important city in the north-east of the Nile Delta (see on 19:11), and Hanes (=Heracleopolis Magna in the classical sources) was two hundred miles farther south, near modern Fayyum. The point of the reference to these two cities is probably to stress that the whole of Egypt, united only recently under the proud new Ethiopian Pharaohs, Shabako and Tirhakah (see on ch. 18), was involved, and their defeat by Sennacherib all the more humiliating.

The short and extremely colourful "Oracle on the beasts of the Negeb" (vv. 6–7) continues the condemnation of Judah's futile approach to Egypt by picturing the envoy's journey through the desert, through a land of trouble and anguish, laden with treasures, no doubt with a view to strengthening their negotiating position. The desert route through the Negeb and across Sinai was perhaps the only route available, if Sennacherib had already defeated the Egyptians and controlled the coastal route ("the way of the sea", 9:1). The six "beasts of the Negeb" beautifully illustrate, on the one hand, the dangers of travel in that area— lions, lionesses, venomous snakes and the fabled fiery serpents that terrorized the Israelites in the wilderness (Num. 21:6)—and, on the other, all the effort and paraphernalia—asses, camels, etc.—required for this desperate operation.

The word in verse 7 translated "worthless" (NEB "vain") is best illuminated by reading the first verses of Ecclesiastes where it occurs five times: "Vanity of vanities, says the Preacher. Vanity of vanities! All is vanity. What does a man gain by all the toil at which he toils under the sun?" The last few words of this verse seem to refer to the subduing of the great sea-monster Rahab, identified here and elsewhere (e.g. Ps. 87:4; Isa. 51:9-10) with Egypt. But the Hebrew is difficult. The word *rahab* in Hebrew can mean "strength, pride", and another possibility is that the prophet is calling, as in verse 15, for "quietness and trust": "therefore have I cried concerning this, Their strength is to sit still" (AV).

The third prophecy in this series (vv. 8-14) follows the conventional judgment pattern of first stating the charge levelled against the accused (vv. 9-11) and then pronouncing sentence (vv. 12-14). The writing in verse 8 then has the force of a legal document to be used as evidence in the future. Like 8:1 and 8:16, this throws little, if any, light on the process of recording the words of the prophets. In later times, however, such verses came to have eschatological significance, "the time to come", for example, being interpreted as "the latter time, the time of the end" (cf. Dan 12:9).

The accusations in this prophecy are rather more general than those in the previous two, and less closely related to the politics of late eighth-century Jerusalem. "Rebellious people" (the Hebrew word is not the same as in verse 1) is a favourite expression of Ezekiel, and means those who "have eyes to see, but see not, who have ears to hear, but hear not" (Ezek. 12:2). So this is a general comment on the prophet's lonely role in society (cf. 6:9-11). It is interesting that his prophecy is described as "the instruction [*torah*] of the Lord", as if he had the authority of the priests (e.g. Lev. 6:9, 14, 25). The existence of seers and prophets who "speak smooth things and prophesy illusions" is documented in an illuminating prophecy by one of Isaiah's contemporaries (Micah 3:5-8). There are false prophets in every age (e.g. Jer. 23:9-40): there were some apparently who supported Hezekiah and his government in their misguided policies.

The sentence pronounced by the Holy One of Israel on the men of Judah (vv. 12–14) is in the form of two dramatic similes: the sudden collapse of a high wall, and the shattering of an earthenware pot. Nothing will survive, not so much as a single useful potsherd. In ancient times potsherds (*ostraca*) were commonly used as shovels, scoops and, of course, writing material.

Nowhere perhaps can we hear the voice of the prophet Isaiah more clearly than in the oracle with which the last in this series of prophecies begins:

> In returning and rest you shall be saved;
> in quietness and in trust shall be your strength. (v. 15)

This is what he said in different words to Ahaz in an earlier crisis (7:4, 9). "Rest" appears in a number of memorable contexts (e.g. 11:10 (see commentary); 28:12; 32:18); "quietness" likewise (e.g. 7:4; 28:12; 32:17). "Trust" (12:2; 26:3, 4; 32:17) and "salvation" (12:2, 3; 25:9; 26;1) occur in key-passages. "Returning" is not so easy. Perhaps it meant originally breaking the alliance with Egypt and "returning" to Assyria again with lavish gifts (2 Kings 18:14–16). As it stands, however, it must be interpreted as referring to the rebellious people of verses 9–12 "returning to God" in penitence (cf. 6:10; 19:22).

Curiously enough, this beautiful statement introduces a prophecy of doom, not hope. The people persist in seeing themselves riding to victory on swift Egyptian horses. The prophet sees them fleeing for their lives, pursued by the Assyrians and, in an image exactly parallel to 1:8, he sees Jerusalem, alone of all the cities of Judah (36:1), standing forlorn on top of a hill, like a flagpole. Yet it is Isaiah's vision of "the peace that passes all understanding" that gives us hope in difficult times if only, unlike his first audience, we listen and "return".

BUT THE LORD IS GRACIOUS

Isaiah 30:18–26

> [18]Therefore the Lord waits to be gracious to you;
> therefore he exalts himself to show mercy to you.

For the Lord is a God of justice;
　blessed are all those who wait for him.

¹⁹Yea, O people in Zion who dwell at Jerusalem; you shall weep no more. He will surely be gracious to you at the sound of your cry; when he hears it, he will answer you. ²⁰And though the Lord give you the bread of adversity and the water of affliction, yet your Teacher will not hide himself any more, but your eyes shall see your Teacher. ²¹And your ears shall hear a word behind you, saying, "This is the way, walk in it," when you turn to the right or when you turn to the left. ²²Then you will defile your silver-covered graven images and your gold-plated molten images. You will scatter them as unclean things; you will say to them, "Begone!"

²³And he will give rain for the seed with which you sow the ground, and grain, the produce of the ground, which will be rich and plenteous. In that day your cattle will graze in large pastures; ²⁴and the oxen and the asses that till the ground will eat salted provender, which has been winnowed with shovel and fork. ²⁵And upon every lofty mountain and every high hill there will be brooks running with water, in the day of the great slaughter, when the towers fall. ²⁶Moreover the light of the moon will be as the light of the sun, and the light of the sun will be sevenfold, as the light of seven days, in the day when the Lord binds up the hurt of his people, and heals the wounds inflicted by his blow.

Verse 18 is formally the concluding verse of the prophecy of doom we have just been discussing (vv. 15–17). As in verses 3 and 12 above, "therefore . . ." introduces the sentence pronounced by God after the crimes of the accused have been described. But in this remarkable case, the sentence is one of forgiveness, marvellously elaborated in the prose verses that follow (vv. 19–26). The Lord is still a "God of justice", however (v. 18), as the accompanying condemnation of Assyria illustrates (vv. 27–33), and we are to understand that this divine volte-face in Jerusalem's favour would not be possible if justice had not already been done. In other words, the catastrophic defeat described in verses 16–17 (and also in vv. 3–5 and 12–14) has already taken place: verses 18–33 are addressed to people whose eyes are wet with weeping (v. 19), a hurt and wounded people (v. 26), who have eaten the bread of adversity and drunk the water of affliction, people who have lost sight of God (v. 20).

Verse 18 is about patience, the patience of a loving God who waits for his prodigal sons to return (Luke 15:11–32), and the patience of people who trust him, even in the midst of adversity and affliction. The word used here for "waiting" is not common in Isaiah (only here and 8:17), but the idea is; verse 15 above is a beautiful example (see also 7:4, 9; 26:3; 40:31). The love of God has not featured very prominently so far in Isaiah (14:1; 27:11; cf. 33:2), but becomes an important idea later (e.g. 49:13, 15; 54:7, 8, 10; 55:7; 60:10). The blessing announced at the end of the verse also reappears later:

> But they who wait for the Lord shall renew their strength.
>   they shall mount up with wings like eagles,
> they shall run and not be weary,
>   they shall walk and not faint. (40:31)

The prose amplification of verse 18 begins by applying it to the people of Jerusalem. It is you this prophecy is about, says the prophet. Have patience. The Lord will hear your cry. He will be gracious to you. This process, which can remove Biblical language from its original context, enables us to hear the Old Testament prophets addressing us today, just as we can make the hymns and prayers in the Book of Psalms our own.

The first scene of affliction alluded to is that of prisoners, hidden away from society, barely existing on a diet of bread and water, like the prophet Micaiah ben Imlah in 1 Kings 22:27. The "bread of affliction" perhaps also alludes to Israel's sufferings in Egypt. Although the same word is not used in the Jewish liturgy, it recalls the unleavened bread at the Passover meal: "This is the bread of affliction that our fathers ate in the land of Egypt. All who are hungry, let them come and eat; all who are needy, let them come and celebrate the Passover. Now we are here, but next year in Jerusalem. Now we are slaves, next year free men" (cf. Deut. 16:3; 1 Cor. 11:24). One day, in place of bread and water, there will be a "feast of fat things, a feast of wine on the lees ... and the Lord God will wipe away tears from all faces" (25:6, 8).

The "Teacher" in verse 20 is God, who rewards and punishes

his people like schoolchildren (Job 5:17), but who is to them a source of wisdom and life (Prov. 8:32-36). Like Moses and the elders on Mount Sinai (Exod. 24:9-11) and all those invited to the eschatological feast on Mount Zion (Isa. 24:23; 25:6), your eyes will see God, and your ears hear his voice. So the blindness and deafness of the prophet's audience (6:9-10; 29:9-10) will finally be cured. The comforting word of God in verse 21 is addressed to someone in a dilemma. Unsure which way to turn, he hears a voice behind him, saying, "I will support and protect you whichever way you turn." In the easily misrepresented words of Martin Luther, "Sin boldly, but more boldly believe."

The first action of the new "pupils" will be to dispose of all the glittering idols that have come between them and their "Teacher". The elaborate terminology, like that in several later treatments of the subject (e.g. 40:19-20; 41:7; 44:9-20), reflects the fascination that idols, and indeed material possessions in general, inevitably have for us. The word translated "unclean things" (NEB "foul discharge") alludes to those chapters of Leviticus (12-15) in which various types of ritual impurity are discussed, and meticulous regulations laid down to prevent contamination. Idols are like that, says the prophet. They contaminate. They are obstacles on the "Way". In the new age they will be removed.

The author moves on now to paint an idyllic picture of a land of plenty. Instead of the "bread of adversity" (v. 20) there will be "grain (the same Hebrew word as that translated 'bread' in v. 20), the produce of the ground, which will be rich and plenteous." The Hebrew for "plenteous" is the word translated "fat things" in the description of the eschatological feast (25:6). Instead of the "water of affliction" (v. 20) there will be streams of running water on every hillside. There will be plenty of open land for the cattle to graze on; the grain prepared for the oxen and the asses in their stalls will be as tasty (with added salt or sorrel, probably) and as finely winnowed as it would be for the rest of us.

Finally, there will be no more darkness, because the moon will be as bright as the sun, and the sun by day will increase its brightness sevenfold. The last words of verse 26 suggest that, like the paradisiacal scene in 11:6–9, this description is not primarily about animals and the countryside. It is about an age of peace and security, in which everyone has plenty of living-space and as much as he needs to eat and drink. It will be a caring society (v. 24), and one from which all black despair, all dark secrets and shady deals will be banished (v. 26). Even the shadow of death will no longer hang over us (cf. 25:8). In that day the wounded and diseased (1:5–6), the afflicted and broken-hearted (61:1) will be healed. We must try to see beyond the details of the imagery—the oxen and the asses, the shovels and forks, the dazzling astronomy—to appreciate the sheer delight of this celebration of faith, hope and love.

"The day of the great slaughter, when the towers fall" (v. 25b) strikes a jarring note in the midst of the celebrations, but reminds us that evil is a reality in the world and will have to be dealt with one day. Heaven is scarcely conceivable without hell, at any rate in the artist's imagination as much as the prophet's (see on 25:10–12). The fall of the towers could be taken literally to refer to the ultimate destruction of the world's wicked cities—Tyre, Damascus, Samaria, Babylon, Rome—and a return to simple rural values (Hos. 2:14–15). But more likely the "towers" stand for the proud and arrogant (Isa. 2:15), including no doubt the Tower of Babel:

> Then they said, "Come, let us build ourselves a city, and a tower with its top in the heavens, and let us make a name for ourselves . . ." (Gen. 11:4)

THE BURNING ANGER OF THE LORD

Isaiah 30:27–33

27Behold, the name of the Lord comes from far,
   burning with his anger, and in thick rising smoke;
his lips are full of indignation,
   and his tongue is like a devouring fire;
28his breath is like an overflowing stream
   that reaches up to the neck;

to sift the nations with the sieve of destruction,
    and to place on the jaws of the peoples a bridle that leads astray.

²⁹You shall have a song as in the night when a holy feast is kept; and
gladness of heart, as when one sets out to the sound of the flute to go to
the mountain of the Lord, to the Rock of Israel. ³⁰And the Lord will
cause his majestic voice to be heard and the descending blow of his arm
to be seen, in furious anger and a flame of devouring fire, with a
cloudburst and tempest and hailstones. ³¹The Assyrians will be terror-
stricken at the voice of the Lord, when he smites with his rod. ³²And
every stroke of the staff of punishment which the Lord lays upon them
will be to the sound of timbrels and lyres; battling with brandished arm
he will fight with them. ³³For a burning place has long been prepared;
yea, for the king it is made ready, its pyre made deep and wide, with
fire and wood in abundance; the breath of the Lord, like a stream of
brimstone, kindles it.

Picking up the theme introduced in the grisly verse 25, the
prophet now goes on to encourage his beleaguered, suffering
people with an extraordinarily cruel and violent description of the
doom that awaits their enemies. They will soon be singing and
rejoicing as they watch the Assyrians writhing under the blows
from the rod of God's anger. Perhaps the image of the divine
Teacher is still in mind from verse 20: he guides and encourages
his own people, but mercilessly disciplines those who reject his
teaching or lord it over their weaker classmates. When considering such bitterness, which can figure even in the same context as
some of the most exalted religious poetry ever written (Psalm 137
and Isaiah 49 are astounding examples: look at the last verses of
each), we must remember two things. First, such passages were
composed in time of extreme adversity, and people driven to such
extremes of bitterness and hate deserve our sympathy, not our
condemnation. Who of us can honestly say we have never had
such vengeful, "unchristian" feelings? Their appearance in the
canon of scripture does not justify them: but it illustrates how
complete a picture of human nature it contains. These are real
people, like ourselves.
    The second observation to be made on such vindictive out-
bursts is that, while they may certainly have been composed in a

particular historical situation and originally directed at actual
people—in this case the Assyrians—by the time the texts reached
their present form that situation no longer obtained, the Assyrian
empire had long since disappeared, and the prophecy is directed
instead at evil powers in general. So the Assyrians, the Babylonians, the Canaanites, the Philistines, the Midianites, are now
symbols of evil, and this kind of violent attack on them is an
expression of faith in God's power to overcome it. It can be
applied to any situation where the forces of good are ranged
against the forces of evil. In our meaner, this-worldly moments,
we identify our actual enemies, military, political or social, in
these passages, and pray that God will give us victory over
them—smiting them in his furious anger, burning them, destroying them. At other times, on a higher plane, we can use this
language to express our faith in God's power to conquer sin, both
here and now, strengthening our own feeble efforts, and on that
day still to come when he will separate the sheep and the goats
(Matt. 25:31–46; cf. Dan. 12:1–4), and, after a bloody war,
dispose of the devil and his hosts with savage efficiency (Rev.
19:11–20:15). In other words Isaiah 30:27–33 is no longer literally about the Assyrians, any more than Revelation 18 is literally
about the Babylonians.

The language and imagery draw heavily on earlier texts, many
of them Isaianic. "The name of the Lord", a Deuteronomic
expression (e.g. Deut. 12:5, 11), reminds us that this is a God
who revealed his name in a burning bush (Exod. 3), and a God
who can be called upon, summoned by name in time of need
(Gen. 4:26). The fire here is not only the fire that accompanied
God's appearance to Moses (Exod. 3) and the Israelites at Sinai
(Exod. 19:18; Deut. 4:36; Heb. 12:18), but also the fire that
purges and purifies (e.g. 6:13; 9:18–19; 10:17; Deut. 13:16; 17:7;
19:19 etc.). The "overflowing stream" in verse 28 is a direct
allusion to 8:8. There it was the Assyrians flooding Judah "even
to the neck"; here they are given a taste of their own medicine (cf.
Ps. 9:15; 57:6). Two final images have little connection with what
goes before. The nations will be shaken through a sieve, and
destroyed; they will be caught, like horses in a field, and led away
to their destruction (cf. 37:29)

Meanwhile God's people will celebrate their liberation as if it was the night of the Passover or the Feast of Booths (Deut. 16:13–15). Perhaps the author also has in mind the night when "the people who walked in darkness saw a great light . . ." (9:2–3). Psalm 122 fills in the background to verse 29: "I was glad when they said to me, Let us go to the house of the Lord". The "Rock" that will provide shelter for Israel during the storm that is about to break over the Assyrians (2:10, 19, 21) is an image familiar to us already (17:10; 26:4).

The next image is a spectacular storm hurled at the Assyrians by God (vv. 30–31): "his majestic voice" refers to thunder, and the "descending blow of his arm" to lightning. Where the lightning strikes, "a flame of devouring fire" appears. The skies pour down torrents of rain and hail. It will be like the day on which the kings of Canaan were defeated "at Taanach, by the waters of Megiddo":

> From heaven fought the stars,
>   from their courses they fought . .
> The torrent Kishon swept them away,
>   the onrushing torrent, the torrent Kishon.
>   March on, my soul, with might! (Judg. 5:19–21)

The terror of the Assyrians is due not only to the storm itself, but to the fact that they recognize in it the chastisement of the Lord. They who for years have been savagely beating the Lord's people with "the rod of his anger" (10:5) are now at the receiving end of the same punishment (cf. 10:12–19).

It has been suggested that the musical accompaniment referred to in verse 32 has some cultic significance. The word translated "brandished arm" (RSV) occurs in cultic contexts in the sense of "sacrifice" (lit. "wave offering": e.g. Lev. 7:30; Num. 8:11), and verse 33 contains a reference to Topheth, a place on the outskirts of Jerusalem where human sacrifices were offered (e.g. 2 Kings 23:10; Jer. 7:31–32). But the grammar of verse 32, especially the last clause, is hard to understand. Perhaps the music simply represents the stat of the victory celebrations (cf. Exod. 15:20; 1 Sam. 18:6–7; Ps. 150).

The final conflagration takes place on Topheth. It had been planned long ago—a way of emphasizing God's overarching control of Israel's destiny. The text as it stands means that only the king of Assyria, often singled out for special mention in Isaianic texts (e.g. 7:17, 20; 8:7; 10:12) is to be ceremoniously burned on the great pyre in Topheth. But again the text is difficult, and an intriguing suggestion is that we should read "to Molech" instead of "to the king" (Heb. *la-melech*). The horrific scene then conjured up is one in which the Assyrian victims are sacrificed to the god Molech, "the abomination of the Ammonites" (1 Kings 11:7). But is it not unthinkable that Yahweh should make sacrifices to a pagan deity?

The chapter ends with fire and brimstone, reminiscent of the miraculous fire with which the pyre on Mount Carmel was kindled in Elijah's contest with the prophets of Baal (1 Kings 18), and also of the destruction of Sodom and Gomorrah (Gen. 19:24). The fall of Assyria's capital, Nineveh, is described in similar detail in the little Book of Nahum (see especially 1:6, 8). Maybe the present passage was composed round about the same time. However that may be, the language and imagery transcend the actual event, and provide the basis for those lurid medieval representations of hell-fire . . . a fate bv no means reserved for Assyrians.

WOE TO THOSE WHO GO DOWN TO EGYPT FOR HELP!

Isaiah 31:1–9

> [1]Woe to those who go down to Egypt for help
>   and rely on horses,
> who trust in chariots because they are many
>   and in horsemen because they are very strong,
> but do not look to the Holy One of Israel
>   or consult the Lord!
> [2]And yet he is wise and brings disaster,
>   he does not call back his words,
> but will arise against the house of the evildoers,
>   and against the helpers of those who work iniquity.

³The Egyptians are men, and not God;
    and their horses are flesh, and not spirit.
When the Lord stretches out his hand,
    the helper will stumble, and he who is helped will fall,
    and they will all perish together.

⁴For thus the Lord said to me,
As a lion or a young lion growls over his prey,
    and when a band of shepherds is called forth against him
is not terrified by their shouting
    or daunted at their noise,
so the Lord of hosts will come down
    to fight upon Mount Zion and upon its hill.
⁵Like birds hovering, so the Lord of hosts
    will protect Jerusalem;
he will protect and deliver it,
    he will spare and rescue it.

⁶Turn to him from whom you have deeply revolted, O people of
Israel. ⁷For in that day every one shall cast away his idols of silver and
his idols of gold, which your hands have sinfully made for you.
⁸"And the Assyrian shall fall by a sword, not of man;
    and a sword, not of man, shall devour him;
and he shall flee from the sword,
    and his young men shall be put to forced labour.
⁹His rock shall pass away in terror,
    and his officers desert the standard in panic,"
says the Lord, whose fire is in Zion,
    and whose furnace is in Jerusalem.

The "Woe" prophecy with which chapter 31 opens (vv. 1–3) is the
clearest and most moving expression of the prophet's conviction
that a policy that relies on Egypt is doomed. So thoroughly
characteristic is it of Isaiah's thought and style that we can confidently picture the scene in the year 701 B.C. when he spoke these
words in Hezekiah's palace and, like Cassandra before the fall of
Troy, no one listened to him: "Prophesy not to us what is right",
they said; "speak to us smooth things, prophesy illusions . . . let us
hear no more of the Holy One of Israel!" (30:10–11). But his
words still stand: Trust in God, not in men.

"Going down" to Egypt has the meaning of leaving Jerusalem, leaving the land of Israel; the opposite, "going up to Jerusalem", is used of pilgrims (Jer. 31:6), returning exiles (Ezra 1:3), and in modern times immigrants to Israel. Here it is certainly more than just another reference to envoys from Judah making a last effort to get help from the Pharaoh (cf. 30:1–5). It is perhaps significant that another familiar passage where Egyptian horses, chariots and horsemen are mentioned, in that order, is Exodus 15—and then "the Lord brought back the waters of the sea upon them" (15:19).

Verse 1 contains four words for "faith", all Isaianic: "rely" is the word translated "lean" in 10:20; "trust" appears in two great hymns (12:2; 26:3–4) as well as in the account of Hezekiah's crisis of faith in chapters 36–37 (e.g 36:4,5,6; 37:10—RSV "rely"); "looking to the Holy One of Israel", rather than to the work of their hands, comes in 17:7–8; and "consulting, seeking the Lord" rather than "idols and sorcerers" (19:3; 9:13; 8:19) is a favourite prophetic idiom: e.g.

> Seek the Lord while he may be found,
>   call upon him while he is near . . .
>
> (55:6; cf. 11:10; Amos 5:4,6,14)

The word "faith" does not occur more than a couple of times in the Old Testament, as a glance at any concordance will show, but faith itself runs through the whole Bible from beginning to end, and is especially prominent in the Book of Isaiah.

The politicians trust their own wisdom: they think a military solution will work, with Egyptian help. The prophet says, with bitter irony, "God is wise too; his solutions always work" (v. 2). Calling them "evildoers" (same word as "disaster") and "those who work iniquity" conjures up all kinds of sinister forebodings: these are idioms moulded by frequent use in the Psalms (e.g. 64:2; 92:7, 9; 94:4–7; 141:3–4, 9–10).

The opposition between men and flesh on the one hand, and God and spirit on the other sums up the prophet's warning in a profound religious statement of faith. The easiest way to explain the verse is in negatives: without God, man is nothing; without the spirit, flesh is nothing. "Spirit" (Heb. *ruach*) is not just the breath of life, although it includes that (e.g. Ps. 104:29–30; Ecc. 12:7): there is another word for "breath" (Gen. 2:7). "Spirit" is also a source of energy, will power and joi de vivre. It plays a prominent role in the legends of Israel's heroes, Gideon (Judg. 6:34), Samson (Judg. 14:19; 15:14), David (1 Sam. 16:13) and the rest. There is also the spirit of prophecy (e.g. Num. 11:25; 1 Sam. 10:10; Isa. 42:1; 61:1), and the spirit of wisdom and understanding (Isa. 11:2) . . . all from God alone, and worth relying on absolutely. Egypt meanwhile was crushingly defeated by Sennacherib at the battle of Eltekeh—the "helper" stumbled; anyone who, like Judah, relied on them for help fell, and they all perished together. All God had to do to sweep away the horses, chariots and horsemen of Egypt, was to "stretch out his hand" (cf. 5:25; 9:12,17,21; 10:4).

The other part of this chapter is a rather heterogeneous collection of short prophecies linked by the common theme of Jerusalem's survival. It begins with a note by the prophet himself ("said to me"). The short prophecy in verse 4 which it introduces is enigmatic as well as original, and this suggests that the introductory formula here takes us back into the genuine prophetic experience. The vision is a very effective one: a vicious lion devouring a sheep, growling defiantly; nothing can distract it or frighten it, not even when all the local shepherds join forces to drive it off. Amos 3:12 adds some gory details to the picture. Here, as in Amos, the lion is the Lord of hosts (cf. Amos 1:2), and his prey must be Mount Zion. The unusual expression "fight upon Mount Zion" (i.e. against) alludes to the scene just described: Zion feebly struggling under the weight of a savage enemy. Such a vision expresses the prophet's fears in an unusually dramatic way, especially as no doubt by this time the Assyrians had defeated Egypt, destroyed all the cities of Judah (36:1) and were closing in on Jerusalem.

But then a curious thing happens, not for the first time in these texts. Verse 5 abruptly changes the image to one of gentle protection—of birds hovering over their young (Deut. 32:11; Ps. 91:4)—and immediately takes us through the Assyrian crisis to miraculous deliverance beyond it:

He shall not come into this city, says the Lord. For I will defend this
city to save it, for my own sake and for the sake of my servant David.
(37:34–35)

Then "fighting upon, against" becomes "doing battle for Mount
Zion" (NEB), or more likely "fighting on Mount Zion", that is
fighting alongside the people of Jerusalem, against the Assyrians.
Verse 9 contains the same idea: it represents the Lord as a fire on
Mount Zion, driving the enemy back with its intense heat and so
protecting Jerusalem. Long after the tragedy of 701 B.C., when all
Judah was laid waste and Jerusalem left like a "booth in a vineyard" (1:8), the legend of Jerusalem's miraculous survival grew
and transformed many of Isaiah's prophecies (see especially chs.
36–37). This is a beautiful example of that process, where a
growling lion is transformed, stops tearing its prey to pieces and
starts instead to protect it gently ("like birds hovering"), and
shepherds are bent on destroying its prey, instead of rescuing it.

Before completing the picture of Jerusalem's victory by describing the defeat of the Assyrians, the chapter issues a short
appeal to the people of Israel: "Turn to God . . . leave your idols
behind" (vv. 6–7). Why here? "Turning to God" is one way to
avoid disaster (see especially Jonah 3:5–10). On the one hand the
appeal comes here as a response to the offer of protection and
deliverance (in verse 5); but, on the other, in a context of military
threats and crises, to Jerusalem and her enemies, repentance will
provide some kind of protection. On the silver and gold idols, see
on 30:22.

Like chapter 30, this prophecy also ends in death and fire.
Assyria will be struck down by some supernatural agent ("the
angel of the Lord", as it is called in 37:36), and put to flight.
Prisoners of war will be put to forced labour, like the Ammonites
under David (2 Sam. 12:31). "Their rock", that is, their strength
or their leaders, will let them down; their officers will run away.
The fire in Zion is a torch or a beacon, a sign of hope to God's
people, a sign of death and destruction to his enemies. The
mention of a "furnace" (or an "oven"; cf. Ps. 21:9; Mal. 4:1;
Lam. 5:10) adds the notion of intense heat to the picture. In the

distance Jerusalem had looked so easy to destroy. When they got closer it turned out to be a blazing, scorching fire that they could not approach: "The light of Israel will become a fire, and his Holy One a flame . . ." (10:17). Even angels have to shield their faces from God's glory (6:2); how much more the "evildoers" and "those who work iniquity" (v. 2)!

A KINGDOM OF RIGHTEOUSNESS AND PEACE

Isaiah 32:1–20

¹Behold, a king will reign in righteousness,
    and princes will rule in justice.
²Each will be like a hiding place from the wind,
    a covert from the tempest,
like streams of water in a dry place,
    like the shade of a great rock in a weary land.
³Then the eyes of those who see will not be closed,
    and the ears of those who hear will hearken.
⁴The mind of the rash will have good judgment,
    and the tongue of the stammerers will speak readily and distinctly.
⁵The fool will no more be called noble,
    nor the knave said to be honourable.
⁶For the fool speaks folly,
    and his mind plots iniquity:
to practise ungodliness,
    to utter error concerning the Lord,
to leave the craving of the hungry unsatisfied,
    and to deprive the thirsty of drink.
⁷The knaveries of the knave are evil;
    he devises wicked devices
to ruin the poor with lying words,
    even when the plea of the needy is right.
⁸But he who is noble devises noble things,
    and by noble things he stands.

⁹Rise up, you women who are at ease, here my voice;
    you complacent daughters, give ear to my speech.
¹⁰In little more than a year
    you will shudder, you complacent women;
for the vintage will fail,
    the fruit harvest will not come.

[11]Tremble, you women who are at ease,
    shudder, you complacent ones;
strip, and make yourselves bare,
    and gird sackcloth upon your loins.
[12]Beat upon your breasts for the pleasant fields,
    for the fruitful vine,
[13]for the soil of my people
    growing up in thorns and briers;
yea, for all the joyous houses
    in the joyful city.
[14]For the palace will be forsaken,
    the populous city deserted;
the hill and the watchtower
    will become dens for ever,
a joy of wild asses,
    a pasture of flocks;
[15]until the Spirit is poured upon us from on high,
    and the wilderness becomes a fruitful field,
    and the fruitful field is deemed a forest.
[16]Then justice will dwell in the wilderness,
    and righteousness abide in the fruitful field.
[17]And the effect of righteousness will be peace,
    and the result of righteousness, quietness and trust for ever.
[18]My people will abide in a peaceful habitation,
    in secure dwellings, and in quiet resting places.
[19]And the forest will utterly go down,
    and the city will be utterly laid low.
[20]Happy are you who sow beside all waters,
    who let the feet of the ox and the ass range free.

In spite of the variety of styles and images, this chapter has a remarkable unity of content and structure. It contains familiar Isaianic themes—the righteous king (11:1ff.), the eyes that see not and the ears that hear not (6:9), the humiliation of proud women (3:16–4:1), the ruin of a city (24:10–13; 25:2), quietness and trust (7:4; 26:2–4; 30:15), and so on. But there is also some traditional wisdom teaching that could have come straight out of Proverbs or Ecclesiastes—the fool in high places (Ecc. 10:6–7), the danger of lying words (Prov. 18:4–8), the value of a good king (e.g. Prov. 21:1), the formula "Happy are you . . ." (e.g. Prov. 3:13; 8:32,34; Ecc. 10:17), and the like. Yet however diverse the origins of the separate strands in this chapter, together they constitute a single richly-textured picture of a new society, where the poor will be protected, fools and knaves restrained, and the vulnerable complacency of the affluent replaced by quietness and security for ever.

There is no suggestion that the "messianic" prophecy (vv. 1–2) originally had a particular "messiah" in mind, for example, Zerubbabel who raised hopes of national revival after the exile (Hag. 2:20–23; Zech. 4; Ezra 3–5). People in every age, particularly an age when a government's policies are characterized by injustice and crass stupidity, entertain such hopes of a better world, and make visions like Isaiah 32 their own. "Righteousness" (*tsedek* in Hebrew) includes "justice", but goes beyond it in the direction of "victory" and "salvation" (see on 1:26). The images in verse 2 are all familiar from Isaiah and the Wisdom literature: the stormy blast of the ruthless (e.g. 25:4), the streams of water in the desert (Prov. 21:1; Job 6:15–20; Psalm 1:3), the protection of a great rock (e.g. 31:9), the "weary" (e.g. 28:12; 29:8; Prov. 25:25, RSV "thirsty").

Verse 3 picks up the recurring theme of unreceptiveness from Isaiah's vision in the Temple: the rare word translated "closed" occurs only here and in 6:10 (and 29:9). In the new age people will listen to the word of God and be wise; hardened hearts will melt. In Ezekiel's words, "I will take the stony heart out of their flesh and give them a heart of flesh, that they may walk in my statutes..." (11:19–20).

In ancient Wisdom tradition, "rashness, hastiness" (v. 4) is one of "six things which the Lord hates" (Prov. 6:18; cf. 7:22–23; 25:8). Ecclesiastes links this with his advice on careful speaking: "Be not rash with your mouth, nor let your heart be hasty to utter a word before God... therefore let your words be few" (Ecc. 5:2). Thus, although the actual word "stammerer" happens to appear only here in the Hebrew Bible, the importance of clear, well-disciplined speech is very frequently emphasized throughout the Wisdom literature: e.g. "Death and life are in the power of the tongue, and those who love it will eat its fruits" (Prov. 18:21; cf. 14:3). All kinds of harmful speaking are criticized: e.g. gossip (Prov. 16:28; 18:8), lying in a court of law (19:5), revolutionary talk, even in secret (Ecc. 10:20); while reticence (Prov. 13:3), gentle words (15:1), "a word in season" (15:23) or the like are recommended over and over again. In the Isaianic new age wisdom will prevail. The very rare word translated "distinctly" in this verse recalls the "clear heat in sunshine" (18:4), one of the most beautiful Isaianic images for the quiet, crystal-clear wisdom of God.

The next four verses turn to another typical "wisdom" theme, the topsyturviness of society: e.g.

> There is an evil which I have seen under the sun, as it were an error proceeding from the ruler: folly is set in high places, and the rich sit in a low place. I have seen slaves on horses, and princes walking on foot like slaves. (Ecc. 10:5–7)

"Fools" in the Wisdom literature are not necessarily people with a low IQ. The term means primarily untrained; hence the continual appeal to come and learn. "Fools" are those who are not fit to govern (Prov. 8:5; 9:4). "Noble", on the other hand, means both "prince, aristocrat" (e.g. Num. 21:18; Prov. 19:6), and "princely, noble" (in character and training): e.g. "Fine speech is not becoming to a fool; still less is false speech to a prince" (Prov. 17:7). In an ideal society the two come together (v. 8).

The damage caused by "fools in high places" needs little comment. Much of Isaianic prophecy has been concerned with the crimes and stupid policies of the rulers of Judah, from the ruthless exploitation of the poor in chapters 1–5 to the short-sighted policies of "those who go down to Egypt for help" in chapters 28–31. "Ungodliness" (v. 6) is another wisdom term: e.g. "With his mouth the godless man would destroy his neighbour, but by knowledge the righteous are delivered" (Prov. 11:9). As we saw in 9:17 and 10:6, it implies alienation from God and man.

As in 3:16–4:1, the "women who are at ease" in Zion (cf. Amos 4:1; 6:1) represent in these bitter prophecies the luxury and, at the same time, the vulnerability of an affluent society (vv. 9–14). Their fear and humiliation stand for the fear and humiliation of the whole city; their sufferings are the sufferings of every household (v. 13); as they are stripped of their fine raiment and carried off into ignominious captivity, so the palace is emptied of its treasures and the populous city deserted (v. 14). Surely the "fruitful vine" (v. 12) refers to thriving family life (Ps. 128:3) and "the soil of my people growing up in thorns and briers" (v. 13) to the break-up of society in Jerusalem: "for the vineyard of the Lords of hosts is the house of Israel, and the men of Judah are his pleasant planting" (5:7).

"The joyful city"—"joy of all the earth" (Lam. 2:15)—has to be destroyed before it can become again "the city of righteousness" (cf. 1:21–26), because its joy was built on complacency. But, with exquisite subtlety, the prophet adds to his description of the end of the old Jerusalem two final details, which lead us from desolation to hope, from death to life: the innocent joy of wild asses, symbols of freedom and independence (Gen. 16:12), and the peaceful grazing of a flock of sheep (v. 14). The end of one scene is the beginning of the next: for "we are his people, and the flock of his pasture" (Ps. 100:3; 95:7; 79:13).

It remains to describe some of the characteristics of the new age (vv. 15–20), the "gifts of the Spirit" as they have been called. First, prosperity: the wilderness will produce fruit-trees like an orchard or a vineyard (*carmel* in Hebrew), and the fruit-trees will produce timber like the forests of Lebanon (cf. 29:17; 35:1–2). Justice and righteousness will take root there, and the fruit that they yield will be peace, quietness and trust for ever. God's people will make their home there in security, happiness and freedom. Much of the force of these verses is lost in translation: for example, the words translated "at ease" and "complacent" in verse 9 reappear in verses 15–20 as "trust", "quiet [resting places]" and "secure [dwellings]". "Righteousness" suggests "victory, salvation" as well as justice (see above); "peace" includes "abundance, health, forgiveness" as well as the absence of war; and the word "resting places" starts off a whole chain of ideas and images associated with the promised land (see on 28:12).

The effect of the final scene is heightened by verse 19: while hail beats down on the forest (28:17; 30:30) and the city (Babylon?, "the city of chaos" (24:10)? or the old Jerusalem (vv.

13–14)?) is thrown down, you will be free to sow wherever you wish, and to leave your animals unattended, without fear of cattle-thieves or wild beasts. The Book of Isaiah began with the ox and the ass in their stable, better able to recognize their lord than "my people Israel" (1:3). Let us end this first volume of our commentary with the coming down of the Spirit upon us, the salvation of "my people Israel", and (v. 20) the freeing of the ox and the ass from their stable.

FURTHER READING

R. E. Clements, *Isaiah 1–39* (New Century Bible) (Oliphants, 1982)

O. Kaiser, *Isaiah 1–12* (Old Testament Library) (Westminster 1983)

    Isaiah 13–39 (Old Testament Library) (Westminster 1974)

G. Von Rad, *The Message of the Prophets* (SCM Press, 1972)

John F. A. Sawyer, *Prophecy and the Prophets* (Oxford University Press, 1984)